IT SERVICE MANAGEMENT

an introduction

*it*SMF

THE IT SERVICE
MANAGEMENT FORUM

Colofon

Title:	IT Service Management, an introduction
Editors:	Jan van Bon (Inform-IT, chief editor)
	Georges Kemmerling (Quint Wellington Redwood, editor)
	Dick Pondman (ISES International, editor)
Quality audit:	Hal Dally (Fujitsu Consulting)
	Klaas Hofkamp (IBM)
	Glenn LeClair (Fujitsu Consulting)
	Dave Pultorak (Pultorak & Associates)
	Mart Rovers (Interprom-USA)
	Philip Stubbs (Sheridan College, Ontario Canada)
Publisher:	Van Haren Publishing
	(info@vanharen.net)
Publication of:	*it*SMF-Canada
ISBN:	90-806713-47
Editions:	First impression, first edition, May 2002

Design & Layout:
DTPresto Design & Layout, Zeewolde-NL

Foreword

Looking back over the past 20 years, it is interesting to note how greatly the IT world has changed. Yet, at its core, the methods to manage and deliver IT services have essentially remained constant. From the orderly and secure approach to operating a mainframe environment to the chaos and open approach to running client server and internet enabled applications and infrastructures, we always come back to the basic business principles required to maintain and ensure delivery of consistent service levels. These principles are the essence of the ITIL support and delivery processes.

The ITIL processes are the core capabilities, which allow us to deliver services that align to the business goals at levels we are able to measure and maintain. IT Service Management, based on the ITIL processes, is key to enabling the delivery of high availability and high quality IT services that meet the needs and demands of the business.

This publication - *IT Service Management – an Introduction* - captures the essence of the ITIL best practice as it applies to the key support and delivery processes, while adding valuable practical knowledge and experience regarding the application of the ITIL theory in a North American context.

*it*SMF Canada (IT Service Management Forum) is proud to have participated as the quality review team in producing this edition of *IT Service Management – an Introduction,* based on the original work published by our colleagues at the *it*SMF Netherlands National Chapter. In keeping with the directives of the International *it*SMF community to *"make IT Service Management expertise accessible to a broader audience"*, itSMF Canada will continue to partner with our global membership to provide pertinent, up-to-date publications related to the field of IT Service Management.

Abbey L. Wiltse
National Chair, Marketing and Communications, *it*SMF Canada

May 2002

Contents

Chapter 1

Introduction

In recent decades IT developments have had a major impact on business processes. The introduction of the PC, LAN, client/server technology and the Internet has enabled organizations to
bring their products and services to markets more quickly. These developments have ushered in
the transition from the industrial to the information age. In the information age, everything has
become faster and more dynamic. Traditional hierarchical organizations often find it difficult to
respond to rapidly changing markets, which has lead to a trend towards less hierarchical and
more flexible organizations. Similarly, emphasis within organizations has shifted from vertical
functions, or departments to horizontal processes that run across the organization, and decision-
making authority is increasingly granted to personnel at a lower level. IT Service Management
operating processes were developed against this background.

In the 1980s, the quality of the IT services provided to the British government was such that the
then CCTA (Central Computer and Telecommunications Agency, now Office of Government
Commerce, OGC) was instructed to develop an approach for efficient and cost-effective use of
IT resources by ministries and other British public sector organizations. The aim was to devel-
op an approach independent from any supplier. This resulted in the **Information Technology
Infrastructure Library™ -ITIL.** ITIL[1] grew from a collection of best practices observed in the
IT service industry.

ITIL gives a detailed description of a number of important IT practices, with comprehensive
checklists, tasks, procedures and responsibilities which can be tailored to any IT organization.
Where possible, these practices have been defined as processes covering the major activities of IT
service organizations. The broad subject area covered by the ITIL publications makes it useful
to refer to them regularly and to use them to set new improvement objectives for the IT organization. The organization can grow and mature with them.

A number of other IT Service Management frameworks have been developed on the basis of
ITIL, generally by commercial organizations. Examples concern Hewlett & Packard -HP ITSM
Reference model, IBM -IT Process Model, Microsoft -MOF and many others. This is one of the
reasons why ITIL has become the de facto standard for describing a number of fundamental
processes in IT Service Management. This adoption and adaptation of ITIL directly reflects the
ITIL philosophy, and is a welcome development as ITIL has become a force for industry alignment that is sorely needed in todays heterogeneous and distributed IT environment.

The broader adoption of ITIL has been hampered by the lack of a basic, but effective introduc-
tory self-study guide. The materials provided for ITIL courses are often too narrow as they are
developed specifically for each course. This publication is aimed at anyone involved in IT Service
Management or interested in the subject. Given the broad target group, the IT Service
Management Forum (*it*SMF) provides the perfect channel as a non-profit industry organization.
The objectives of the *it*SMF and this publication are similarly compatible.

The mission statement of the *it*SMF:

> *'The objective of the itSMF is to promote current IT Service Management expertise and practices,
> as an independent, not-for-profit organization.'*

*it*SMF implements this by organizing conferences, publishing a magazine, setting up working
parties, and issuing publications. The itSMF also aims to recruit more members.

Correspondingly, the *it*SMF statement with respect to this book:

> *'Making IT Service Management expertise accessible to a broader audience.'*

Thus, the objectives related to the book are :
1. To contribute to the mission of the *it*SMF by publishing an accessible and practical reference book on IT service management, which can also be used when studying for the ITIL examinations.
2. To adopt ITIL as the de facto standard and common framework for the book.
3. To stay current by adopting relevant new terms, expertise and methods which make IT Service Management more accessible, and regularly publishing new editions.
4. To ensure that the text is independent by disregarding vendor publications.

Given the rapid developments in this field, the ITIL books can not always describe the latest developments. ITIL is primarily a collection of best practices developed in the industry, and theory and practice are not always in step. When writing this book we aimed to incorporate current developments in the field, without substantially diverting from the ITIL publications. Thus, this book can be used both as a self-study guide to prepare for the official ITIL examinations, and as a general introduction to the broader area of IT Service Management. This publication does not address the planning and implementation of ITIL processes. In chapter 2 'The background to IT Service Management' it does however address, in a more general way, relevant matters in IT Service Management, in terms of quality, processes and policies.

The first edition of this book is based upon an *it*SMF publication in the Netherlands, developed as an introduction to IT Service Management. That work was based on management summaries and descriptions in official ITIL publications, with permission of the OGC. *it*SMF-Canada set up the Quality Audit group, which monitors the quality of the publication and ensures the content speaks to the North American user community. The last detailed review of the draft in May 2002 was done by Karen Ferris, KMF Advance. Given the desire for a broad consensus in the ITIL field, new developments, additional material and contributions from ITIL professionals are welcome. They will be discussed by the editors and where appropriate incorporated into new editions.

Jan van Bon,
Editor in chief,
May 2002

Please address feedback on this document to the editors of 'IT Service Management, an introduction', c/o Inform-IT, P.O. Box 23, 9841 PA Grijpskerk, the Netherlands, e-mail: jvbon@wxs.nl.

---

[1] ITIL is a registered trademark of CCTA/OGC.

Chapter 2

IT Service Management - background

This chapter addresses issues such as services, quality, organization, policy and process management. These concepts provide the backdrop for the development of a systematic approach to IT Service Management.

The IT Service Management processes described in this book (also referred to as IT Management) are best understood against the background of the concepts about organizations, quality and services which influenced the development of the discipline. Familiarity with these terms also helps to understand the links between the various elements of the IT Infrastructure Library (ITIL). ITIL is by far the best-known description of IT Service Management and is therefore used as the foundation for this book.

This chapter introduces the following subjects:

- **Services and quality:** This section addresses the relationship between the quality experienced by the customer's organization and users, and quality management by the provider of the IT services.
- **Organization and policies:** This section addresses concepts such as vision, objectives, and policies, and discusses issues such as planning, corporate culture and Human Resource Management. This section also discusses the coordination between the business processes of a company and the IT activities.
- **Process management:** This section addresses the control of IT service processes.

2.1 Services and quality

Organizations are often greatly dependent on their IT services and expect the IT services not only to support the organization, but also to present new options to implement the objectives of the organization. Furthermore, the high expectations of customers of IT services tend to change significantly over time.

Providers of IT services can no longer afford to focus on technology and their internal organization, they now have to consider the quality of the services they provide and focus on the relationship with their customers.

> *The provision of IT services refers to the full management - maintenance and operation - of the IT infrastructure.*

Before buying a **product** in a store, we normally assess the quality such as its appearance, usefulness and robustness. In a store, the customer has few opportunities to influence the product quality. This is because the product is produced in a factory. By effectively controlling the production plant, the manufacturer will try to deliver a fairly constant quality. In this example, manufacture, sales and consumption of the product are quite separate.

However, **services** are provided through interaction with the customer. Services cannot be assessed in advance, but only when they are provided. The quality of a service depends to some extent on the way in which the service provider and the customer interact. In contrast to the manufacturing process, customer and provider can still makes changes when the services are being delivered. How the customer perceives the service and what the provider thinks they supply, both depend largely on their personal experiences and expectations.

> *The process of providing a service is a combination of production and use, in which the provider and customer participate simultaneously.*

The perception of the customer is essential in the provision of services. Customers will generally use the following questions to assess the quality of the service:
• Does the service meet the expectations?
• Can I expect a similar service the next time?
• Is the service provided at a reasonable cost?

Whether or not the service fulfills the **expectations** depends primarily on how effectively the deliverables were agreed on in a dialog with the customer, rather than on how well the supplier provides the service.

A **continuing dialog** with the customer is essential to refine the services and to ensure that both the customer and the supplier know what is expected of the service. In a restaurant, the waiter will first explain the menu, and ask if everything is satisfactory when serving a new course. The waiter actively coordinates supply and demand throughout the meal. And this experience with customers is then used to improve future customer contact.

The **quality** of a service refers to the extent to which the service fulfills the requirements and expectations of the customer. To be able to provide quality, the supplier should continuously assess how the service is experienced and what the customer expects in the future. What one customer considers normal will be considered as a special requirement by another customer. And eventually a customer will get used to something considered special at the start. The results of the assessment can be used to determine if the service should be modified, if the customer should be provided with more information, or if the price should be changed.

> *Quality is the totality of characteristics of a product or service that bear on its ability to satisfy stated and implied needs (ISO-8402).*

Reasonable costs may be considered as a derived requirement. Once it has been agreed on what is to be expected of the service, the next step is to agree on the cost. At this stage the service provider has to be aware of the costs they incur, and the current market rates for comparable services.

A customer will be dissatisfied about a service provider who occasionally exceeds the expectations but disappoints at other times. Providing a **constant quality** is one of the most important, but also one of the most difficult aspects of the service industry.

For example, a restaurant will have to purchase fresh ingredients, the chefs will have to work together to provide consistent results, and hopefully there are no major differences in style among the waiting staff. A restaurant will only be awarded a three-star rating when it manages to provide the same high quality over an extended period. This is not always the case: there are changes among the waiting staff, a successful approach may not last, and chefs leave to open their own restaurants. Providing a constant high quality also means that the component activities have to be coordinated: the better and more efficiently the kitchen operates, the more quickly the guests can be served.

Thus, when providing a service, the overall quality is the result of the quality of a number of component processes that together form the service. These component processes form a chain, and the

links affect each other and the quality of the service. Effective coordination of the component processes requires not only adequate quality when performing each process, but also consistent quality.

2.1.1 Quality assurance

Supplying products or services requires activities. The quality of the product or service depends
greatly on the way in which these activities are organized. Deming's quality circle (Figure 2.1)
provides a simple and effective model to control quality. The model assumes that to provide
appropriate quality, the following steps must be undertaken repeatedly:
- **Plan:** what should be done, when should it be done, who should be doing it, how should it
  be done, and by using what?
- **Do:** the planned activities are implemented.
- **Check:** determine if the activities provided the expected result.
- **Act:** adjust the plans based on information gathered while checking.

Effective and timely intervention means that the activities are divided into processes with their
own plans and opportunities for checking. It must be clear who is responsible in the organization and what authority they have to change plans and procedures, not for only for each of the
activities, but also for each of the processes.

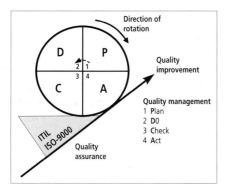

Figure 2.1 Deming's Quality Circle

---

*Dr. Edward Deming was an American statistician brought to Japan by General Douglas
MacArthur after the Second World War to help rebuild the destroyed economy. He had developed
theories about the best possible use of expertise and creativity in organizations in the United States
in the 1930s, but because of the Depression his ideas were not accepted in the US. However, his optimization methods were successfully adopted in Japan.*

Some of Deming's typical statements:
- *'The customer is the most important part of the production line.'*
- *'It is not enough to have satisfied customers, the profit comes from returning customers and
  those who praise your product or service to friends and acquaintances.'*
- *'The key to quality is to reduce variance.'*
- *'Break down barriers between departments.'*
- *'Managers should learn to take responsibility and provide leadership'*
- *'Improve constantly.'*
- *'Institute a vigorous program of education and self-improvement.'*
- *'Institute training on the job.'*
- *'The transformation is everybody's job.'*

Quality management is the responsibility of everyone working in the organization providing the service. Every employee has to be aware of how their contribution to the organization affects the quality of the work provided by their colleagues, and eventually the services provided by the organization as a whole. Quality management also means continuously looking for opportunities to improve the organization and implementing quality improvement activities.

Quality assurance is a policy matter within the organization. This is the complete set of the measures and procedures used by the organization to ensure that the services provided continue to fulfill the expectations of the customer and the relevant agreements. Quality assurance ensures that improvements resulting from quality management are maintained.

A **quality system** is the organizational structure related to responsibilities, procedures and resources for implementing quality management.

The ISO 9000 series of standards is often used to develop, define, assess and improve quality systems.

ISO 9000 quality standard:

Some organizations require their suppliers to hold an ISO 9001 or ISO 9002 certificate. Such a certificate proves that the supplier has an adequate quality system whose effectiveness is regularly assessed by an independent auditor.

ISO is the International Organization for Standardization. A quality system that complies with the ISO standard ensures suppliers that
- the supplier has taken measures to be able to provide the quality agreed with the customers;
- the management regularly assesses the operation of the quality system, and uses the results of internal audits to implement improvement measures where necessary;
- the suppliers' procedures are documented and communicated to those affected by them;
- customer complaints are recorded, dealt with in a reasonable time, and used to improve the service where possible;
- the supplier controls the production processes and can improve them.

An ISO certificate does not provide an absolute guarantee about the quality of the service provided, however, it does indicate that the supplier takes quality assurance seriously and is prepared to discuss it. The new ISO 9000 series of standards, ISO-9000-2000, puts even greater emphasis than the previous standard on the ability of an organization to learn from experience and to implement continuous quality improvement.

2.1.2 Organizational maturity

Experience with improving the quality of IT services has shown that it is rarely sufficient to structure and define current practices. The causes of a mismatch between the service provided and the customer's requirements are often related to the way in which the IT organization is managed. A permanent quality improvement demands a certain degree of maturity of the organization.

The European Foundation for Quality Management (EFQM) model (Figure 2.2) can be useful in determining the maturity of an organization. It identifies the major areas to be considered when managing an organization.

Deming's Quality Circle is incorporated in the EFQM model. Based on the outcomes from the result areas actions are taken (strategy, policies). These actions serve to underpin the planning (e.g. the structure of the processes) which should then lead to the desired results. The EFQM identifies nine areas.

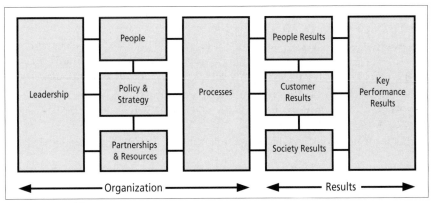

Figure 2.2 EFQM model

As an additional tool, the Dutch quality organization, INK, divided the EFQM model into stages indicating to what extent a company has implemented Total Quality Management, either in a particular area, or in general.

There are five stages:

- **Product-focused** - also known as ad hoc, output-focused; everyone in the organization works hard (but their efforts show little direction).
- **Process-focused** - also known as 'we know our business'; the performance of the organization is planned and repeatable.
- **System-focused** - or 'cooperation between departments'.
- **Chain-focused** - also known as 'external partnership'; the organization is focused on the value it adds in the supplier–customer chain it forms a part of.
- **Total quality-focused** - also known as 'heaven on earth'; the organization has reached the stage where a continuous and balanced focus on improvement has become second nature.

The areas covered by the EFQM model can be combined with the levels of organizational maturity. Questionnaires can be used to determine how mature the organization is in each of these areas. Internal or external auditors can carry out such an assessment.

When an organization determines its maturity, it can develop a strategy for improvement that can then be further developed into a plan. The plan, based on the model and covering a period of one year, describes what improvement should be made to specific aspects in each area and how. By repeating this process of self-assessment and planning, every year the organization becomes more aware how it is maturing. Major advantages of this approach are that the organization can improve its quality step by step, that the intermediate results are visible, and that the management can steer the organization on the basis of its strategy.

There are many other health checks and types of self-assessment in addition to the EFQM approach. Some focus primarily inward. One should bear in mind that improvements to parts of the internal organization might only have a limited effect on the results, for example if there is no improvement in the relationship with the customers, employee satisfaction and leadership, or if the strategy and policy of the organization is unclear.

In the IT industry, the process maturity improvement process is the best known in the context of the Capability Maturity Model (CMM). This process improvement method was developed by the Software Engineering Institute (SEI) of Carnegie Mellon University. CMM is concerned with improving the maturity of the software creation processes. CMM includes the following levels:

- **Initial** - the processes occur ad hoc.
- **Repeatable** - the processes have been designed such that the service quality should be repeatable.
- **Defined** - the processes have been documented, standardized and integrated.
- **Managed** - the organization measures the results and consciously uses them to improve the quality of its services.
- **Optimizing** - the organization consciously optimizes the design of its processes to improve the quality of its services, or to develop new technology or services.

Maturity models based on the CMM levels of maturity have also been developed for IT Service Management.

Developing and maintaining a quality system which complies with the requirements of the ISO 9000 (ISO-9000-2000) series can be considered a tool for the organization to reach and maintain the system-focused (or 'managed' in IT Service CMM) **level of maturity.** These ISO standards emphasize the definition, description and design of processes.

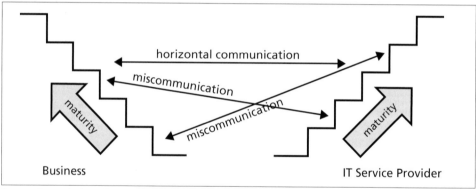

Figure 2.3 Communication and maturity levels: customer and supplier.

When assessing the maturity of an organization, we cannot restrict ourselves to the service provider. The level of maturity of the customer (Figure 2.3) is also important. If there are large differences in maturity between the supplier and the customer, then these will have to be considered to prevent a mismatch in the approach, methods and mutual expectations. Specifically, this affects the communication between the customer and the supplier. It is advisable to bring both organizations to the same level of development, and to operate at that level, or to adjust the communication in line with the lower level.

2.2 Organization and policies

The preceding sections clearly illustrated that service quality is closely associated with the quality of an organization and its policies. This section will discuss several important aspects of organization and policies that are relevant to process management.

2.2.1 Vision, objectives and policies

An organization is a form of cooperation between people. Any organization, from a darts club to a multinational company, depends on a concept of why it is worth cooperating in the organization. This **vision** might be that you could make money-selling PCs. However, to be attractive to all stakeholders (e.g. customers, investors, personnel) an organization will have to communicate why they should do business with you, for example because you are the best, cheapest or most fun. Thus, you will want to build up a suitable image. Just think of slogans such as 'Let's make things better' or 'You'll never walk alone'.

To communicate its vision, the organization can be defined in the form of a **Mission Statement** (Figure 2.4). The mission statement is a short, clear description of the objectives of the organization and the values it believes in.

The **objectives** of the organization describe in greater detail what it wants to accomplish. Good objectives have five essential elements: they have to be **S**pecific, **M**easurable, **A**ppropriate, **R**ealistic and **T**ime-bound (SMART).

The **policy** of the organization is the combination of all decisions and measures taken to define and realize the objectives. In its policies, the organization will prioritize objectives and decide how the objectives will be reached. Of course, priorities may change over time, depending on the circumstances. The clearer the organization's policies are to all stakeholders, the less needs to be defined about how personnel are supposed to do their work. Instead of detailed procedures, personnel can independently use the policies as their guideline. Clearly formulated policies contribute to a flexible organization, as all levels in the organization can respond more quickly to changing circumstances.

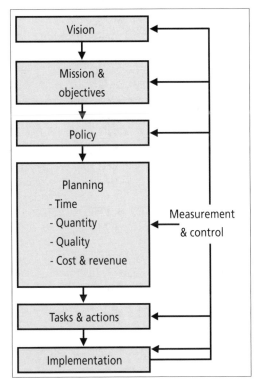

Figure 2.4 Vision, objectives and policies

Implementing policies in the form of specific activities requires **planning**. Plans are usually divided into stages to provide milestones where progress can be monitored. For example, the policies can be used to draw up an annual plan, which is then used to develop the budgets. An annual plan can be developed in greater detail into departmental plans, quarterly plans or project plans. Each of these plans contains a number of elements: an activity schedule, the required resources, and agreements about the quality and quantity of the products or services to be delivered.

Realization of the planned activities requires **action**. Actions are allocated to personnel as **tasks**, or outsourced to external organizations.

When translating the mission of the organization into objectives, policies, planning and tasks, there is the risk that after some time, the mission, objectives or policies are forgotten. It is therefore important that at every stage we **measure** if the organization is still moving in the right direction, and to take remedial action where necessary.

Thus, we have to measure if the organization or processes fulfill the objectives, and there are various methods available for this. One of the most common methods in business is the **Balanced Score Card,** or BSC. In this method, the objectives of the organization or process are used to define **Critical Success Factors** (CSF). CSFs are defined for a number of areas of interest or perspectives: customers/market, business processes, personnel/innovation and finance. The parameters determined to measure if the CSFs meet the standard are known as **Key Performance Indicators** (KPI). Where necessary, these can be subdivided into Performance Indicators (PI).

> *Key Performance Indicators, or KPIs, are parameters for measuring progress relative to key objectives or Critical Success Factors (CSF) in the organization.*

The outcome of the measurements and changing circumstances can lead to **modification** of the processes, tasks, plans, and policies, and even to a change in the objectives, mission and vision of the organization. The more matured the organization is, the better it deals with such changes. If the IT department supports the interests of the business, the objectives of the IT department will be derived from the business objectives. The IT department, for example, might have the following objective: 'To contribute to the competitive strength of the business'. The specific objectives of the IT department will then be developed on the basis of this general objective. Depending on the nature of the business, objectives will be defined for the IT department with respect to safety, accessibility, response speed, technical sophistication, and so forth.

2.2.2 Planning horizon

When considering the policies and planning of an IT department, we should be aware of the links between planning for the business as a whole, the application systems and the technical infrastructure. When planning the network and applications of a business, the IT department will have to stay ahead of the overall planning to ensure that the business has an IT infrastructure in which it can develop. Figure 2.5 gives an example of the links between the various plans.

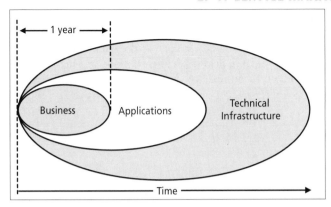

Figure 2.5 Planning horizons

Technical infrastructure has the longest planning horizon and in its support role it has fewer clear links with the substantive business activities. It takes time to develop a technical infrastructure and the fact that information systems and the business depend on the technical infrastructure, limits the speed at which changes can be implemented. Furthermore, developing a technical infrastructure demands significant investment and the period over which it can be depreciated have to be considered.

The planning horizon is shorter for **applications** as they are designed for specific business purposes. Application life cycle planning is primarily based on the business functions to be provided by the system, after which the underlying technology is considered.

Business plans, based on the organization's strategy, normally cover one calendar or financial year. Budget, planning and progress reports all fall within this period. In some markets, the planning cycle time has become even shorter as the cycle time for product development is also being cut. Planning should address four elements:
• **Time** - this is the easiest factor to determine. It is defined by a starting date and ending date, and is often divided into stages.
• **Quantity** - the objectives have to be made measurable to monitor progress. Terms such as 'improved' and 'quicker' are insufficient for planning purposes.
• **Quality** - the quality of the deliverables (results) should be appropriate for the objective.
• **Costs and revenues** - the deliverables must be in proportion to the expected costs, efforts and revenues.

Differences between the planning horizons occur not only between areas, but also between the various levels of activities and processes (strategic, tactical and operational). This will be addressed in greater detail later in this book.

2.2.3 Culture
Organizations that want to change, for example to improve the quality of their services, will eventually be confronted with the current organizational culture. The organizational culture, or corporate culture, refers to the way in which people deal with each other in the organization; the way in which decisions are made and implemented; and the attitude of employees to their work, customers, suppliers, superiors and colleagues.

Culture, which depends on the standards and values of the people in the organization, cannot be controlled, but it can be influenced. Influencing the culture of an organization requires leadership in the form of a clear and consistent policy and a supportive personnel policy.

The corporate culture can have a major influence on the provision of IT services. Businesses value innovation in different ways. In a stable organization, where the culture places little value on innovation, it will be difficult to adjust its IT services in line with changes in the organization of the customer. If the IT department is unstable, then a culture which values change can pose a serious threat to the quality of its services. In that case, a free for all can develop where many uncontrolled changes lead to a large number of faults.

2.2.4 Human Resource Management

Personnel policy plays an important and strategic role in fulfilling the long-term objectives of an organization (see also the EFQM model). It can also be used as an instrument to change the corporate culture. The objective of modern personnel management is to optimize the performance of all personnel of the organization, for which it uses instruments such as recruitment and selection, training and career development, motivation and reward.

Human Resource Management (HRM) is the major form of modern personnel management. Human Resource Management is based on two premises:
• Personnel management should contribute to the objectives of the organization. If organizations have to respond better and more quickly in an environment which changes ever more quickly, then this will affect the deployment, quality and number of personnel.
• Giving employees in the organization the opportunity to develop and use their skills will benefit the organization.

There are three approaches to HRM:
• **The hard approach** sees human resources as means of production which have to be organized as effectively and efficiently as possible. As the corporate strategy is determined by economic, technical and market factors, the same applies to personnel policy. This approach places different values on employees. Some core employees are strategically more important than peripheral employees who are easily replaceable. For example, a company might choose to permanently employ only core personnel, and for the rest use a pool of contract personnel.
• **The soft approach** emphasizes that making the best possible use of human potential and opportunities will benefit the business. Modern employees are highly educated, ambitious and prepared to invest a lot in their work. For this reason, their potential must be identified early and developed continuously (career development, training policy). When selecting its strategy and policy, the business must base its choices on the talent and potential of its employees.
• **The integrated approach** looks at the shared interests of personnel and management in an organization. To reach the objectives of the organization there will have to be good inflow, movement and outflow of personnel. Changes in the market and the organization (e.g. developments in technology) lead to constant changes in the need for skills.

All aspects of personnel policy have to be carefully coordinated. The movement of employees in the organization, determining and developing skills (competence), and promoting mobility in the internal labor market are becoming increasingly important in organizations.
The quality of service provided by an organization will benefit if the best use is made of the potential of its employees. This facilitates continuous improvement. Instruments for quality management in personnel policy include:
• **Policy Deployment** - communicating to each employee how and to what extent their task contributes to realizing the objectives of the organization. An important condition for the suc-

cess of policy deployment is that it also extends to all layers of management.

- **Empowerment** - giving employees the opportunity to organize and implement their task in consultation with the organization. The degree of empowerment determines the extent to which employees can be held responsible for the quality of the work they provide.
- **Accountability** - as the result of policy deployment and empowerment. If an employee has been explained what is expected of them, and if they have had the opportunity to arrange and implement the task as they wanted, then they can be held accountable for it. This could be used as a basis for assessing and rewarding employees. The reward may be material (salary) or immaterial, for example appreciation, new opportunities for development and career opportunities.
- **Competence Management** - this is both a means to use the competence available in an organization as effectively as possible, and as a way to systematically develop the competence the organization needs. This approach charts the competence required by the processes and projects as well as the competence of the employees. When organizing employees, the focus is not only on obtaining a good match between the required and available competence, but also on the opportunities to develop competence, transfer expertise, and learn skills. Mentors or coaches may support employees. Setting up skills groups can also support the exchange of experience and encourage the development of new competence.

2.2.5 IT Customer Relationship Management

The quality of IT services largely depends on good relationships with the customers of the IT organization. These relationships provide the basis for making and updating agreements. IT Customer Relationship Management (CRM) addresses maintaining a relationship with customers and coordinating with customer organizations, at the strategic, tactical and operational levels. Figure 2.6, a diagram of customer relationships, illustrates the horizontal communication between the customers and the IT organization, regarding support and coordination. The vertical communication concerns policies, and control and reporting.

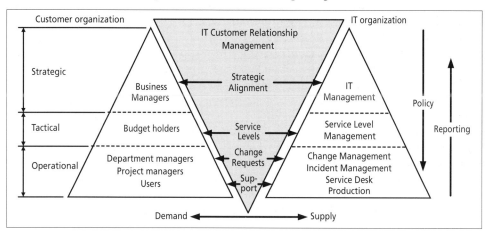

Figure 2.6 IT Customer Relationship Management

In IT Customer Relationship Management, the major challenge is to ensure that there are good and effective relationships between the IT organization and the customer organization at all levels. However, the extent of IT Customer Relationship Management will be different at each level. One of the elements in customer relationships is the Service Desk, and the control of the Service Levels can be based on Service Level Management. In these areas, IT Customer Relationship Management will primarily play a supportive role, for example, by organizing surveys among customers and users, providing information, and so forth.

*The **user** is the 'hand on the keyboard' user, the employee who uses IT services for their routine activities.*

*The **customer** is the 'pay the bills' customer, the person who is authorized to conclude an agreement with the IT organization about the provision of IT services (for example a Service Level Agreement, or SLA) and who is responsible for ensuring that the IT services are paid for.*

Obviously the 'pay the bills' customer can also play the role of the 'hands on the keyboard' user in many situations.

IT Customer Relationship Management plays an important role in developing the Strategic Alignment between the IT organization and the organization purchasing the IT services. In practice, this is primarily a matter of staying in touch with the customer organization, and exploring the options for linking the strategic objectives of both organizations. This can provide the basis for a long-term relationship, in which the IT organization focuses on the customer and proposes IT solutions that the help the customer reach their business objectives. Given the dynamic nature of both the customer organization and the IT organization, the rate of change in both organizations should also be coordinated.

The agreements with the customer about the services to be provided are then developed into service level proposals through Service Level Management. For example, if the customer wants to introduce an Intranet, then the availability, user support, implementation of change requests and cost all have to be agreed. These agreements are laid down in a Service Level Agreement (SLA).

If the customer organization wants changes (expansion or modification) to the IT services that fall within the agreements laid down in the SLA, then a **Request For Change** will be submitted. Change Management then processes the request. Changes outside the current agreements are introduced into the Service Level Management process.

In most cases, users can contact a **Service Desk** for such operational requests and questions, and to report problems.

Figure 2.6 not only provides information about the horizontal and vertical communication, but also about the **planning horizon** of the processes. Coordination at a strategic level has a planning horizon of several years. Service Level Management concerns agreements at the tactical level, with a planning horizon of approximately one year. Change Management, Service Desk and Incident Management all concern the operational level, with a planning horizon of months, weeks, days or even hours.

2.3 Process Management

Every organization aims to realize its vision, mission, objectives and policies, which means that appropriate activities have to be undertaken. To return to the example of the restaurant, appropriate activities include buying vegetables, bookkeeping, ordering publicity material, receiving guests, cleaning tables, peeling potatoes, and making coffee.

With just such an unstructured list, something will be left out and we will easily become confused. It is therefore a better idea to structure the activities. Preferably they should be arranged such that we can see how each group of activities contributes to be objectives of the business, and how they are related.

Such groups of activities are known as **processes**. If the process structure of an organization is clearly described, it will show:
• What has to be done.
• What the expected result is.
• How we measure if the processes deliver the expected results.
• How the results of one process affect those of another process.
The questions in Figure 2.7 arise constantly in the process-based approach typical of modern IT Service Management. The tools to answer these questions are shown on the right.

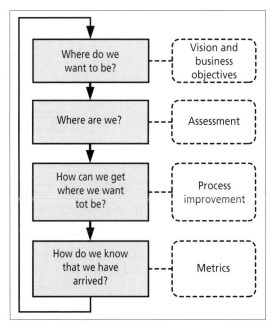

Figure 2.7 Process improvement model

2.3.1 Processes

When arranging activities into processes, we do not use the existing allocation of tasks, nor the existing departmental divisions. This is a conscious choice. By opting for a process structure, we can often show that the certain activities in the organization are uncoordinated, duplicated, neglected, or unnecessary.

*A **process** is a logically related series of activities conducted toward a defined objective.*

Instead, we look at the objective of the process and the **relationships** with other processes. A process is a series of activities carried out to convert input into an output (Figure 2.8). We can associate the **input** and **output** of each of the processes with **quality characteristics and standards** to provide information about the results to be obtained by the process. This produces chains of processes which show what goes into the organization and what the result is, as well as monitoring points in the chains to monitor the quality of the products and services provided by the organization.

The standards for the output of each process have to be defined such that the complete chain of processes meets the corporate objective, if each process complies with its process standard. If the result of a process meets the defined standard, then the process is **effective**. If the activities in the process are also carried out with the minimum required effort and cost, then the process is efficient. The aim of process management is to use planning and control to ensure that processes are effective and **efficient**.

We can study each process separately to optimize its quality. The **process owner** is responsible for the process results. The **process manager** is responsible for the realization and structure of the process, and reports to the process owner. The **process operatives** are responsible for defined activities, and these activities are reported to the process manager.

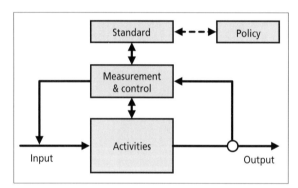

Figure 2.8 Process diagram

The logical combination of activities results in clear transfer points where the quality of processes can be monitored. In the restaurant example, we can separate responsibility for purchasing and cooking, so that the chefs do not have to purchase anything and possibly spend too much on fresh ingredients that do not add value.

The management of the organization can provide control on the basis of the quality of the process as demonstrated by data from the results of each process. In most cases, the relevant **performance indicators** and standards will already be agreed upon. The day-to-day control of the process can then be left to the process manager. The process owner will assess the results based on a report of performance indicators and whether they meet the agreed standard. Without clear indicators, it would be difficult for a process owner to determine whether the process is under control, and if planned improvements are being implemented.

Processes are often described using **procedures** and **work instructions**.

> A **procedure** is a description of logically related activities, and who carries them out. A procedure may include stages from different processes. A procedure defines who does what, and varies depending on the organization.
>
> A set of **work instructions** defines how one or more activities in a procedure should be carried out.

Figure 2.9 shows the process model based on the ITIL approach which forms the foundation for the IT Service Management processes described in this book.

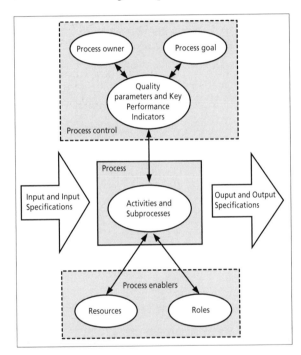

Figure 2.9 Generic ITIL process model

2.3.2 Processes and departments

Most businesses are hierarchically organized. They have departments that are responsible for a group of employees. There are various ways of structuring departments, for example by customer, product, region or discipline. IT services generally depend on several departments, customers or disciplines. For example, if there is an IT service to provide users with access to an accounting program on a central computer, this will involve several disciplines. The computer center has to make the program and database accessible, the data and telecommunications department has to make the computer center accessible, and the PC support department has to provide users with an interface to access the application.

Processes that span several departments can monitor the quality of a service by monitoring certain aspects of quality, such as availability, capacity, cost and stability. A service organization will then try to match these quality aspects with the customer's demands. The structure of such processes can ensure that good data is available about the provision of services, so that the planning and control of services can be improved.

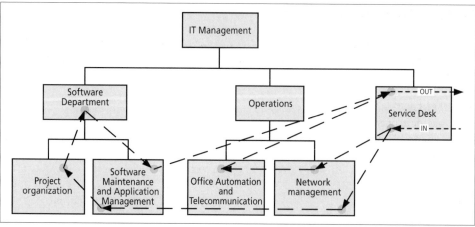

Figure 2.10 Processes and departments (example)

Figure 2.10 shows a basic example of the combinations of activities in a process (indicated by the dashed lines).

2.3.3 IT Service Management

IT Service Management is primarily known as the process and service-focused approach of what was initially known as IT Management. In this chapter we demonstrated that processes should always have a defined objective. The objective of IT Service Management processes is to contribute to the quality of the IT services. Quality management and process control form part of the organization and its policies.

In a process-focused approach we also have to consider the situation within an organization (policies, culture, size, etc.).

ITIL, the best known approach to IT Service Management, does not prescribe the type of organization, but instead describes the relationships between the activities in processes, which are relevant to any organization. This provides a framework for exchanging experiences between organizations. This approach also provides a framework for learning from the experience of dynamic organizations.

Chapter 3

Introduction to ITIL

This chapter describes the structure and objectives of the IT Infrastructure Library (ITIL) and the organizations that contribute to maintaining ITIL as the best practice standard for IT Service Management.

3.1 Background

ITIL was developed in recognition of the fact that organizations are becoming increasingly dependent on IT to fulfill their corporate objectives. This increasing dependence has resulted in a growing need for IT services of a quality corresponding to the objectives of the business, and which meet the requirements and expectations of the customer. Over the years, the emphasis has shifted from the development of IT applications to the management of IT services. An IT application (sometimes referred to as an information system) only contributes to realizing corporate objectives if the system is available to users and, in the event of fault or necessary modifications, it is supported by maintenance and operations.

In the overall life cycle of IT products, the operations phase amounts to about 70 to 80% of the overall time and cost, the rest is spent on product development (or procurement). Thus, effective and efficient IT Service Management processes are essential to the success of IT. This applies to any type of organization, large or small, public or private, with centralized or decentralized IT services, with internal or outsourced IT services. In all cases, the service has to be reliable, consistent, of a high quality, and of acceptable cost.

IT Service Management addresses the provision and support of IT services tailored to the needs of the organization. ITIL was developed to disseminate IT Service Management best practices systematically and cohesively. The approach is based on service quality and developing effective and efficient processes.

ITIL offers a common framework for all the activities of the IT department, as part of the provision of services, based on the IT infrastructure. These activities are divided into processes, which provide an effective framework to make IT Service Management more mature. Each of these processes covers one or more tasks of the IT department, such as service development, infrastructure management, and supplying and supporting the services. This process approach makes it possible to describe the IT Service Management best practices independently from the actual organizational structure of the entity.

Many of these best practices are clearly identifiable and are indeed used to some extent in most IT organizations. ITIL presents these best practices coherently. The ITIL books describe how these processes, which have sometimes already been identified, can be optimized, and how the coordination between them can be improved. The ITIL books also explain how the processes provide a framework for common terminology within the organization. They help to define the objectives and to determine the required effort.

By using a process approach, ITIL primarily describes what must be included in IT Service Management to provide IT services of the required quality. The structure and allocation of tasks and responsibilities between functions and departments depends on the type of organization, and these structures vary widely among IT departments and often change.

The description of the process structure provides a common point of reference that changes less rapidly, which can help maintain the quality of IT services during and after reorganizations and among suppliers and partners as they change.

The list below identifies some advantages and disadvantages of ITIL. This list is not intended to be definitive, but is provided here as a basis for considering the advantages or disadvantages of ITIL and the different ways in which organizations use ITIL.

Advantages of ITIL to the customer/user:
- The provision of IT services becomes more customer-focused and agreements about service quality improve the relationship.
- The services are described better, in customer language, and in more appropriate detail.
- The quality and cost of the services are managed better.
- Communication with the IT organization is improved by agreeing on the points of contact.

Advantages of ITIL to the IT organization:
- The IT organization develops a clearer structure, becomes more efficient, and more focused on the corporate objectives.
- The management is more in control and changes become easier to manage.
- An effective process structure provides a framework for the effective outsourcing of elements of the IT services.
- Following the ITIL best practices encourages a cultural change towards providing service, and supports the introduction of a quality management system based on the ISO-9000 series.
- ITIL provides a uniform frame of reference for internal communication and communication with suppliers, and standardization and identification of procedures.

Potential problems of ITIL:
- The introduction can take a long time and significant effort, and requires a change of culture in the organization. An over ambitious introduction can lead to frustration because the objectives are never met.
- If process structures become an objective in themselves, the service quality may be adversely affected. In that case, procedures become bureaucratic obstacles that are avoided where possible.
- There is no improvement due a lack of understanding about what processes should provide, what the performance indicators are, and how processes can be controlled.
- Improvement in the provision of services and cost reductions are insufficiently visible.
- A successful implementation requires the involvement and commitment of personnel at all levels in the organization. Leaving the development of the process structures to a specialist department may isolate that department in the organization and it may set a direction that is not accepted by other departments.
- If there is insufficient investment in support tools, the processes will not be done justice and the service will not be improved. Additional resources and personnel may be needed if the organization is already overloaded by routine IT Service Management activities.

These potential problems could of course be overcome. ITIL was developed in view of the advantages. Many of the best practice suggestions aim to prevent such problems, or to help solve them should they occur.

3.2 Organizations

3.2.1 OGC (CCTA)

ITIL was originally a CCTA product. CCTA was the Central Computer and Telecommunications Agency of the UK government. As of 1 April 2001, the CCTA has been amalgamated with the OGC (Office of Government Commerce), which is now the new owner of ITIL. The objective of the OGC is to help its customers in the UK public sector update their procurement activities and improve their services by making the best possible use of IT and other instruments. 'OGC aims to modernize procurement in government, and deliver substantial value for money improvements.' The OGC promotes the use of 'best practices' in many areas (e.g. project management, procurement and IT Service Management). The OGC publishes several series (libraries) of books written by UK and international experts from a range of companies and organizations.

The OGC IT Infrastructure Library consists of a number of clear and thorough 'Codes of Practice' to provide efficient and effective IT services.

3.2.2 itSMF

The Information Technology Service Management Forum (*it*SMF), originally known as the Information Technology Infrastructure Management Forum (ITIMF), is the only internationally recognized and independent user group dedicated to IT Service Management. It is owned and operated solely by its membership. The *it*SMF is a major influence and contributor to Industry Best Practice and Standards worldwide.

The first chapter of *it*SMF was set up in the UK in 1991. The Dutch itSMF (*it*SMF - The Netherlands) was the next chapter, set up in November 1993. There are now *it*SMF chapters in countries such as South Africa, Belgium, Germany/Austria/Switzerland, Canada, the United States, and Australia, which cooperate in *it*SMF International. Website addresses of the chapters can be found in Appendix B2.

*it*SMF chapters promote the exchange of information and experience which enables IT organizations to improve the services they provide. They organize seminars, conferences, special subject evenings, and other events about current IT Service Management subjects. They also publish newsletters and operate a website for information sharing. Task forces also contribute to the development of ITIL.

3.2.3 EXIN and ISEB

The Dutch foundation "Exameninstituut voor Informatica" (EXIN) and the UK "Information Systems Examination Board" (ISEB) jointly developed a professional certification system for ITIL. This was done in close cooperation with the OGC and *it*SMF. EXIN and ISEB are nonprofit organizations that cooperate to offer a full range of ITIL qualifications at three levels:
• Foundation Certificate in IT Service Management
• Practitioner Certificate in IT Service Management
• Manager Certificate in IT Service Management

The certification system is based on the requirements for effectively fulfilling the relevant role within an IT organization. To date, Foundation Certificates have been awarded to over 50,000 IT professionals in over 30 countries.

The Foundation Certificate is intended for all personnel who have to be aware of the major tasks in the IT organization, and the relationships between them. The Foundation examination covers the Service Desk function, and the processes for Incident Management, Problem Management, Change Management, Configuration Management, Release Management, Service Level Management, Availability Management, Capacity Management, IT Service Continuity Management and Financial Management for IT Services. After obtaining the Foundation Certificate, the Practitioner and Manager examinations can be taken. Practitioners are trained on a practical level how to perform specific ITIL processes or tasks in such processes, for one process such as Incident Management, Change Management, and Service Level Management. Managers are trained on a theoretical level how to control all the processes as listed under the Foundation certificate, how to advise about the structure and optimization of the processes, and how to implement them.

Today, ITIL represents much more than a series of useful books on IT Service Management. The framework of best practice in IT Service Management is an entire industry of organizations, tools, education and consulting services, related frameworks, and publications. Since the 1990s, ITIL is not only considered to be the framework, but also the approach and philosophy shared by those using ITIL best practices in their work. A range of organizations is now cooperating internationally to promote ITIL as the de facto standard in IT Service Management.

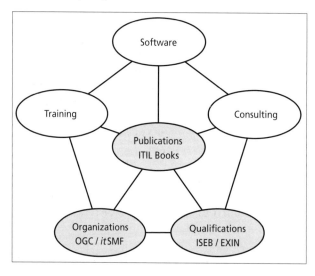

Figure 3.1 ITIL environment (source: OGC)

Figure 3.1, the ITIL environment, shows that the organizations involved also provide feedback between current practice (white ellipses) and theory (gray ellipses) to keep ITIL up-to-date. Furthermore, extensions and alternatives have been developed, some of which may be considered as IT Service Management methods in their own way. These alternatives often address the needs of certain groups or organizations whose specific problems are not adequately covered by ITIL.

The unique aspect of ITIL is that it offers a generic framework based on the practical experience of a global infrastructure of professional users.

3.3 The ITIL books

Each of the ITIL books addresses part of the framework. Each provides an outline description of what is needed to organize IT Service Management.

ITIL defines the objectives and activities, and input and output of each of the processes found in an IT organization. However, ITIL does not give a specific description of how these activities should be implemented, as this will be different in every organization. The emphasis is on an approach that has been proven in practice, but that, depending on the circumstances, may be implemented in a number of ways. ITIL is not a method, instead it offers a framework for planning the most common processes, roles and activities, indicating the links between them and what lines of communication are necessary.

ITIL is based on the need to supply high-quality services, with an emphasis on customer relationships. The IT organization will have to fulfill the agreements with the customer which means maintaining good relationships with customers and partners such as suppliers.

Part of the ITIL philosophy is based on quality systems, such the ISO-9000 series, and Total Quality frameworks, such as that of the EFQM. ITIL supports such quality systems with a clear description of the processes and best practices in IT Service Management. This can significantly reduce the time required to obtain ISO certification.

Originally, ITIL consisted of a large number of sets of books, each of which described a specific area of the maintenance and operation of IT infrastructure. Ten books describing Service Support and Service Delivery were considered as the core of ITIL. There were approximately 40 other books on supplementary subjects that related to IT Service Management, from cabling to managing customer relationships. However, the original series of books in the Infrastructure Library mostly approached IT Service Management from the IT perspective. The Business Perspective Set was introduced to bridge the gap between the business and the IT organization. Even more, certain aspects of ITIL had a slightly dated approach.

The core ITIL books have now been revised and published as two books, one on Service Support, and one on Service Delivery. This has eliminated significant overlap and occasional inconsistencies in the earlier series and has improved cohesion. It also illustrates the above vision of IT Service Management more clearly.

As of the publication of this book, the updating of the full series of ITIL publications shown in figure 3.2 has not been completed yet.

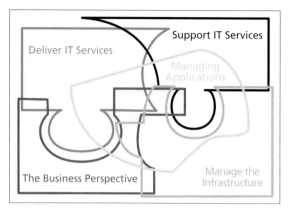

Figure 3.2 ITIL jigsaw puzzle (source: OGC)

The basic structure of ITIL is illustrated in figure 3.2, which uses a set of jigsaw puzzle pieces as an analogy.

The ITIL puzzle shows the five main elements addressed by the ITIL books. Each of these elements interfaces with the other four, and overlaps them to some extent.
The five elements are:
• Service Support
• Service Delivery
• The Business Perspective
• ICT Infrastructure Management
• Applications Management

The first two elements were published in 2000 and 2001 respectivley. The three following elements are under preparation at the time of this publication.
There is a sixth element, Planning to Implement Service Management, planned for publication at April 2002. This book explains the steps necessary to identify how an organization might expect to benefit from ITIL, and how to set about reaping those benefits.
The ITIL puzzle has also been compared with tectonic plates, or colliding and overlapping continents. Not only is a difficult to identify the boundaries exactly, there is also clearly friction and stress. This impression is confirmed by what happens in many organizations. It is at these boundaries in particular, that management problems occur. Although such problem cannot be prevented, we can, just as with earthquakes, prepare for them, and learn how to deal with them.
In this chapter, we will introduce the ITIL series of publications using the main elements of the ITIL puzzle. By the end of 2002 the original set of books, the first elements of which appeared in 1989, should have been replaced by six new ITIL books. However, many of the best practices to be described in the new books were also included in the current ITIL series. For more information, see the references in Appendix D and the lists on the OGC and EXIT web sites.

3.3.1 Business Perspective
The ITIL books in the Business Perspective Set describe many issues related to understanding and appreciating IT services as an integrated aspect of managing a business.
The Business Perspective Set, and the Business Perspective book, which will eventually replace the set, address:
• Business Continuity Management
• Partnerships and outsourcing
• Surviving changes
• Adapting the business to radical changes

Other ITIL books address some of these topics, in addition to those in the Business Perspective Set.

Managing Facilities Management

Managing Facilities Management addresses the management of contracts between the IT organization and Facilities Management companies. The Facilities Management suppliers may be responsible for the operation of all or part of the IT infrastructure. However, the IT organization bears the ultimate responsibility for the services provided to the customer. This book describes what measures the IT organization can take to accept responsibility for agreements about Service Levels, and to monitor the services provided by the facilities suppliers.

Managing Supplier Relationships

To some extent, Managing Supplier Relationships is similar to Customer Relationship Management, but now covering the relationship between the IT organization and its suppliers. A good relationship with suppliers is not just a matter of contractual agreements and contacts; it primarily concerns a businesslike form of cooperation which contributes to the current and future provision of IT services and objectives of the IT organization.

The nature and content of the contacts can distinguish relationships with suppliers. These may be to discuss the long-term prospects of existing relationships, to promote communication, or to investigate the range offered by various suppliers.

The major tasks of the Managing Supplier Relationships process include selecting suppliers, assessing the performance of suppliers, and determining the way in which the IT organization handles supplier contacts.

3.3.2 Service Delivery

As indicated above, Service Support and Service Delivery are considered to be at the heart of the ITIL framework for IT Service Management. The ITIL book on Service Delivery describes the services the customer needs, and what is needed to provide these services.

The following subjects are addressed in the Service Delivery set:
• Service Level Management
• Financial Management for IT Services
• Capacity Management
• IT Service Continuity Management
• Availability Management

Security Management (with reference to the ITIL book on Security Management) was added to this introduction book, but it is not part of the Service Delivery set.

The complex interrelationship between the processes described in the books on Service Support and Service Delivery is almost impossible to show in a diagram. The simplified diagram in Figure 3.3 illustrates the main outlines.

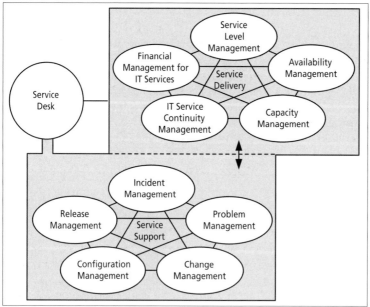

Figure 3.3 Service Support and Service Delivery

Service Level Management

The objective of Service Level Management is to make clear agreements with the customer about the IT services, and to implement these agreements. Consequently, Service Level Management needs information about the customer needs, facilities provided by the IT organization, and the financial resources available.

Service Level Management addresses the service provided to the customer (Customer Focus). By creating services based on the needs of the customer (demand pull) rather than solely on the basis of what is currently technically feasible (supply push), the IT organization can improve customer satisfaction. The chapter on Service Level Management in the Service Delivery book describes:

- How clearly defining the agreements in a Service Level Agreement can optimize the IT services at a cost that can be justified to the customer.
- How the service can be monitored and discussed.
- How the service can be supported by Underpinning Contracts with suppliers to the IT organization.

Financial Management for IT Services

Financial Management addresses the prudent provision of IT services. For example, Financial Management provides information about the costs incurred while providing IT services. This enables a proper consideration of costs and benefits (price and performance) when deciding on changes to the IT infrastructure or IT services. The identification, allocation, forecasting and monitoring of the costs, as discussed in the chapter on Financial Management in the Service Delivery book, are all covered by the term 'costing', which in the current revision of ITIL is referred to as Budgeting and Accounting. These activities support cost awareness (what cost is incurred where?) and can also be used in drawing up budgets. With respect to the revenue stream of the IT organization, Financial Management for IT Services describes various charging methods, including setting goals for charging and determining pricing, as well as budgeting aspects.

Capacity Management
Capacity Management is the process of optimizing the cost, timing of acquisition, and deployment of IT resources, to support the agreements made with the customer. Capacity Management addresses resource management, performance management, demand management, modeling, capacity planning, load management and application sizing. Capacity Management emphasizes planning to ensure that the agreed Service Levels can also be fulfilled and future.

Availability Management
Availability Management is the process of ensuring the appropriate deployment of resources, methods and techniques, to support the availability of IT services agreed with the customer. Availability Management addresses issues such as optimizing maintenance, and design measures to minimize the number of incidents.

IT Service Continuity Management
This process addresses the preparation and planning of disaster recovery measures for IT services in the event of a business interruption. Known as Contingency Planning in the prior revision of ITIL, it emphasizes the links with all the measures necessary to safeguard the continuity of the customer organization in the event of a disaster (Business Continuity Management) as well as the measures to prevent such disasters. IT Service Continuity Management is the process of planning and coordinating the technical, financial and management resources needed to ensure continuity of service after a disaster, as agreed with the customer.

3.3.3 Service Support
The ITIL book on Service Support describes how a customer can get access to the appropriate services to support their business.
This book covers the following subjects:
• Service Desk
• Incident Management
• Problem Management
• Configuration Management
• Change Management
• Release Management

Service Desk
The Service Desk is the initial point of contact with the IT organization for users. Previously, the ITIL books referred to it as the Help Desk. The major task of the Help Desk was recording, resolving and monitoring problems. A Service Desk can have a broader role (for example receiving Requests For Change) and it can carry out activities belonging to several processes. It is the initial point of contact with the IT service provider for users.

Incident Management
The distinction between incidents and problems is possibly one of the best known, but not always the most popular, contribution made by ITIL to the IT Service Management field. Although this distinction may sometimes be confusing, it has a major advantage in that a distinction is made between the rapid return of the service, and identifying and remedying the cause of an incident.

The Incident Management process aims to resolve the incident and restore the provision of services quickly. Incidents are recorded, and the quality of the incident records determines the effectiveness of a number of other processes.

Problem Management

If a problem is suspected within the IT infrastructure, Problem Management aims to identify the underlying cause. A problem may be suspected because there are incidents, but obviously the objective is to prevent disturbances where possible.

Once the causes have been identified (known errors), a business decision is taken whether to make permanent improvements to the infrastructure to prevent new incidents. Submitting a Request For Change makes this improvement.

Also note that ITIL's definition of Problem Management significantly differs from e.g. the definition the IT industry in North America has given to it in the past.

Configuration Management

Configuration Management addresses the control of a changing IT infrastructure (standardization and status monitoring), identifying configuration items (inventory, mutual links, verification and registration), collecting and managing documentation about the IT infrastructure and providing information about the IT infrastructure to all other processes.

Change Management

Change Management addresses the controlled implementation of changes to the IT infrastructure. The objective of the process is to determine the required changes, and how they can be implemented with a minimum adverse impact on the IT services, while at the same time ensuring the traceability of changes, by effective consultation and coordination throughout the organization. Changes are made in consultation with the status monitoring activities of Configuration Management, at the request of the customer organization, Problem Management and several other processes. Changes are implemented by following a specific path of definition, planning, building and testing, acceptance, implementation and evaluation.

Release Management

A release is a set configuration items (CIs) that are tested and introduced into the live environment together. The main objective of Release Management is to ensure the successful rollout of releases, including integration, testing and storage.

Release Management ensures that only tested and correct versions of authorized software and hardware are provided. Release Management is closely related to Configuration Management and Change Management activities. The actual implementation of changes is often carried out through Release Management activities.

3.3.4 IT Infrastructure Management

IT operational management processes will be addressed in a new ITIL book on ICT Infrastructure Management. This book will cover:
• Network Service Management
• Operations Management
• Management of Local Processors
• Computer Installation and Acceptance
• Systems Management

IT Infrastructure Management also includes Environmental Management.

Network Services Management

The Network Services Management process addresses planning and controlling communications networks. These include telephone systems and LAN and WAN networks.

The ITIL module Network Services Management also addresses the long-term communications needs of the organization. In essence, it describes how the ITIL best practices can be applied in a network environment.

Operations Management
Computer Operations Management (Computer Operations) addresses the management of computer hardware and systems software, including mainframes and midrange systems, but also file servers, to ensure that the agreed Service Levels are provided.

Management of Local Processors
The Management of Local Processors process addresses management operations at decentralized sites. The objective is to support the provision of IT services at the user site. This specifically includes making agreements about the activities of various processes (especially the processes to support IT services) when IT services are being provided at multiple locations. A good definition of responsibilities is important to optimize the service.

Computer Installation and Acceptance
Computer Installation and Acceptance primarily concerns guidelines for planning the acceptance, installation and eventual removal of large computer hardware in the IT infrastructure. These guidelines are a development of the activities in the Change Management and Release Management processes.

Systems Management
To date, the ITIL books have not covered Systems Management. In future, it will be covered by the new book on IT Infrastructure Management.

Environmental Management
Environmental Management concerns managing the environment of the IT infrastructure (power supply, cooling, etc.). One of the tasks of this process is to set up and maintain climate-controlled computer and network rooms.

3.3.5 Applications Management
The ITIL book on Application Management will address the relationship between management and the software lifecycle. This includes issues such as Software Lifecycle Support and Testing an IT service for Operational Use. A major issue in Applications Management is effectively responding to changes in the business. Here, clearly defining the requirements and implementing a solution that meets the needs of the customer organization is paramount.

Software Lifecycle Support
Software Lifecycle Support aims to define the approach for supporting the entire software lifecycle, in consultation with those responsible for software development. The way in which software is designed, built, tested, introduced, operated, maintained, and eventually decommissioned, is extremely important in IT services. In every stage of the software lifecycle, there have to be agreements between those developing and those operating the IT infrastructure. The selection of Software Lifecycle models can have a significant impact on the IT services.

Testing an IT Service for Operational Use
The objective of Testing an IT Service for Operational Use is to ensure that the proper operation of newly or modified IT services is tested before they enter operations. Various testing phas-

es are undertaken such as system testing, installation testing, user acceptance testing, to determine if the developed application works, is correctly installed, interfaces with the rest of the IT infrastructure, and offers the users the functions agreed with the customer.

3.3.6 Management and organization

The ITIL series also includes some books on subjects at the strategic level, the Managers Set. Developing policies and long-term planning of IT services are specifically addressed in the books on Quality Management, IT Service Organization and Planning and Control for IT Services.

Quality Management for IT Services

Quality Management for IT Services addresses setting up and maintaining a coherent quality system, based on the IT Service Management processes described in other ITIL books. This book describes the introduction of a quality management system (based on the ISO-9000 series of standards) in an IT organization, and the evaluation of an existing quality management system. The relationship between the ISO standards and ITIL modules is also identified. Quality Management activities include defining and implementing the quality policy, and managing the quality system, including audits.

IT Services Organization

IT Services Organization addresses the structure of the IT organization. This ITIL book describes how the organization can be analyzed and assessed, particularly in terms of tasks, authority and responsibility. A framework is provided for dealing with organizational changes, based on the process descriptions in the other ITIL books. Major activities in this process include determining and defining the organizational structure and role and function descriptions.

Planning and Control for IT Services

Planning and Control for IT Services aims to provide a coherent system of planning, reporting and control for the IT organization, to ensure that the organization fulfills the objectives and requirements based on the business strategy and the strategy of the IT organization. This includes coordinating the planning and reporting of the various IT Service Management processes (for example in the form of annual plans and quarterly reports).

3.3.7 Other processes addressed

Although they are not actually ITIL modules in the Service Delivery set or the Service Support set, there are two processes that are addressed by reference to other modules, or through a culmination of other processes. IT Customer Relationship Management is a process that is drawing more and more attention, but it still is not covered in a specific ITIL module yet. Security Management has been published in ITIL in 1999, but it is not officially part of the Service Delivery set. Security is covered in this book in a separate chapter.

IT Customer Relationship Management

The best practices of many organizations show that it is advisable to apply cohesion and structure to relationships with the customer organization at several levels. The IT Customer Relationship Management activities involve several processes (see also section 2.2.5). The Service Desk is the first point of contact for users. However, the customer, who has commissioned the service, will initially contact IT Customer Relationship Management. IT Customer Relationship Management provides a bridge between the IT organization, which has traditionally taken a technical approach, and the customers who want to fulfill their business objectives. IT Customer Relationship Management is not part of the Service delivery set and is not elaborated in this introduction book.

Security Management

The objective of Security Management is to protect the IT infrastructure against unauthorized use (such as unauthorized access to data). This is based on security requirements laid down in Service Level Agreements, contractual requirements, legislation, and policy, and a basic level of security. When updating the Service Delivery part of ITIL it was decided that the recently published book on Security Management did not have to be replaced. The ITIL book on Service Delivery does not address security management, but refers to the ITIL Security Management book.

3.3.8 Planning and implementation

There is now much experience throughout the world with planning and implementing programs to optimize IT Service Management. A future ITIL book will be devoted to this subject.

In essence, the concept of planning and implementing changes in IT Service Management processes is shown in the process improvement model (in chapter 2). In practice, the situation illustrated by this model is often obscured by the way in which important decisions are taken in organizations, which may be affected by historical and political issues. It is therefore necessary for management to commit to the improvement program (Management Commitment), and for them to understand the organizational culture. You should also be aware that there will generally already be processes that meet the needs of the organization, albeit only partly. Ignoring this will engender resistance from the very people needed to align these processes better with the business needs and the experience gained with IT Service Management.

Analyzing the needs of the organization and implementing the required solution will necessitate a temporary organization to set this up. This could be considered as one project, or as a series of projects in an improvement program. One advantage is that it will provide the organization with clear decision points where it can decide to terminate, continue, or modify the project. In this context, the ITIL books recommend the adoption of PRINCE2 (Projects IN Controlled Environments, 2nd version) to manage such projects.

Each project is based on an analysis of the current situation, the desired situation, and the path in between. In most cases, the alternatives will be compared on the basis of:
• Advantages to the organization
• Risks, obstacles and potential problems
• Transition costs and long-term costs
• Costs of continuing the current approach

Identifying the potential alternatives may well be a project in itself.

Experience shows that you should be aware that ITIL is no magic formula. Do not expect miracles. You should be particularly wary of so-called ITIL implementation projects that have a hidden agenda, such as a reorganization or merger. ITIL describes the best practice for improving IT Service Management, it is not an organizational cookbook. ITIL primarily provides a frame of reference for process structures in the IT organization and, to a much lesser extent, a guideline for the structure of that organization. If a project aims to improve the organization as such, it is advisable to involve experts in this field.

A baseline measurement or health check can provide a good start for process improvements. Such an assessment of the IT Service Management processes can help identify the strengths and weaknesses of the organization, and define clear objectives for an improvement project. After some time the measurement can be repeated to show the progress of the project or program.

Chapter 4

Incident Management

4.1 Introduction

Incident Management has a reactive task, i.e. reducing or eliminating the effects of (potential) disturbances in IT services, thus ensuring that users can get back to work as soon as possible. For this reason, incidents are recorded, classified and allocated to appropriate specialists, incident progress is monitored, and incidents are resolved and they are closed. Because this requires close contacts with the users, the focal point of the incident management process is usually on the Service Desk function, which serves as a front office for the "back-office" of underlying specialist departments and suppliers. Incident Management is essential to the other ITIL processes as it provides valuable information about infrastructure errors.

Figure 4.1 below gives an example of Incident Management as a horizontal process in the organization that provides effective management and controls the incident workflow.

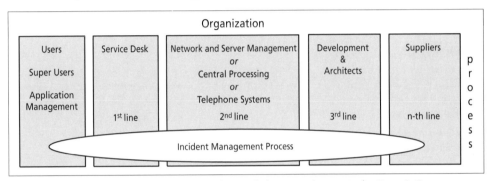

Figure 4.1 Position of the Incident Management process in relation to the functions or departments of an IT organization

4.1.1 Terminology

Incident
ITIL uses a broad definition of 'incident', so that almost all calls can be recorded and monitored as incidents.

The ITIL Service Support book defines an incident as:

> *An incident is any event which is not part of the standard operation of a service and which causes, or may cause an interruption to, or a reduction in the quality of that service.*

In the context of ITIL, incidents include not only hardware and software errors, but also Service Requests.

> *Service Request - request from a user for support, delivery, information, advice or documentation, not being a failure in the IT infrastructure.*

Examples of Service Requests:
- Functional question or request for information
- Status inquiry
- Password reset
- Requests for batch jobs, restores and password authorizations
- Database extraction

To be able to discriminate the 'true' incidents from the 'service request incidents' it is wise to assign a specific category to the service requests. It is also important to note that a Service Request is not the same as a Request For Change (RFC):

> *Request For Change - Form, or screen, used to record details of a request for a change to any Configuration Item (CI) within an infrastructure or to procedures and items associated with the infrastructure.*

An RFC is completed when changes to the infrastructure are made, e.g. the replacement of registered components, installation of a PC, etc. These are not incidents but changes.

Impact, urgency and priority

When several incidents are being dealt with at the same time, priorities have to be set. These priorities are based on the seriousness of the error to the business and the user. In consultation with the user, and in accordance with the provisions of the SLA, the Service Desk assigns the priority, which determines the order in which incidents are dealt with. When incidents are escalated to second-line (tier two), third-line (tier three) or higher level support, then the same priority is maintained, or it may be adjusted in consultation with the Service Desk.

Of course, each user will think that their incident has the highest priority, but user requirements are often subjective. To make an objective assessment, the following criteria are discussed with the user:
- **Impact of the incident:** extent of the deviation from the normal service level, in terms of the number of users or business processes affected.
- **Urgency of the incident:** the acceptable delay to the user or business process.

The priority is determined on the basis of urgency and impact. The number of people and the amount of resources that can be devoted to an incident are defined for each priority. For incidents with the same priority, the required effort can determine the order in which they are dealt with. For example, an incident that is easily resolved may be dealt with before an incident requiring a greater effort.

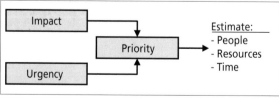

Figure 4.2 Determining the impact, urgency and priority

Incident Management has options for reducing the impact or urgency, such as swapping hardware or assigning another print queue. The impact and urgency may also change during the life of an incident, for example when it affects more users or during critical periods.

Impact and urgency can be combined in a matrix, such as in Table 4.1.

priority / resolution time	IMPACT		
URGENCY	**high**	**medium**	**low**
high	critical / < 1 hour	high / < 8 hours	medium / < 24 hours
medium	high / < 8 hours	medium / < 24 hours	low / < 48 hours
low	medium / < 24 hours	low / < 48 hours	planning / planned

Table 4.1 Example of a priority coding system

Escalation

If an incident cannot be resolved by first-line support within the agreed time, then more expertise or authority will have to be involved. This is known as escalation, which is determined by the priorities and resolution times discussed above.

We distinguish between functional and hierarchical escalation:
- **Functional escalation** (horizontal) – functional escalation means involving more specialist personnel or access privileges (technical authority) to solve the incident, and departmental boundaries may be exceeded.
- **Hierarchical escalation** (vertical) – hierarchical means that a vertical move is made (to higher levels) throughout the organization because the authority (organizational authority, powers) or resources required for resolution are insufficient.

The Incident Manager aims to reserve capacity in advance for functional escalation in the line organization, so that incident resolution does not require regular hierarchical escalation. In all cases, the line organization has to provide adequate resources for the process.

First-, second- and Nth-line support

Incident routing, or functional escalation, was introduced above. The routing is determined by expertise, urgency and authority. First-line support (also known as tier 1 support) is normally provided by the Service Desk, second-line by the management departments, third-line by the software developers and architects, and the fourth-line support by suppliers. The smaller the organization, the fewer escalation levels there are. In larger organizations, the Incident Manager may appoint Incident Coordinators in relevant departments to support him or her. For example, the Coordinators act as the interface between the process and the line organization. They each coordinate their own support teams. Figure 4.3 illustrates the escalation process.

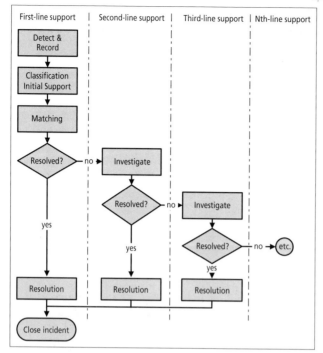

Figure 4.3 Incident escalation (source: OGC).
Note: 'Nth-line' is also known as 'Tier N'

4.2 Objective

The objective of Incident Management is to return to the normal service level, as defined in the SLA, as soon as possible, with the smallest possible impact on the business activity of the organization and the user. Incident Management should also keep effective records of incidents to measure and improve the process, and report to other processes.

4.2.1 Benefits

- For the business as a whole:
  - More timely resolution of incidents resulting in reduced business impact.
  - Improved user productivity.
  - Independent, customer-focused incident monitoring.
  - Availability of SLA-focused production information.

- For the IT organization:
  - Improved monitoring, allowing performance against SLAs to be more accurately measured.
  - Useful management and SLA reporting by effective use of the available information.
  - Better and more efficient use of personnel.
  - No lost or incorrectly registered incidents and service requests.
  - More accurate CMDB, as it is essentially being audited while incidents are registered in relation to CIs.
  - Improved user and customer satisfaction.

Failing to implement Incident Management may result in the following adverse effects:
As nobody is responsible for monitoring and escalating incidents, incidents may become unnecessarily severe and reduce the level of service; users are referred repeatedly to other authorities, without the incident being resolved.

Specialists are constantly interrupted by phone calls from users, which means they cannot do their work properly. Consequently, several people may be working on the same incident, waste time unnecessarily, and come up with conflicting solutions.

There is a lack of management information about the user domain and services.

Due to the above problems, the costs incurred by the customer and the IT organization will be higher than needed.

4.3 The process

Figure 4.4 shows the input and output of the process, and its activities.

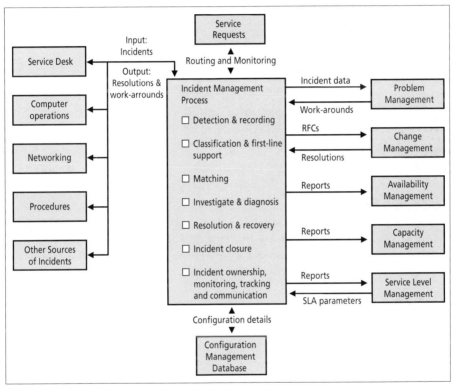

Figure 4.4 Position of the Incident Management process

4.3.1 Process Input

Incidents can arise from any part of the infrastructure and are often reported by users, but incidents may also be detected by other departments besides the Service Desk, and automatically through detection systems that have been set up to trap application and technical infrastructure events.

4.3.2 Configuration Management

The Configuration Management Database (CMDB) plays an important part in Incident Management as it defines the relationships between resources, services, users and Service Levels. For example, Configuration Management shows who is responsible for an infrastructure component, so those incidents can be routed more effectively. It also helps to decide on operational matters, such as diverting print queues and moving users to a different server. During incident registration, the configuration details are linked to the incident record to provide better information about the error. Where necessary, the status of the relevant components in the Configuration Management Database can be updated.

4.3.3 Problem Management

Problem Management has requirements for the quality of incident recording to facilitate the identification of any underlying errors. Problem Management assists Incident Management by providing information about problems, known errors, work-arounds and Quick Fixes.

4.3.4 Change Management

Incidents can be resolved by implementing changes, for example by replacing a monitor. Change Management provides Incident Management with information about scheduled changes and their status. Furthermore, changes can cause incidents if the changes are incorrectly implemented or contained errors. Incident Management will provide information to Change Management about these incidents.

4.3.5 Service Level Management

Service Level Management monitors the agreements with the customer about the support to be provided. Incident Management must be familiar with the Service Level Agreement (SLA) so that this information can be used when communicating with users. The incident records can be used to generate reports to determine if the agreed level of service is indeed being provided.

4.3.6 Availability Management

To measure aspects of the availability of services, Availability Management uses the incident records and the status monitoring provided by Configuration Management. A service can be assigned the status 'down', just like a CI in the CMDB. This information can be used to determine the actual availability of a service and the response time of the supplier. This capability requires time-stamping of actions taken in the progression of incidents, from the initial detection to closure.

4.3.7 Capacity Management

Capacity Management is concerned with incidents that relate to its imperative, such as incidents caused by a shortage of disk space or by slow response time. These incidents may be signalled to the Incident Management process by a system manager or by the system itself, on the basis of events.

Figure 4.5 illustrates the steps included in the process:
- **Incident acceptance and Recording** - the call is accepted and an incident record is created.
- **Classification and initial support** - the incident is coded by type, status, impact, urgency, priority, SLA, etc. The user may be given suggestions to solve the issue, even if only temporarily.
- If the call concerns a **Service Request** the relevant procedure is initiated.
- **Matching** - it is investigated if the incident is known, and possibly related to a problem or known error, and if there is a solution or a work-around.
- **Investigation and Diagnosis** - if there is no known solution then the incident is investigated.
- **Resolution and Recovery** - once the solution has been found, the issue can be resolved.
- **Closure** - the user is asked if they are satisfied with the solution and then the incident can be closed.
- **Progress monitoring and tracking** - the entire incident cycle is monitored, if it appears that an incident cannot be resolved in time, then escalation will occur.

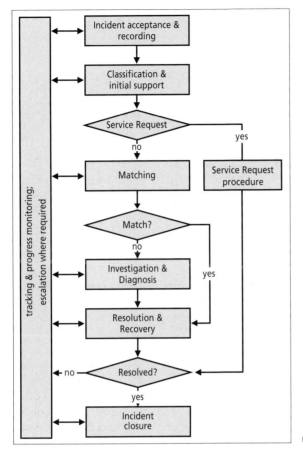

Figure 4.5 Incident Management process

4.4 Activities

4.4.1 Acceptance and recording

In most cases incidents will be recorded by the Service Desk where they are reported. All incidents should be recorded immediately when they are reported, for the following reasons:
- Recording backlogs are rarely correctly caught up with.
- The progress of an incident can only be monitored if it is recorded.
- Recorded incidents assist with the diagnosis of new incidents.
- Problem Management can use recorded incidents to uncover the causes.
- It is easier to determine the impact if all calls have been recorded.
- Without recording, compliance with the agreed service levels cannot be monitored.
- Recording incidents immediately can prevent situations where either several people are working on the same problem, or nobody is doing anything to progress the incident to closure.

The place where the incident is noticed determines who reports it. Incidents can be noticed as follows:
- **Noticed by a user:** who reports the incident to the Service Desk.
- **Detected by a system:** when an application or technical infrastructure event is trapped, such as when a critical threshold is exceeded, the event is logged as an incident in the incident recording system, and where necessary routed to a support group.

- **Noticed by a Service Desk agent:** who ensures that the incident is recorded.
- **Noticed by someone in another IT department:** who records the incident in the incident recording system or reports it to the Service Desk.

Recording the same incident twice must be avoided. Hence, when recording an incident it is checked if there are similar open incidents:

- **If so (and they concern the same incident),** the incident information is updated or the incident is recorded separately and linked to the main incident; the impact and priority can be amended if necessary and information about the new user is added.
- **If not (not the same as an open incident),** then a new incident is recorded.

In both cases, the rest of the process is the same, although the following steps in first case are much simpler .

The following activities are undertaken when recording an incident:

- **Assigning an incident number:** in most cases the system automatically assigns a unique incident number. The user is often informed of the number so they can refer to it in later communications.
- **Recording basic diagnostic information:** time, symptoms, user, person dealing with the issue, location and information about the affected service and/or hardware.
- **Supplementing incident information:** with other relevant information about the incident (e.g. from a script or interview procedure) or from the CMDB (generally on the basis of the relationship defined in the database).
- **Alerting:** if there is an incident with a high impact, such as failure of an important server, then the other users and management departments are warned.

4.4.2 Classification

Incident classification aims to determine the incident category to facilitate monitoring and reporting. The more extensive the classification options, the better. However, this also demands a higher level of commitment from personnel. Sometimes it is attempted to combine several classification aspects in a single list, such as type, support group and origin. This is often confusing. It is better to use several short lists. This section addresses issues relevant to classification.

Category

First, incidents are assigned to a category and subcategory, for example on the basis of the suspected origin of the incident or relevant support group:

- **Central processing** - access, system, application.
- **Network** - router, segment, hub, and IP address.
- **Workstation** - monitor, network card, disk drive, keyboard.
- **Use and Functionality** - service, capacity, availability, back-up, manual.
- **Organization and Procedures** - order, request, support, communication.
- **Service Request** - request by the user to the Service Desk for support, delivery, information, advice or documentation. This may be covered by a separate procedure or dealt with in the same way as real incidents.

Priority

Next, the priority is assigned, to ensure that the support groups will pay the required attention to the incident. Priority is a number based on the Urgency (How fast does it need to be fixed?) and Impact (How much damage will there be, if not fixed soon). Priority = Urgency * Impact.

Service
A list may be used to identify the service(s) related to the incident, with reference to the relevant SLA. This list will also supply the escalation times for the related service as determined by the SLA.

Support group
If the Service Desk cannot solve the incident immediately, it is determined which support group should deal with the incident. This routing is often based on the category. When defining the categories, the structure of the support groups may have to be considered. Appropriate incident routing is essential for effective Incident Management. One of the Key Performance Indicators for quality of the Incident Management Process should therefore be "the number of calls routed incorrect".

Timelines
On the basis of the priority and the SLA, the caller will be informed about the estimated maximum time to resolve the incident (cycle time), and when they can call again. These timelines are recorded in the system.

Incident reference number
The caller is informed of the incident number for future reference.

Workflow position (status)
The incident status indicates its position in the incident workflow. Examples of categories include:
• New
• Accepted
• Planned
• Assigned
• Active
• Suspended
• Resolved
• Closed

4.4.3 Matching
After classification it is investigated if a similar incident has occurred previously, and if there is a solution or work-around. If the incident has the same symptoms as a problem or a known error, then the incident can be linked to it.

4.4.4 Investigation and Diagnosis
The Service Desk or support team routes incidents, for which no solution is available or which go beyond the expertise of the agent, to another support team with more expertise and technical competence. The support group will then investigate and resolve the incident, or route it to another support group.

During the resolution process, different agents can update the incident record with the current status and information about the actions, reviewed classification, time, and agent identification.

4.4.5 Resolution and Recovery
After successfully completing the analysis and solving the incident, the agent records the solution in the system. For some solutions, a Request For Change (RFC) will have to be submitted

to Change Management. In the worst case, if no solution is found, then the incident remains open.

4.4.6 Closure

Once a solution, which is satisfactory to the user, has been implemented, the support group routes the incident back to the Service Desk. The person who reported the incident is then contacted to verify that it has indeed been resolved. The incident can be closed if they confirm that it is solved correctly; otherwise the process is restarted at the appropriate place.

During closure, the final category, priority, affected service(s), and causative component (CI) must also be updated.

4.4.7 Progress tracking and monitoring

In most cases, the Service Desk, as the owner of all incidents, is responsible for progress monitoring. In that case, the Service Desk should also inform the user about the status of their incident. User feedback may be appropriate after a status change, such as further routing, a change in the expected cycle time, and escalation. During tracking and monitoring there may be functional escalation to other support groups, or hierarchical escalation to force decisions on the resolution.

4.5 Process control

Process control is based on the reports to the various target groups. The Incident Manager is responsible for these reports, and also for drawing up a distribution list and a reporting calendar. The reports may be highly detailed and customized for the following functions:

- **Incident Manager** - report required for:
  - Identifying missing links in the process
  - Identifying conflicts with agreements
  - Keeping track of the process
  - Identifying trends
- **IT Line Management** - report for the support group management; should facilitate control within each department. This requires information about:
  - Incident resolution progress
  - Incident cycle time in the various support groups
- **Service Level Management** - this report will primarily contain information about the quality of the services provided. The Service Level Manager will receive all information needed for Service Level reports to the customers. Reports to the customers should provide information about whether the agreements with respect to the Service Levels within the Incident Management process have been fulfilled.
- **Process managers of other Service Management processes** - the reports to the managers of other processes will primarily be informative. For example, Incident Management could provide the following information based on the incident records:
  - Number of reported and recorded incidents.
  - Number of resolved incidents, subdivided by resolution time.
  - Status of unresolved incidents and the number of unresolved incidents.
  - Incidents by period, customer group, support group and resolution in accordance with the SLA.
  - Incidents by category and priority, by support group.

4.5.1 Critical success factors

Successful Incident Management requires:

- An up-to-date CMDB to help estimate the impact and urgency of incidents. Alternatively, this information can be obtained from the user, but the information will be less complete, the information might be highly subjective, and this will take more time.
- A Knowledge Base, for example an up-to-date problem/known error database describing how to recognize incidents, and what solutions and work-arounds are available. This also includes supplier databases.
- An adequately automated system for recording, tracking and monitoring incidents.

Close ties with Service Level Management to ensure appropriate priorities and resolution times.

4.5.2 Performance indicators

Assessment of the process performance requires clearly defined parameters and measurable objectives, which are often referred to as Performance Indicators. These are reported on regularly, for example every week, to produce historical data that can be used to identify trends. Examples of such parameters include:

- Total number of incidents
- Average resolution time
- Average resolution time, by priority
- Averages resolved within the SLA
- Percentage of incidents resolved by first-line support (without routing)
- Average support cost per incident
- Resolved incidents per workstation or per Service Desk agent
- Incidents resolved without visiting the user
- Number of incidents (or percentage) with initial incorrect classification
- Number of incidents (or percentage) routed incorrect

4.5.3 Functions and roles

Processes cut horizontally across the hierarchy of the organization. This is only possible if the responsibilities and authorities associated with the implementation are clearly described. To provide flexibility it may be useful to use an approach based on roles. In smaller organizations, or to reduce costs, roles may be combined for example Change Management and Configuration Management.

Incident Manager

In many organizations, the role of the Incident Manager is assigned to the Service Desk Manager. The Incident Manager is responsible for:

- Monitoring the effectiveness and efficiency of the process
- Controlling the work of the support groups
- Making recommendations for improvement
- Developing and maintaining the Incident Management system

Support group personnel

- First-line support is responsible for recording, classifying, matching, routing, resolving and closing incidents.
- The other support groups are primarily involved in investigation, diagnosis, and recovery, all within the set priorities.

4.6 Costs and problems

4.6.1 Costs
Costs associated with Incident Management include initial implementation costs, such as defining the process, training and instructing personnel, and the selection and purchase of tools to support the process. Selecting the tools can be time-consuming. There are also running costs associated with the personnel and use of the tools. These costs depend greatly on the Incident Management structure, scale of the activities, responsibilities, and the number of sites.

4.6.2 Problems
The introduction and implementation of Incident Management can be affected by the following problems:
- **Users and IT staff bypassing Incident Management procedures** - if users resolve errors by themselves, or directly contact specialist staff, without following the procedures, the IT organization will not get information about the service level and the number of errors. Similarly, management reports will not adequately describe the situation.
- **Incident overload and backlog** - if there are an unexpectedly large number of incidents, there will be insufficient time and the incidents will not be recorded effectively. This happens because before entering the information properly the next user has to be served. Incidents are not clearly described and the procedures for allocating and routing incidents are not properly followed up. Consequently, resolution becomes inefficient and the workload increases even more. If the number of open incidents increases greatly, a procedure for deploying spare capacity within the organization can prevent overloads.
- **Escalations** - in Incident Management, incidents that are not resolved quickly enough may escalate. Too many escalations may have an adverse impact on the specialists who are thereby distracted from their regular work.
- **Lack of a Service Catalog and Service Level Agreements** - if the services and products that are supported are not clearly defined, then it is difficult for Incident Management to refuse to help users.
- **Lack of commitment** - resolving incidents using a process-based approach normally requires changes to the culture and a higher level of commitment from personnel. This may engender serious resistance within the organization. Effective Incident Management requires real staff commitment, not just involvement.

Chapter 5

Problem Management

5.1 Introduction

As you read in the preceding chapter, Incident Management takes action if there is an incident, and stops activities once the situation has been recovered. This means that the root cause of the incident is not always uncovered, and the incident may recur.

Problem Management investigates the infrastructure and the available registrations, including the Incident Database, to identify the underlying causes of actual and potential errors in the provision of services. These investigations are needed because the infrastructure is complex and distributed, and the links between incidents may not be obvious. For example, several errors may lie at the base of a problem, while several problem definitions may be associated with the same error. First we have to identify a cause. Once the underlying cause has been identified, the problem becomes a known error. A Request For Change (RFC) may then be raised to eliminate the cause. Even after that, Problem Management continues to track and monitor known errors in the infrastructure. For this reason, information is recorded about all identified known errors, their symptoms, and the solutions available.

5.1.1 Definitions of 'problem' and 'known error'

Figure 5.1 shows the relationship between a problem, known error and RFC, and defines these terms.

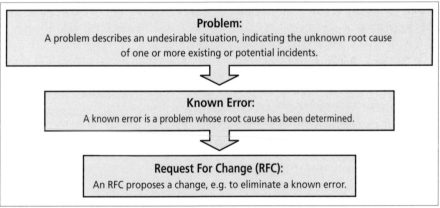

Figure 5.1 Relationship between problems & known errors (source: OGC)

5.1.2 Relationship with Incident Management

Problem Management supports Incident Management by providing work-arounds and quick fixes, but does not have responsibility for resolving the incident. Incident Management aims to solve an error quickly, by whatever means possible, including a work-around, while Problem Management takes the time to identify the cause and eliminate it. An incident can never 'become' a problem. However, in addition to the incident, a related problem can be defined. Thus, the investigation of the problem can lead to a solution for the current incident if it is still open.

Figure 5.2 shows the relationships between incidents, problems, known errors and changes.

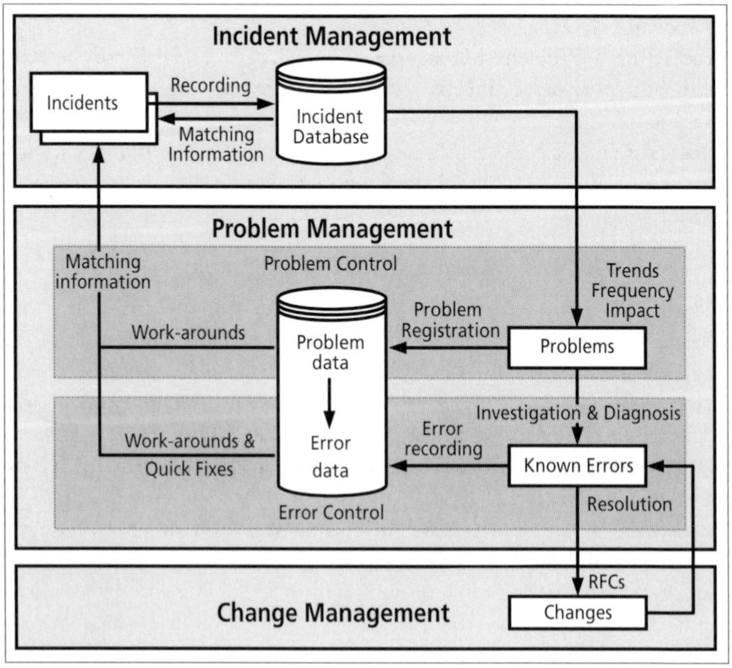

Figure 5.2 Relationships between Incident Management, Problem Management and Change Management

5.2 Objective

The objective of Problem Management is to root out the underlying cause of problems and consequently prevent incidents. Problem Management includes proactive and reactive activities. Reactive Problem Management aims to identify the root cause of past incidents and presents proposals for improvement or rectification. Proactive Problem Management aims to prevent incidents by identifying weaknesses in the infrastructure and making proposals to eliminate them.

Problem Management ensures that:
• Long-term errors are identified, documented and tracked.
• Symptoms and permanent or temporary solutions for errors are documented.
• Request For Changes are raised to modify the infrastructure.
• New incidents are prevented.
• Reports are issued about the quality of the IT infrastructure and the process.

Problem Management can quickly improve the quality of service by significantly reducing the number of incidents and reducing the workload on the IT organization. Some of the advantages include:
• **Improved IT service quality and management** - as errors are documented and/or eliminated.
• **Increased user productivity** - by improving service quality.
• **Increased support personnel productivity** - as solutions are documented, even less experienced Incident Management agents can resolve incidents more quickly and efficiently.
• **Improved IT service reputation** - because the stability of the services is increased, customers are more likely to entrust the IT organization with new business activities.
• **Enhanced management and operational knowledge and learning** - Problem Management

stores historical information that can be used to identify trends, and which can then lead to measures to prevent new incidents. Historical information is also useful for investigation and diagnosis, and when preparing RFCs.

- **Improved incident recording** - Problem Management introduces standards for incident recording and classification to identify problems and their symptoms effectively. This also improves incident reporting.
- **Higher first-line resolution rate** - as Problem Management makes solutions to incidents and problems, and work-arounds available in a knowledge base, first-line support is more likely to be able to solve incidents.

5.3 The process

The inputs to Problem Management are:
- Incident details
- Work-arounds defined by Incident Management
- Configuration details from the Configuration Management Database (CMDB)
- Supplier details about the products used in the infrastructure, including technical details and the known errors for those products)]
- Details about the infrastructure and the way in which it behaves, such as capacity records, performance measurements, Service Level reports, etc.

The major activities of Problem Management are:
- **Problem Control:** defining and investigating problems
- **Error Control:** monitoring known errors and raising RFCs
- **Proactive Problem Management:** Preventing incidents by improving the infrastructure
- **Providing information:** reports on the results and major problems

Outputs include:
- Known errors
- Requests For Change (RFC)
- Up-to-date problem records (updated with information about solutions and/or work-arounds)
- Closed problem record once the cause has been eliminated
- Management information

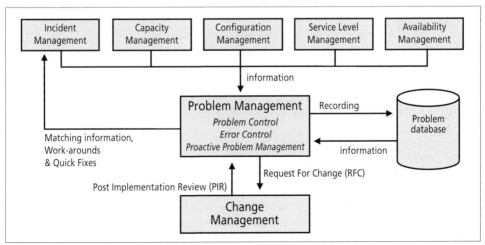

Figure 5.3 Position of the Problem Management process

The following processes are linked to Problem Management:

5.3.1 Incident Management

Incident Management is an important partner of Problem Management. Effective incident records are essential for successful Problem Management as this information is used to identify problems.

Problem Management supports Incident Management. Problem Management studies the problem, and - until a solution for the problem has been found - Problem Management can provide Incident Management with a work-around (found while studying the problem) to deal with the incident. Once the cause has been identified and a known error has been defined, it may be possible to provide a Quick Fix that will prevent further incidents for the time being, or to reduce the damage of an incident. If possible, Problem Management will provide an RFC that will lead to a definitive resolution.
Note: both Incident Management and Problem Management can provide work-arounds.

5.3.2 Change Management

Change Management is responsible for the controlled implementation of changes, including the RFCs proposed by Problem Management to eliminate problems. Change Management is responsible for assessing the impact and required resources, planning, coordinating and evaluating requested changes, and informing Problem Management about the progress and completion of corrective changes. These corrective changes are evaluated in consultation with Problem Management. This results in a Post-Implementation Review (PIR), after which the known errors can be closed by Error Control, and relevant (open) incident records can be closed as well.

5.3.3 Configuration Management

Configuration Management provides essential information about elements of the infrastructure, blueprints, hardware and software configurations, services, and other relationships such as 'is connected to', 'uses', and 'forms part of'. These relationships are vitally important to the Problem Management investigations.

5.3.4 Availability Management

Availability Management aims to plan and realize the agreed availability levels, and provides information to Problem Management. Problem Management supports Availability Management by identifying the causes of unavailability and remedying them. Availability Management addresses the design and architecture of the infrastructure and aims to prevent problems and incidents by optimizing availability planning and monitoring.

5.3.5 Capacity Management

Capacity Management optimizes the utilization of the IT resources. Capacity Management provides essential information to Problem Management that can be used to define problems. Problem Management supports Capacity Management by identifying the causes of capacity-related problems and rectifying them.

5.3.6 Service Level Management

Service Level Management includes negotiating and concluding agreements about the quality of IT services and providing those services. Service Level Management provides information to Problem Management that is used to define problems. The Problem Management procedures should support the agreed quality standards. Problem Management also fulfills this role for Financial Management and IT Service Continuity Management.

5.4 Activities

5.4.1 Problem Control

This activity is responsible for identifying problems and investigating their causes. The imperative of Problem Control is to advance problems to become known errors by diagnosing the unknown underlying cause of the problem. Problem Control activities are shown in Figure 5.4.

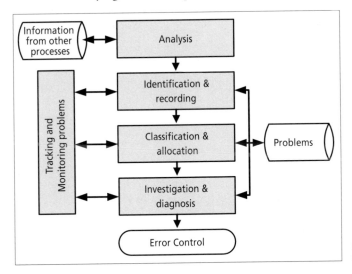

Figure 5.4 Problem Control
(source: OGC)

Problem identification and recording

In principle, any incident with an unknown cause should be associated with a problem. However, this will normally only be worthwhile if the incident occurs repeatedly or is expected to recur, or if there is a single serious incident.

The activity 'identifying problems' is often allocated to Problem Coordinators. However, personnel not primarily involved with problem identification, such as Capacity Management personnel can also identify problems. Their findings should also be recorded as problems.

Problem details are similar to incident details, but in this case there is no need to include information about the user, etc. However, the incidents related to the problem should be identified.

Examples of instances when problems are identified:
• Analysis of incident details indicates that an incident recurs, and leads to a significant volume or trend.
• Analysis of the infrastructure identifies the weak areas where new incidents may arise (also analyzed by Availability Management and Capacity Management).
• A serious incident occurs which requires a permanent solution, as further occurrences should be avoided.
• Service Levels are threatened (capacity, performance, costs, etc.).
• New incidents cannot be linked to an existing problem or known error.
• Recorded incidents cannot be linked to an existing problem or known error.

Trend analysis can uncover areas that need further attention. The additional efforts can be expressed in terms of the cost and benefits to the organization. For example, by identifying the areas that need more support and determining how relevant they are to the services provided.

This assessment can be based on the 'pain factor' of the incidents, which takes into account:
- Cost to the business activities of the incidents
- Number of incidents
- Number of users and business processes affected
- Time and cost of resolving the incidents

Classification and allocation

Problems can be classified by area (category). Identification points to the lowest level CIs that affect the problem. The classification is accompanied by an impact analysis, that is the seriousness of the problem and its effect on the services (urgency and impact). Next a priority is assigned, in the same way as in the Incident Management process. Personnel and resources are then allocated on the basis of the classification, and time is made available to solve the problem.

The classification includes:
- **Category:** identifying the relevant domain, for example hardware or software
- **Impact** on the business process
- **Urgency:** extent to which deferral of the solution is acceptable
- **Priority:** combination of urgency, impact, risk and required resources
- **Status:** problem, known error, resolved

The classification is not static, but may change during the life cycle of a problem. For example, the availability of a work-around or a quick fix may reduce the urgency of the problem, while new incidents may increase in the impact of a problem.

Investigation and diagnosis

Investigation and diagnosis is an iterative phase - it is repeated several times, each time getting closer to the intended result. Often, it is attempted to reproduce the incident in a test environment. More expertise might be needed, i.e. specialists of a support group may assist with the analysis and diagnosis of the problem.

Problems are not only caused by hardware and software. They can be caused by a documentation error, human or procedural error, such as releasing the wrong software version. It might therefore be useful to include procedures in the CMDB and subject them to version control. Most errors can be traced to infrastructure components.

Once the cause of the problem is known, the CI or combination of CIs responsible have been identified, a link can be established between the CI and the incident(s), then a known error can be defined. After that, Problem Management continues with the Error Control activities.

Error sources in other environments

In most cases, errors are only identified in the production environment. However, products from the development environment (external supplier or internal developer) may actually contain known errors (bugs). Note: For a development organization the software development environment is their production environment.

Normally, the development environment and suppliers should specify the errors contained in a specified version. Trade magazines often also provide information about bugs in popular products. Some vendors supply knowledge database for their products that contain the known errors for these products.

If the known error in the supplied product is not too serious, or there is a business imperative to move forward with the release despite this shortcoming, it may be decided to use the developed item in the production environment, and then it is essential that the known errors are included in Error Control. A link is provided to Incident Management to ensure that incidents resulting from the implementation can be recognized quickly. Where necessary, a work-around or quick fix can also be provided. Before starting the implementation, Change Management should decide if these known errors are acceptable. This decision is often taken under considerable pressure as the users are waiting for the new functions.

5.4.2 Error Control

Error Control consists of monitoring and rectifying known errors until they are successfully resolved, where possible and appropriate. Error Control does this by raising a Request For Change to Change Management, and by evaluating the changes in a Post Implementation Review (PIR). Error Control monitors all known errors from their identification through resolution. Error Control may involve many departments and covers both the production and development environments.

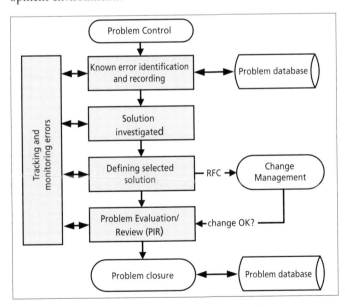

Figure 5.5 Error Control (source: OGC)

Error identification and recording

Once the cause of the problem has been identified and the relevant CI is known, it is assigned the status 'known error' and Error Control starts. In many cases a work-around for the problem will also be known, even if the error comes straight from the development environment. But in other cases it will still be necessary to find a work-around. This can then be communicated to Incident Management if there are still open incidents. The work-around can then also be used in incident matching.

Investigating a solution

Personnel involved in Problem Management assess what is needed to resolve the known error. They compare different solutions, taking into consideration Service Level Agreements, costs and benefits. They determine the impact and urgency of the RFC. All solution activities should be recorded and there should be facilities for monitoring problems (with status known error) and to determine their status.

Emergency fix

During the process, it may be necessary to approve an emergency fix if the known error is causing serious incidents. If an emergency fix or quick fix requires modification of the infrastructure then an RFC will have to be submitted first. If the matter is very serious and delay is unacceptable, the urgent RFC procedure may have to be followed.

Defining the selected solution

The optimum solution was determined in the previous step. However, it may be decided not to fix a known error, e.g. because there may be no business justification for doing so. For example, a company that is experiencing problems with its in-house developed ERP system may have put a moratorium on any code fixes on the existing system, as the company has made the strategic decision to move to SAP by year-end. In this, and similar cases, the cost to make the fix may not outweigh the benefits. In other cases, the impact is acceptable, the incident may be easy to remedy, or its recurrence is unlikely. In some cases it will simply be impossible to remedy the known error without a disproportionate effort. Whatever decision is taken about the known error should be recorded, so that it can be used in Incident Management.

Once a solution has been selected, sufficient information will be available to raise an RFC. Change Management then implements the actual fix of the known error.

Post-Implementation Review (PIR)

The change intended to eliminate the known error has to be reviewed in a Post-Implementation Review (PIR) before the problem can be closed. If the change was successful then the problem can be closed. In the Problem Database, its status is changed to 'resolved'. Incident Management is informed so that incidents associated with the problem can also be closed.
Note: Many organizations implement the process so that the problem can only be closed after the associated incidents have been closed (and thus verified for closure by the customer), otherwise the problem would have to be re-opened if the associated incidents could not be closed.

Tracking and monitoring

This activity monitors the progress of the problems and known errors during all process stages of Problem Control and Error Control. The objectives of this are:
• Determining if the severity or urgency of the problem changes, therefore creating the need to adjust the assigned priority.
• Monitoring the progress of identifying and implementing the solution, and monitoring if the RFC is implemented correctly. For this reason change Management regularly informs Error Control about the progress of the RFCs it has submitted.

Providing information

During the process, information about work-arounds and quick fixes is provided to Incident Management. The users may also be informed. Although the information is provided by Problem Management, the Service Desk disseminates the information. Problem Management

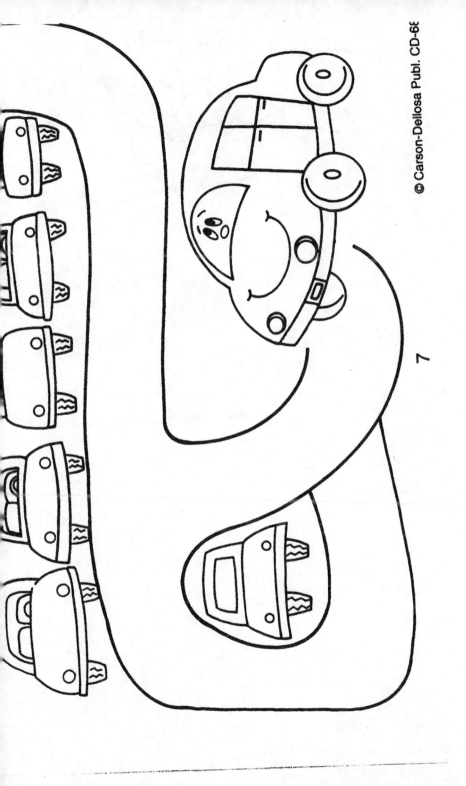

7

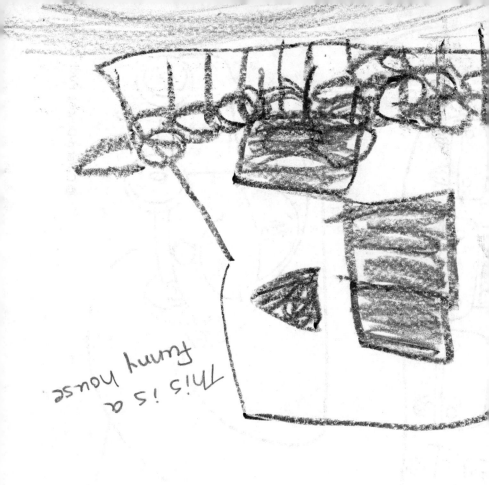

This is a
funny house

This is the sky.

These are flowers.

This is the
Sun.

Help Spence find his car in the parking lot.

uses the CMDB to decide what information should be provided and to whom. The SLA can also provide information about what has to be communicated and to whom.

5.4.3 Proactive Problem Management

In general, Proactive Problem Management is concerned with the quality of the infrastructure. Proactive Problem Management (i.e. preventing problems) concentrates on trend analysis and identifying potential incidents before they occur. This is done by looking at components which are either weak or may be overloaded. If there are several domains, then attempts will be made to prevent errors occurring in one domain from also appearing in other domains. Weaknesses of infrastructure components can be uncovered and investigated.

5.5 Process control

5.5.1 Management reports and Performance Indicators

The success of Problem Management is demonstrated by:
• The reduction in the number of incidents, by resolving problems
• The reduction of time needed to resolve problems
• Decrease of other costs incurred associated with resolution

Process parameters may also be reported for internal management purposes, to assess and control the efficiency of Problem Management.

Problem Management reports can be extensive and cover the following subjects:
• **Time reporting:** divided into Problem Control, Error Control and Proactive Problem Management and by support group and supplier.
• **Product quality:** the incident, problem and known error details can be used to identify products affected by frequent errors, and to determine if suppliers may have relevant contractual obligations.
• **Effectiveness of Problem Management:** details about the number of incidents, before and after solving a problem, recorded problems, number of RFCs raised, and resolved known errors.
• **Relationship between reactive and proactive Problem Management:** increasing proactive intervention instead of reacting to incidents shows an increasing maturity of the process.
• **Quality of the products being developed:** products handed over from the development environment should be of a high quality; otherwise they will introduce new problems. Reports about new products and their known errors are relevant for quality monitoring.
• **Status and Action Plans for open problems:** summary of what has been done so far, and what will be done next to advance top problems, including planned RFCs and required time and resources.
• **Proposals to improve Problem Management:** if the information about the above factors indicates that the process does not comply with the objectives of the Service Quality Plan, then proposals may be made for recording, investigation, proactive activities, and the necessary additional resources. Regular process audits may be carried out to plan and improve the process.

The reports depend on the scope of Problem Management. If the scope extends to products in the development environment, then known errors can be defined and monitored by Problem Management even while the software is being developed.

5.5.2 Critical success factors

Successful Problem Management depends on:

- Effective automated incident records and effective records of the behavior of the infrastructure.
- Feasible objectives and making the best possible use of the expertise of personnel, for example by agreeing on their availability at set times and reserving time to investigate the root causes of problems.
- Effective cooperation between Incident Management and Problem Management is essential. When allocating tasks and activities you should be aware of the conflict between fire fighting by Incident Management and identifying the root causes by Problem Management.

5.5.3 Functions and roles

Processes cut across the functions or departments of the organization and their hierarchy. Effective processes require that the responsibilities and authority associated with their implementation are clearly defined. To provide flexibility, it may be useful to take an approach based on roles. In small organizations, or for financial reasons, roles may be combined for example Problem Management and Service Level Management. The last bullet in 5.5.2 talks explains why many organizations avoid the combination of Service Desk / Incident Manager and Problem Manager.

Problem Manager

The Problem Manager is responsible for all Problem Management activities such as:
- Developing and maintaining Problem Control and Error Control
- Assessing the efficiency and effectiveness of Problem Control and Error Control
- Providing management information
- Managing Problem Management personnel
- Obtaining the resources for the activities
- Developing and improving Problem Control and Error Control systems
- Analyzing and evaluating the effectiveness of Proactive Problem Management

Problem support roles

The responsibilities of personnel with problem support roles include:
- Reactive responsibilities:
  - Identifying and recording problems by analyzing incident details
  - Investigating problems based on their priority
  - Raising RFCs
  - Monitoring the progress of eliminating known errors
  - Advising Incident Management about work-arounds and quick fixes.
- Proactive responsibilities:
  - Identifying trends.
  - Raising RFC
  - Preventing problems spreading to other systems

5.6 Costs and problems

5.6.1 Costs

In addition to the costs of support and diagnosis tools, you have to consider personnel costs. In the past, time was rarely set aside for these activities. Apart from internal IT personnel involved in Problem Management, there are the costs of hiring additional expertise from external suppliers. However, the benefits of these activities should easily outweigh their costs.

5.6.2 Problems

Where possible the following issues should be avoided when implementing Problem Management:

- **Poor link between Incident Management and Problem Management:** if there is a poor link between incident details and problem and known error details, then Incident Management will not be aware of the work-arounds for the problems, and Problem Management will find it difficult to assess and monitor problems. Less documented expertise about the IT infrastructure and less historical data will be available. The success of Problem Management largely depends on creating this link.
- **Poor communication of known errors from the development environment to the live production environment:** software and technical infrastructure transferred to the production environment should be accompanied by details of any known errors. Transitioning the knowledge of known errors at the time of the system deployment prevents wasting the time of the organization chasing after errors that are already known. Thus, there should be effective data exchange between both record-keeping systems, or there should be a unified system.
- **Lack of commitment:** if the previous approach was informal, there may be resistance against a strict Problem Management approach, particularly with respect to documentation and keeping time records. For this reason, personnel involved in Problem Management activities should be informed accurately and effectively of the developments in the implementation of the process.

Chapter 6
Configuration Management

6.1 Introduction

Every IT organization has information about its IT infrastructure. Such information is particularly likely to be available after major projects that are generally followed by an audit and impact analysis. However, the art is in keeping the information up-to-date. Configuration Management aims to provide reliable and up-to-date details about the IT infrastructure. Importantly, these details include not just details on specific items in the infrastructure (Configuration Items, or CIs), but how these CIs relate to one another. These relationships form the basis for impact analysis.

Configuration Management checks if changes in the IT infrastructure have been recorded correctly, including the relationships between CIs, and monitors the status of the IT components, to ensure that it has an accurate picture of the versions of Configuration Items (CIs) in existence.

If Configuration Management is effectively implemented, it can provide information about the following subjects:
- **Financial data and product policy**
  - What IT components are we currently using, how many of each model (version), and how long have we had them?
  - What are the trends in the various product groups?
  - What is the current, depreciated value of the IT components?
  - What IT components can be phased out and which require upgrading?
  - How much will it cost to replace certain IT components?
  - What licenses do we have, and are they adequate?
  - What maintenance contracts should be reviewed?
  - How standardized is our IT infrastructure?
- **Troubleshooting information and impact assessment**
  - What IT components will we need for a disaster recovery procedure?
  - Will the disaster recovery plan still be effective if the configurations are modified?
  - What IT components are affected by a rollout?
  - Which network is equipment connected to?
  - Which software modules are included in each suite?
  - What IT components are affected by a change?
  - What RFCs are under consideration for specific IT components, and what incidents and problems have occurred in the past and are currently relevant?
  - What IT components are responsible for known errors?
  - What IT components have been purchased during a period from a particular supplier?
- **Provision of services and charging**
  - What IT component configurations are essential for certain services?
  - What IT components are in use at a site, and who are they used by?
  - What are the standard IT components which users can order and which we support (product catalog)?

6.1.1 Basic concepts

In the terminology of Configuration Management, IT components and the services provided with them are known as Configuration Items (CIs). Each IT component whose existence and version are recorded is a CI. As shown in Figure 6.1, CIs can include PC hardware, all kinds of software, active and passive network components, servers, central processors, documentation, procedures, services and all other IT components to be controlled by the IT organization.

If Configuration Management is applied to Information Systems rather than Information Technology alone, the CMDB may also be used to store and control details of IT users, IT staff and business units. Those CIs will have to be subject to Change Management as well, for example in staff introduction and exit processes.

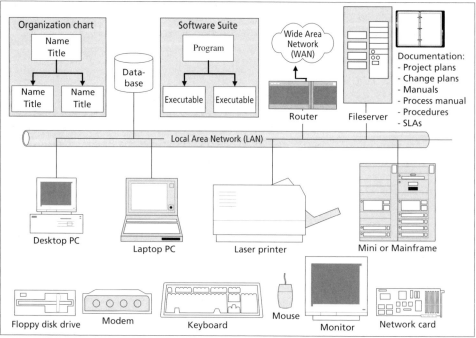

Figure 6.1 Configuration Items

All CIs are included in the Configuration Management Database (CMDB). The CMDB keeps track of all IT components and the relationships between them. In its most basic form, a CMDB could consist of paper forms or a set of spreadsheets.

Development departments often use something like a CMDB for version control of all program modules. Such version control is provided by some development platforms. A CMDB could consist of several physical databases that form a logical entity. It is advisable to optimize the integration.

The CMDB should not be confused with databases for stock management programs or auditing tools. Stock management programs only provide limited information about active hardware and software, network components and environment components. However, the CMDB also shows what the infrastructure should be like if everything is done as planned (see also Change Management), including the documentation. The data in the CMDB is in fact an administration of the authorized configuration of the infrastructure. A list of the differences (deltas) between asset management databases and the CMDB can provide valuable information.

Configuration Management should not be confused with Asset Management.
- **Asset Management** is an accounting process for monitoring depreciation on assets whose purchase price exceeds a defined limit, by keeping records of the purchase price, depreciation, business unit and location. An effective Asset Management system can provide a basis for setting up a Configuration Management system.
- **Configuration Management** goes beyond that, by also keeping information about the relationships between CIs (Configuration Items) and the standardization and authorization of CIs. Configuration Management also monitors feedback about current information such as the status of IT components, their location, and the changes that have been made to them.

6.2 Objectives

Configuration Management aims to assist with managing the economic value of the IT services (a combination of customer requirements, quality and costs) by maintaining a logical model of the IT infrastructure and IT services, and providing information about them to other business processes. Configuration Management implements this by identifying, monitoring, controlling and providing information about Configuration Items and their versions.

The objectives of Configuration Management include:
- Keeping reliable records of details of IT components and services provided by the organization
- Providing accurate information and documentation to support the other Service Management processes

6.2.1 Benefits

Configuration Management contributes to the cost-effective provision of high quality IT services by:
- **Managing IT components** - the IT components are essential to the services. Each element of the services will include one or more CIs and Configuration Management checks what happens to them.
- **High quality commercial services** - Configuration Management assists with processing changes, identifying and solving problems, and supporting users. This reduces the number of errors and therefore also reduces costs by preventing duplication of effort.
- **Effective problem solving** - Configuration Management assists with localizing the affected CIs and manages the modification and replacement of the CIs. Configuration Management also provides information about trends as an input to Problem Management.
- **More rapid processing of changes** - Configuration Management facilitates rapid and accurate impact analysis so changes can be processed more quickly and more effectively.
- **Better control of software and hardware** - the rollout of packages can be combined, possibly also with hardware rollouts, such that the whole combination can be tested in advance. The CMDB and baselines (infrastructure snapshots, recorded positions) can be used to develop test and distribution plans for specific groups. The CMDB also contains details about reliable software versions for back-outs.
- **Improved security** - managing the versions used provides information about the authorized changes to CIs and the use of different software versions. Information from the CMDB can also assist with monitoring licenses.
- **Compliance with legal requirements** - illegal copies will be identified when audit results are compared with the CMDB. This can bring extra benefit, because illegal software can contain viruses. In this way Configuration Management can prevent the introduction of viruses to the

organization. Although, the introduction of illegal and contaminated software by staff may not be easily avoidable for some organizations, the fact that staff know that they will be discovered due to the existence of Configuration Management, CMDB and audits, and the subsequent disciplinary action that will be taken, can certainly discourage this practice. It is the thought that no-one will find out that will encourage staff to break the rules.

- **More precise expenditure planning** - the CMDB can provide information about maintenance costs and contracts, licenses and expiration dates.
- **Better support for Availability Management and Capacity Management** - these processes depend on correct configuration details for analyzing and planning services.
- **A solid foundation for IT Service Continuity Management** - the CMDB, if there is a backup copy of it in a safe place, can play an important part in restoring services after a disaster. The CMDB is also essential in identifying the CIs required for the disaster recovery, including the relevant procedures and the manuals if they are included in the CMDB.
- **Identification of hidden costs** - most personnel keep records about the part of the IT infrastructure they are responsible for. As there are different reasons for collecting this information there will be overlaps. Duplication and inconsistencies also bring additional costs and risks. To facilitate the identification of costs and to reduce the workload of other IT personnel it is recommended that the CMDB become a coordinated process of a limited number of individuals.

6.3 Process

Configuration Management process inputs include information about changes and information from a procurement process. The outputs are the reports to the other processes and to IT management. There is another output. In that Configuration Management provides CMDB data for the other processes to access while undertaking their activities.

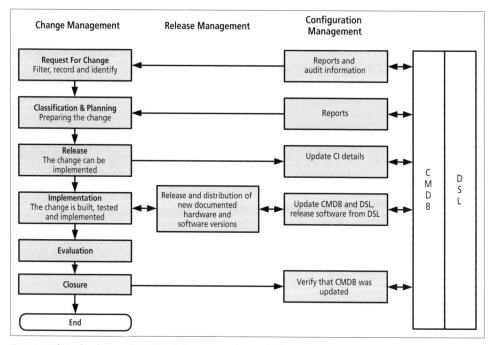

Figure 6.2: Relationships between the CMDB and other processes (source: OGC)

Configuration Management has links with a number of other processes.

6.3.1 Incident Management
Incident Management needs information across the whole infrastructure. When recording incidents, Incident Management needs to access CI information,e.g., to determine the CIs location and owner, to determine if there is a problem or a known error with a work-around associated with the CI, for which customer and what service it is intended for, and by which SLA it is covered.

6.3.2 Problem Management
Problem Management needs information about the complexity of the infrastructure. Problem Management should be able to link problems and known errors to CIs and uses CMDB data to analyze incidents and problems. Verifying the actual configuration of the infrastructure against the authorized configuration in the CMDB can point to deviations or defects in the infrastructure.

6.3.3 Change Management
Change Management uses the CMBD to estimate the impact of the changes to be implemented. Change Management authorizes changes, and changes have to be associated with the relevant CIs. Change Management is responsible for recording RFCs. Thus, Change Management provides the major input for updating the CMDB.

6.3.4 Release Management
Release Management provides information about release plans and versions, such as the planned dates of the major and minor releases. Release Management provides information about implemented changes. Before implementing a change it requests information about CIs such as the status, location, source code, etc.

6.3.5 Service Level Management
Service Level Management needs information about service characteristics, and the relationship between services and the underlying infrastructure. SLM data can also be stored on the CMDB against the CI as an attribute. The Service Level (eg. gold, silver, bronze) can be recorded against the service CI, or the component hardware or software CI.

6.3.6 Financial Management
Financial Management needs information about the use of services; for example who has a PC, and combines this with information from the SLAs to determine the prices to be charged. This process also monitors IT components and investments (Asset Management).

6.3.7 Availability Management
Availability Management uses the CMDB to identify the CIs which contribute to a service, to draw up plans for changes, and to identify weaknesses, for example using Component Failure Impact Analysis (CFIA). The availability of a service (chain of infrastructure components) is only as good as the weakest component (link in the chain). Configuration Management provides information about the composition of the chain, as well as about each of the elements.

6.3.8 IT Service Continuity Management
IT Service Continuity Management uses standard configurations from the CMDB (baselines) to specify disaster recovery requirements and checks that these configurations are available at the disaster recovery site.

6.3.9 Capacity Management

Capacity Management uses data from the CMDB to plan the optimization of the IT infrastructure, to allocate the workload and to develop a capacity plan.

6.3.10 Activities

Although, like the other processes, Configuration Management has a logical workflow, this is not followed so strictly. The activities tend to be carried out in parallel. The sequence shown below is primarily provided for developing the process when introducing it, and processing and implementing new information requirements.

- **Planning:** determining the strategy, policy and objectives of the process, analysis of available information, identifying tools and resources, creating interfaces with other processes, projects, suppliers, etc.
- **Identification:** setting up the process to keep the database up-to-date. The activities include developing a data model for recording all IT infrastructure components, the relationships between them and information about their owner or person responsible for them, status and available documentation. Procedures for new CIs and for changes to CIs must also be developed. As the demands for information are changing on a continuous basis, the identification of configuration data is changing continuously too.
- **Control:** control ensures that the CMDB is always up-to-date by only admitting, recording and monitoring authorized and identified CIs. Control ensures that no CI is added, changed, replaced or removed without appropriate documentation, such as an approved RFC or updated specification.
- **Status monitoring:** storing current and historical details about the status of CIs during their life cycle. Status monitoring can be used to identify changes in the status such as 'under development', 'being tested', 'stock', 'live use', and 'phased out'.
- **Verification:** verification of the Configuration Management Database by audits of the IT infrastructure to verify the existence of recorded CIs and to check the accuracy of the records.
- **Reporting:** to provide information to other processes and to report about the trends and developments in the use of CIs.

These activities will now be discussed in detail.

6.4 Activities

6.4.1 Planning

The aim, objectives, scope and priorities of Configuration Management have to be defined within Service Management and should be aligned with the business objectives. The relevant steps to implement Configuration Management are outside the scope of this book.

6.4.2 Identification

Identification relates to defining and maintaining naming conventions and version numbers of physical components of the IT infrastructure, the relationships between them, and the relevant attributes. Baseline configurations of current and future hardware are described in the form of CI clusters.

The general question about the identification of IT components is:

'What services and associated IT infrastructure components should be controlled by Service Management, and what information do we need for that?'

When developing an identification system, decisions have to be taken about the scope and level of detail of the information to be recorded. An owner or stakeholder has to be identified for each property (characteristic) to be recorded. The more properties that are recorded, the more effort it will take to update the information. The general question above can be detailed to determine the information to be recorded. Examples of such questions are:

- What resources are available for collecting and updating the information?
- How mature are our administrative and logistics processes?
- At what levels are components installed, replaced, developed and/or distributed by the organization, independently of the major component?
- What activities carried out by third parties should be measurable and under control?
- What components will impact the services if they are affected by a fault, and what information is relevant when diagnosing such faults?
- For which components should the status and status history be recorded?
- Of which components are several versions or variants used in the organization?
- Which components may affect the capacity and availability of the services after a change?
- Which high-cost components should be protected against theft or loss?
- What are the current and future information needs of the other processes?
- For which components should information such as the serial number, purchase date, and supplier be available, and what information does the accounting department require?
- What requirements are associated with the provisions of the SLA?
- What information do we need for charging purposes?
- Are our ambitions realistic or should some issues be deferred?

The answers to these questions provide information about a number of activities. A decision has to be made on the scope (breadth) of the CMDB and its level of detail (depth). The depth can be divided into: the number of levels, the relationships to be tracked, naming conventions, and attributes. These areas will be discussed below.

Scope
When setting up a CMDB and when updating the data model, it has to be decided what part of the IT infrastructure should be controlled by Configuration Management. For example, should PDAs, networked copiers and fax machines, keyboards and IT staff, be included, or are they out of scope? The Configuration Management scope affects the scope of diagnoses by Problem Management, impact analysis by Change Management, the verifiability of SLAs, the analysis and planning by Availability Management and impact management, etc.

Additionally, the IT services and their contribution to or impact on the customers' business activities can also be analyzed. Lastly, the agreements made with the users about support and services can be considered.

The scope can be divided into areas with their own requirements and approach. Examples of these areas are workstations, data communication, file, print and application services, central processing, databases and IT systems, and telephone services. To develop each area, a separate project can be set up in the relevant management environment.

The scope of the CMDB can include hardware and software, but also documentation, such as Service Level Agreements (SLAs), procedures, manuals, technical specifications, organization charts, people and project plans. Like other CIs, these documents will be physically present elsewhere, but are entered in the CMDB under their version number, date of publication, author and other information. Hence, these document characteristics can be controlled by Configuration Management and Change Management.

Figure 6.3 Shows the relationships between a service and CMDB components. Underneath this, we find the other CIs required for the service. Keeping track of these relationships makes it easier to determine the impact of incidents on the services. It is also possible to generate a report of all components used for a service. This information can then be used to plan improvements to the service. The CI 'service' can also have relationships with other CIs such as agreements with the customer in the form of a Service Level Agreement. Service B is completely outside the scope. This figure shows that not all CIs that contribute to "service A" are covered by the scope of the CMDB, which means that service A cannot be fully supported.

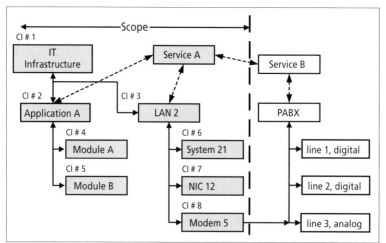

Figure 6.3 CMDB scope
(source: OGC)

After determining the number of areas in the scope we can identify the CI life cycle elements to be included by the scope. Are CIs included in the CMDB while their status is 'under development' or 'on order', or are they only included once they have been incorporated in the infrastructure? The advantage of including products under development is that their specifications cannot be changed without consultation and that their transfer to the management environment will be smoother. The status monitoring activity of Configuration Management will be affected by this choice, but it may also broaden the scope of Configuration Management in terms of the product life cycle.

Level of detail
Determining the level of detail for each type of CI is an important aspect of setting up Configuration Management. One size definitely does not fit all. This determines the information available about the CIs. To determine the level of detail, a plan is drawn up of the relationships between the CIs to be covered and the depth of the CMDB, and the names and attributes to be covered.

When determining the depth and the relationships to be covered, the requirements, associated workload and available resources must be carefully balanced. The number of relationships increases exponentially with the number of levels.

CI relationships

The relationships between CIs are useful for diagnosing errors and predicting the availability of services. Many different logical and physical relationships can be recorded.

- **Physical relationships:**
  - *Forms part of:* this is the parent/child relationship of the CI, e.g. a floppy disk drive forms part of a PC, and a software module forms part of a program.
  - *Is connected to:* e.g. a PC connected to a LAN segment.
  - *Is needed for:* e.g. hardware needed to run an application.
- **Logical relationships:**
  - *Is a copy of:* copy of a standard model, baseline or program.
  - *Relates to:* a procedure, manuals and documentation, a SLA, or customer area.
  - *Is used by:* e.g. a CI needed for providing a service, or a software module which is called by a number of programs.

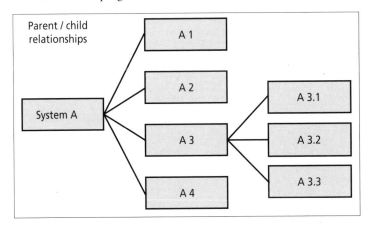

Figure 6.4 CI parent/child relationships (source: OGC)

Depth

When defining the levels of the system, a hierarchy of components and elements is created. The parent CIs are selected and the number of CI levels used for detailing are defined. The highest level is formed by the IT infrastructure itself. The lowest level is the most detailed level at which control must be exercised. Incorporating a CI in the CMDB is only useful if the control of it and related information is beneficial to other ITIL processes.

A relevant consideration for level and depth is that any CI registered on the CMDB has to go through the formal Change Management process in order for a change to that CI to be effected. Therefore, recording the mouse on the CMDB means that any request for a new mouse has to go through Change Management as an RFC as opposed to a Service Request. This is usually a good rule of thumb and a wake-up-call for some organizations going to too low a level of detail.

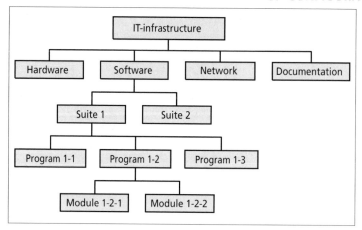

Figure 6.5 CMDB breakdown
(source: OGC)

The following general considerations apply to the definition of the CMDB.
• The more levels, the more information must be handled. This increases the workload and results in a larger and more complex CMDB.
• The fewer levels, the less control and information there is about the IT infrastructure.

If the CMDB has too little detail, the changes to underlying components cannot be monitored effectively. In that case, any change to the components of a parent CI will result in the creation of a variant[2] of the parent CI. For example, a PC available with two types of hard disk will occur as Variant A and Variant B. If there are many changes to child components, the variant numbering will become complex and difficult to maintain. However, if there are more underlying levels then the variants can be maintained at the appropriate level. More attributes can also be recorded for the child components, and known errors can be associated with them, and during diagnosis questions can be asked such as: 'Which driver is needed for this hardware option?', 'Which segment is the network interface card connected to?' and 'Which programs use this library?'.

Naming conventions
Each CI should have a unique and systematic name to ensure it can be distinguished from other CIs. The most basic option is a simple numbering system, possibly divided into ranges for each area. New numbers can be generated when a new CI is created. If possible, the names should be meaningful, to support communicatin with users.

The naming conventions can also be used for physically labeling CIs, so that they are easily identifiable during audits, maintenance and incident recording. Some of the naming conventions recommended by ITIL include:
• Physical labels for hardware should be easily accessible and readable by users, and should be difficult to remove. It could be agreed with third party service providers that support contracts refer to the labels. A user should also be able to read out a label when reporting an incident.
• Controlled documents, such as SLAs, procedures, and organization charts should be marked with a CI number, version number and a version date.

---

[2] Variants are used if there are several forms of a CI that co-exist; i.e. there is a parallel relationship. Versions exist, for example, if both an old and new version of a CI is used at the same time, i.e. there is a serial relationship. The effective use of these two concepts assists change planning. If each variant is then developed separately, separate version number systems should be introduced for each variant. This is undesirable as it makes the IT infrastructure more complex and increases the maintenance effort. In most cases it is advisable to continue to develop the source of all variants and where possible use the new version to create the required variants.

- Copies of software should be stored in the DSL (Definitive Software Library), see the chapter on Release Management. All software should have a CI number, and where possible, installed software should also have a CI number, version number, and copy number.

Attributes

In addition to the structure of CI levels, relationships, and naming conventions, the detailed development of the CMDB also includes attributes. Attributes are used to store information relevant to the CI. The following attributes may be used when setting up a CMDB.

ATTRIBUTE	DESCRIPTION
CI number/label or bar code number	Unique identification of the CI. This is frequently a record number allocated automatically by the database. Although not all CIs can be physically labeled, they all have a unique number.
Copy or serial number	Supplier's identification number in the form of a serial number or license number.
Audit tool identification number	Audit tools often use their own identifiers that may be different for each area. This attribute provides the link to this environment.
Model number/catalog reference	Unique identification used by the supplier in the catalog. Each version of a model has a different number, e.g. PAT-NL-C366-4000-T.
Model name	Full model name, which often includes a version identifier, e.g. 'PII MMX 400 MHz'.
Manufacturer	Manufacturer of the CI.
Category	Classification of the CI (e.g. hardware, software, documentation, etc.).
Type	Description of the CI-type, provides for the details about the category, e.g. hardware configuration, software package, or program module.
Warranty expiry date	Date when the warranty expires.
Version number	Version number of the CI.
Location	Location of the CI, e.g. the library or media where software CIs reside, or the site/room where hardware CIs are located.
Owner responsible	Name and/or designation of the owner or person responsible for the CI.
Responsibility date	Date the above person became responsible for the CI.
Source/supplier	The source of the CI, e.g. developed in-house, bought in from supplier X, etc.
License	License number or reference to the license agreement.
Supply date	Date on which the CI was supplied to the organization.
Accepted date	Date on which the CI was accepted and approved by the organization.
Status (current)	Current states of the CI, e.g. 'under test', 'live', 'phased out'.
Status (scheduled)	The next scheduled status of the CI, with the date and indication of the required action.
Cost	Cost of acquisition of the CI.
Residual value after depreciation	Current value of the CI after depreciation.
Comment	Text field for comments, e.g. to describe how one variant differs from another.

Table 6.1 Examples of attributes.

It depends on the Service Management tool if the relationship with incidents, etc. is included in the CMDB as a CI attribute or in another way. Generally, the numbers of the relevant CIs are included in the incident record, problem record and change record. Whatever approach is selected, relationships have to be maintained between the CI and the following records:

ATTRIBUTE	DESCRIPTION
RFC numbers	RFC number(s) currently or formerly open for the CI.
Change numbers	Change number(s) currently or formerly open for the CI.
Problem numbers	Problem number(s) currently or formerly open for the CI.
Incident numbers	Incident number(s) related to the CI.

Table 6.2 Other records related to CIs.

As discussed earlier, maintaining the relationships between CIs form an important element of Configuration Management. Depending on the type of database, these relationships may be included as CI attributes, or in a separate table.

ATTRIBUTE	DESCRIPTION
Parent CI relationships	Key or CI number of the parent CIs.
Child CI relationships	Key or CI number of the child CIs.
Other relationships	Relationships between the CI and other CIs, apart from the parent and child relationships referred to above, e.g. this CI 'uses' or 'is connected to'.

Table 6.3 Relationship attributes

Some databases have a field option to record changes of the field contents to provide a historical log. This can be useful for the 'Current status' fields to obtain information about downtime, repairs and maintenance. It can also be useful to track the ownership history.

Apart from the attributes discussed above, it can be necessary to keep lists of attributes with technical information for each CI type. Each type will have different features. For example, for a PC: hard disk capacity, BIOS manufacturer and BIOS version, RAM, IP number, etc. Many System Management systems will record this information, in which case it is sufficient to provide a link to the CI type record to prevent duplication of the information. However, you should remember that these systems provide the current information, without indicating if the results are from an approved change or an unauthorized situation.

Pick lists can be used to facilitate entering and updating attributes. Links can also be created to other reliable sources, for information about locations, users, departments, telephone numbers, budget holders, and budget numbers. There are many options, but the workload for maintaining these files must always be considered.

Baselines
A configuration baseline is a snapshot of a group of CIs taken at a specific point in time. A configuration baseline can be used as:
• An authorized/supported product that may be incorporated in the IT infrastructure (these baselines are included in the product catalog).
• Standard CIs for recording cost information (cost items).
• Starting points for the development and testing of new configurations.
• As a back-out if there are problems with new configurations after changes.
• As a standard for supplying configurations to users, e.g. a 'standard workstation'.
• As a starting point for supplying new software.

A standard workstation is a common example of a baseline. By limiting the number of different standard workstations it becomes easier to estimate the impact and required resources for rolling out new functions and improvements, and to test them. The baselines can also be used to set a policy for combining and planning changes, e.g. for Packaged Releases. Baselines help to reduce management costs and facilitate project planning.

A product catalog is another useful application of baselines. This catalog lists the certified configurations which may be used in the IT infrastructure, and which users can request. In that case, a new CI is a copy from the catalog, with a number and label.

Before a new model or product can be added to the infrastructure it has to be included in the catalog. This requires three decisions:
• **Business:** does it serve the business interests of the user?
• **Finance:** are the support costs acceptable?
• **Impact:** is the impact on the service acceptable?

Recording
The CMDB is initially populated with information from the financial records and existing IT infrastructure records and supplemented with technical data from suppliers. Only information with an identified stakeholder is recorded, and the organization must be committed to recording it (i.e. it must be prepared to update the information).

6.4.3 Status monitoring
The life cycle of a component can be divided into a number of stages, and a status code can be assigned to each stage. This depends on the characteristics of the IT infrastructure that the organization wants to record. Keeping a record of the date of each status change can provide useful information about the life cycle of a product: order time, installation time, and the maintenance and support it needs.

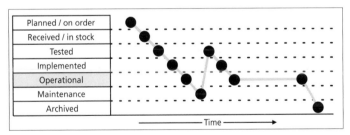

Figure 6.6 Example of CI status monitoring (source: OGC)

The status of a component can also determine what may be done with it. For example, if the status of non-operational spares is tracked, this hardware may not be deployed elsewhere without consultation, for example as part of a disaster recovery plan. A change in the status of a CI may be due to an authorized or unauthorized change or to an incident.

The following status classification could be used:
• **New CIs**
  - In development/on order
  - Tested
  - Accepted

- **Existing CIs**
  - Received
  - RFC open for the CI, new version has been requested
  - The change has been approved and included in the plans, a new CI and documentation (which is also a CI) will be provided
  - Undergoing maintenance
  - Down
- **Archived CIs**
  - Phased out
  - Deleted
  - Removed
  - Stolen
  - Sold or lease expired
  - In archival storage awaiting donation, sale, or destruction
  - Destroyed
- **All CIs**
  - In stock
  - Order has been received, or changed version available
  - Under test
  - Released for installation
  - Live (active), the CI is being used
  - Spare

6.4.4 Control

The information must be managed effectively to keep the CMDB up-to-date. Whenever an activity changes the recorded characteristics of a CI, or the relationships between CIs, the change should be recorded in the CMDB. Note: changes to characteristics of CIs can only be made by a change authorized by Change Management; Incident Management can only change the status of an existing CI.

Configuration Management controls all IT components received by the organization and ensures that they are recorded in the system. Hardware can be recorded when it is ordered or delivered, and software can be recorded when it is included in the Definitive Software Library (DSL).

One of the control tasks is ensuring that CIs are only recorded if they have been authorized and included in the product catalog. For this reason, Configuration Management maintains close ties with suppliers, Incident Management, Problem Management and Change Management.

If changes coordinated by Change Management are made in the IT structure then Configuration Management has to include this information in the CMDB. Although the ITIL publications are unclear about this, in practice, recording RFCs comes under the responsibility of Change Management. Changes are the major source of information about infrastructure changes and for updating the CMDB. As such, Configuration Management imposes certain requirements on the maturity of other processes in the organization, particularly Change Management, production and the purchasing department.

To ensure that the actual situation reflects the authorized CMDB, the following actions are

monitored:
- CI is added
- CI changes its status, e.g. 'up' or 'down' (useful for Availability Management)
- CI changes owner
- CI changes in relationship to another CI
- CI is removed
- CI gets other relationships with a service, documentation or other CIs
- CI license is renewed or modified
- CI details are updated after an audit

6.4.5 Verification and audits

Audits are used to verify if the current situation still reflects the details in the CMDB. For example, audit tools can automatically analyze workstations and report on the current situation and status of the IT infrastructure. This information can be used to check and update the CMDB. Audits may be carried out in the following situations:
- After the implementation of the new CMDB
- Six months after implementation
- Before and after major changes
- After disaster recovery
- At any other convenient time

The following questions are asked during an audit:
- Are all RFCs, in all stages of implementation, recorded in the CMDB, and is this controlled by Configuration Management?
- Is the CMDB still up-to-date, and if not, why? And what is the impact on Change Management (actual impact analysis of planned changes)?
- Does the naming of new CIs comply with the naming conventions?
- Are variants used correctly?
- Have the baseline configurations been recorded correctly, and are they immediately available?
- Do the contents of the Definitive Software Library (DSL) and the Definitive Hardware Store (DHS) correspond with the information in the CMDB? If not, why not?

Audits can also be carried out randomly, or if the Configuration Manager thinks that the information may not be correct. If there is a link with the audit tools, then audits or delta reports can be generated almost daily for the relevant area.
Audit tools should not be allowed to automatically update the CMDB when discrepancies are found. All discrepancies indicate that Change Management processes have been bypassed and therefore must be investigated.

6.5 Process control

6.5.1 Management reports and performance indicators

Configuration Management reports can include the following elements:
- Information about the quality of the process
- Number of observed differences between the records and the situation found during an audit (deltas)
- Number of occasions on which a configuration was found to be unauthorized
- Number of occasions on which a recorded configuration could not be located

- Attribute level differences uncovered by audits
- Time needed to process a request for recording information
- List of CIs where more than a given number of incidents or changes were recorded
- Statistical information about the structure and composition of the IT infrastructure
- Growth data and other information about IT infrastructure developments
- Summaries, reports and proposals for improvement, like recommendations for changes in the scope and level of CIs tracked by Configuration Management, due to business, technical, market price, and other relevant changes
- List of the personnel costs when implementing the process

6.5.2 Critical success factors

A condition for successful Configuration Management is that appropriate information is received to keep the database up-to-date. This means that the links with Change Management must be strictly maintained. There should always be a stakeholder for the characteristics to be recorded.

When introducing the process it is essential that the implementation is divided into stages correctly. Attempts to introduce the required recording suddenly, generally fail because the discipline required for Configuration Management cannot be suddenly instilled. The records maintained before the introduction of the process should be phased out to prevent duplication. When introducing the process, it is important to promote some clear advantages of Configuration Management (Quick Wins). It is also important that the recording elements of the process are allocated to personnel who not only have the required skills but also the appropriate attitude.

6.5.3 Functions and roles

Processes cut across the hierarchy of the organization. This is only possible if the responsibilities and authority associated with their implementation are clearly defined. To provide flexibility, it may be useful to take an approach based on roles and responsibilities. In small organizations, or for financial reasons, roles may be combined for example Change Management and Configuration Management. The tasks of the Configuration Manager could include:
- Propose changes to the scope and level of detail of Configuration Management
- Ensuring that the Configuration Management process is communicated throughout the organization
- Providing personnel and training for the process
- Developing the identification system and naming conventions
- Developing the interfaces to other processes
- Evaluating existing systems and implementing new systems
- Planning and implementing the population of the CMDB
- Creating reports
- Organizing configuration audits

6.6 Costs and problems

6.6.1 Costs

The costs of the introduction and implementation of Configuration Management largely depend on its scope and level of detail. These costs include the costs of hardware, software and personnel. The costs of hardware and software depend on:
- Additional hardware required, and its configuration

- Additional software required and its configuration
- License fees based on number of users
- Application and database design, population, customization and implementation
- Database development
- Database maintenance
- Additional personnel costs associated to the process

The personnel costs depend primarily on the size of the organization and level of detail of the CMDB.

6.6.2 Problems

The IT organization should make a clear commitment to the characteristics of the IT infrastructure to be recorded, and it should provide the necessary resources for this form of management. The organization should also commit itself to the use of the CMDB and should incorporate any relevant data and data structures from any relevant databases used before the introduction of the CMDB into the CMDB.

The following problems may affect successful implementation:
- **Wrong CMDB scope or CI level of detail** - if the CMDB scope is too small, important parts of the infrastructure won't be easily checked, fixed, secured, or restored. If the CMDB scope is too large, the cumbersomeness of the database will be an obstacle that slows down all service management processes. If there are too many levels, attributes, and relationships, it will take a great effort to maintain the CMDB. Too little detail can mean recording insufficient information about the CIs and related incidents, problems, known errors and RFCs.
- **Inadequate manual systems** - some organizations want to keep paper records for as long as possible and only purchase automated tools when this becomes unfeasible. This can introduce delays, confusion, and a shortage of personnel and resources. It is better to select a tool earlier, on the basis of the functional requirements.
- **Affect of urgent changes** - there will always be situations where changes have to be implemented quickly. This often happens outside normal office hours. If the CMDB is also relevant in this situation, it is advisable to immediately record the change in the CMDB, but the person responsible may not be present. If this can wait till the next working day then the change records and the CMDB should be updated as soon as possible.
- **Over ambitious schedules** - if the schedule for the changes (RFCs) does not allow time for implementing Configuration Management, then the work will be delayed and Configuration Management will appear to be the bottleneck. Realistic schedules should be drawn up on the basis of past experience.
- **Management acceptance** - because Configuration Management is a relatively new process that is not always clearly visible, people may be hesitant to accept it. There must be sufficient commitment for its successful implementation. Hence, the Configuration Manager must promote the process and inform the rest of the organization about it. Experience shows that the process costs will be much lower if Configuration Management is introduced as a separate discipline with dedicated staff and a manager responsible for the process.
- **Bypassing the process** - personnel in a hurry will try to bypass Configuration Management. If this situation still exists, even after providing all the information about the disadvantages of bypassing the process, disciplinary measures may have to be taken.

Chapter 7
Change Management

7.1 Introduction

The rapid development of IT technology and the business market means that change is now a matter of course. However, experience shows that incidents affecting business applications are often related to changes. The causes for such incidents are numerous: they may be caused by carelessness, a lack of resources, insufficient preparation, poor impact analysis, and inadequate testing or teething problems. If the incidents related to changes are not brought under control, the IT service provider, and consequently the business itself, can spiral out of control. The number of incidents rises, with each incident requiring fire fighting, which in turn may easily lead to new incidents. The daily planning often fails to take the increasing pressure of work into account. This in turn has an impact on the routine operation and maintenance of IT services.

Change Management aims to manage the process of change and consequently limit incidents related to changes. The motto of Change Management is:

> *Not every change is an improvement, but every improvement is a change.*

Figure 7.1 shows the cycle of changes as a process supplied with proposals for new developments and improvements (Service Delivery and Problem Management), changes (requests made to Change Management) and solutions (Problem Management):
- **Innovation and improvement** - the introduction of new services and new technical capability in the IT infrastructure will be responsible for some of the new, long-term errors in the IT infrastructure.
- **Changes** - anything from a minor installation to the relocation of a mainframe; if done carelessly, changes will introduce long-term errors in the IT infrastructure.
- **Corrective measures** - aim to correct the newly introduced long-term errors.

Change Management operates like a thermostatic control between **flexibility** (allowing changes which may lead to long-term errors) and **stability** (allowing changes to remedy long-term errors). Corrective measures reduce the number of incidents, as a result of which the pressure of work will also fall. Returning to the thermostatic control analogy, the water temperature is analogous to the rate of change and innovation the organization can cope with. Newer homes are being fitted with showers with thermostatic controls which automatically compensate for any changes in water pressure. Consequently, if someone turns on the cold water tap elsewhere in the house, the person in the shower will not get scalded.

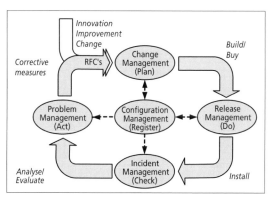

Figure 7.1 Inputs to the change process

85

7.1.1 Basic terms

Change authorities

There are two authorities in Change Management:

- **The Change Manager:** the person responsible for filtering, accepting and classifying all Requests For Change (RFC). In a large organization, the Change Manager may be supported by Change Coordinators who represent him or her by liaising with the various areas of the organization. Change Management is also responsible for obtaining the required authorization. To some extent, the process already has the authorization by declaration, but it may be necessary to approach the IT Management (e.g. Steering Committee or Executive Committee) for some of the changes. The Change Manager is also responsible for planning and coordinating the implementation of the changes.

- **The Change Advisory Board (CAB):** this consultative body meets regularly to assess and plan changes. Normally, only the more significant changes are presented to the CAB. A CAB/EC (Emergency Committee) should be appointed with the authority to make emergency decisions. The Board's membership is flexible and includes representatives from all major IT sections:
  - Change Manager (chair)
  - Service (Level) Manager
  - Representatives of the Service Desk and Problem Management
  - Line Managers
  - Business Managers (or their representatives) from the customer environment
  - User group representative(s)
  - Applications Development representatives
  - Software and Systems managers
  - Supplier Representatives

Process scope

The scope of Change Management is determined together with the scope of Configuration Management, as Configuration Management provides the information to assess the impact of changes. After implementing the change, Configuration Management will update the CMDB. If the CMDB keeps track of mice and keyboards, then replacing a keyboard counts as a change. Determining the scope is a dynamic activity, as the scope can change and therefore the need for information from the CMDB will also change. Hence, the scope should be reviewed regularly, and the CMDB data model should be updated correspondingly.

To ensure that Change Management and Configuration Management cooperate effectively, the changes and related information for the CMDB have to be recorded. It could be assumed that a number of routine management tasks, which are clearly defined and covered by procedures (standardized), need not be controlled by Change Management. Examples of such routine activities include mounting backup tapes, creating user IDs. In that case, the activities are not processed as changes, but at most are classified as Service Requests under Incident Management. A careful assessment of routine operations can be useful to prevent Change Management becoming too bureaucratic.

One way of handling this is to define so called pre-authorized changes (or 'category 0') which are registered (preferably by the requester themselves) into the change database, but do not require effort from Change Management procedures. For example, if there are fourteen steps that are usually followed when a new employee is hired (establish an account, set up his or her workstation, set up e-mail, etc.), this type of routine occurrence does not require the scrutiny that significant changes to the infrastructure do. As a result, these kinds of standard changes become a repeatable template and are treated as pre-authorized Service Requests.

7.2 Objective

The objective of Change Management is to ensure that standard methods and procedures are used, such that changes can be dealt with quickly, with the lowest possible impact on service quality. All changes should be traceable, in other words, one can answer the question, "what changed"?

7.2.1 Advantages

To be able to provide IT services effectively, the organization should be able to deal with a large number of changes smoothly and responsibly.

Specific advantages of Change Management include:
• Reduced adverse impact of changes on the quality of IT services.
• Better estimates of the costs of proposed changes.
• Fewer changes are reversed, and any back-outs that are implemented proceed more smoothly.
• Enhanced management information is obtained about changes, which enables a better diagnosis of problem areas.
• Improved user productivity through more stable and better IT services.
• Improved IT personnel productivity, as they are not distracted from their planned work by urgent changes or back-out procedures.
• Increased ability to accommodate frequent changes without creating an unstable IT environment.

7.3 The process

The Change Management process approves or rejects each RFC. The process is facilitated by the Change Manager, but actual decisions about more significant changes are taken by the Change Advisory Board (CAB). The CAB has members from many parts of the organization, as well as customers and suppliers. Configuration Management is responsible for providing information about the potential impact of the proposed change.

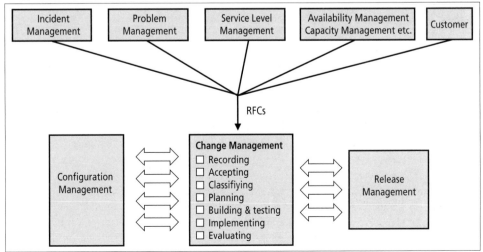

Figure 7.2 Position of Change Management

Inputs for Change Management include:
- RFCs
- CMDB information (specifically the impact analysis for changes)
- Information from other processes (Capacity Database, budget information, etc.)
- Change planning (Forward Schedule of Change: FSC)

Process outputs include:
- Updated change planning (Forward Schedule of Change: FSC)
- Triggers for Configuration Management and Release Management
- CAB agenda, minutes and action items
- Change Management reports

Change Management has the following relationships with other processes.

7.3.1 Incident Management
Incident Management has a two-sided relationship with Change Management. On the one hand, Change Management puts through changes requested by Incident Management to take away the effect of an incident, or changes requested by Problem Management that eliminate the root cause of incidents. On the other hand, despite the many precautions, the implementation of changes still can lead to incidents. These may be related to poor implementation, or to users who were not adequately prepared for the change. Relevant personnel in Incident Management must be informed of the implementation of changes, so that they can quickly identify and remedy any related incidents.

7.3.2 Configuration Management
Change Management and Configuration Management are tightly coupled processes, so much so that the two processes can effectively be integrated, a step recommended in the ITIL Service Support guidance.
Changes are recorded under the control of Configuration Management, and impact analysis of changes is also done by Configuration Management. Configuration Management identifies the relationships between the CI (in the change being addressed) and other CIs, to show what is affected by the change.

7.3.3 Problem Management
The relationship between Change Management and Problem Management is much like that between Change Management and Incident Management. On the one hand changes are often requested to solve problems. On the other hand, if the implementation of changes is not adequately controlled, the changes can introduce new problems.

7.3.4 Release Management
Changes often result in the development and distribution of a new set of applications or technical infrastructure. This is implemented by Release Management. The rollout of the new versions of such systems is controlled by Change Management.

7.3.5 Service Level Management
Service Level Management is involved in determining the impact of the changes on services and business processes. Depending on the situation, Service Level Management may be represented on the CAB. If a change has a major impact or high risk, its implementation and the timeframe will always have to be discussed with the customer. Change Management reports to Service Level

Route 591 — Deer Valley

Look for RAP D service this fa

Check www Va eyMetro org periodica y for updates

Monday-Friday PM/Northbound
Lunes a Viernes, por la tarde hacia el Norte

See fo d out map for routes serving this area

Para las rutas que funcionan en este área, vea el mapa desplegable.

Waha a Ln

Union Hi s Dr

A

23rd Ave
21st Ave

Utopia Rd

B

Be Rd

19th Ave

C

Downtown Phoenix

Adams St

Washington St

Jefferson St

17

N
W
S
E

Route 591 — Deer Valley

Monday-Friday AM/Southbound
Lunes a Viernes, por la mañana hacia el Sur

23RD AVE AT UNION HILLS	19TH AVE AT WAHALLA	BELL/I-17 (DEER VALLEY)	JEFFERSON AT 17TH AVE	JEFFERSON AT 3RD ST
600a	605a	615a	650a	659a
624a	629a	639a	714a	723a
640a	646a	656a	736a	745a

WASHINGTON AT 3RD ST	ADAMS AT 18TH AVE	BELL/I-17 (DEER VALLEY)	19TH AVE AT WAHALLA	23RD AVE AT UNION HILLS
415p	421p	456p	507p	512p
435p	441p	516p	527p	532p
455p	455p	536p	547p	553p
520p	526p	601p	612p	618p

* These timepoints are estimated arrival times and should not be used to coordinate transfers.

* *Estos horarios de paradas son estimaciones sobre las horas de llegada y no deben usarse para ccordinar los transbordos.*

♿ *Las sillas de ruedas tienan acceso a todos los autobuses*

Management in the form of a Projected Service Availability (PSA) report. In this report, Change Management lists the changes to the agreed SLAs and the impact of the Forward Schedule of Changes (FSC) on the service availability.

7.3.6 Availability Management
Availability Management initiates changes that aim to improve service availability. It is verified if the intended improvement is actually obtained. Availability Management will often be involved in estimating the potential impact of changes, as such an impact could affect the availability of the service.

7.3.7 Capacity Management
The Capacity Manager should primarily be concerned with the cumulative effect of changes over an extended period, such as an increase in response time and the need for more storage capacity. On the basis of the Capacity Plan, Capacity Management will regularly propose enhancements and changes in the form of RFCs.

7.3.8 IT Service Continuity Management
Prevention measures and recovery plans that ensure the continuity of the services have to be monitored at all times, as infrastructure changes could make a plan unworkable or superfluous. Change Management works closely together with IT Service Continuity Management to ensure that IT Service Continuity Management is aware of all changes that could affect recovery plans and can take steps to ensure recovery can be completed.

7.3.9 Change Management activities
Change Management uses the following activities to process changes:
- **Submission** - not included in the Change Management activities, but supported by this process, as Change Management is responsible for ensuring that all changes are adequately recorded.
- **Acceptance** - filtering the RFCs and accepting them for further consideration.
- **Classification** - sorting the RFCs by category and priority.
- **Planning** - consolidating changes, planning their implementation and the required resources.
- **Coordination** - coordinating the building, testing and implementation of the change.
- **Evaluation** - determining if each change was successful and drawing conclusions for the next event (learning).

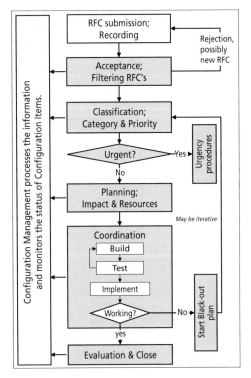

Figure 7.3 Change Management activities

7.4 Activities

7.4.1 Recording

Firstly, all RFCs have to be recorded or logged. When an RFC is submitted to solve a problem, then the number of the known error must also be recorded.

What constitutes an RFC?

Not every request for a modification is treated as a change: some routine management tasks that are clearly defined and covered by procedures (standardized) but do involve modifications can be dealt with as Service Requests (e.g. 'category 0' changes, see 7.1.1). This results in the following classification of changes:

- **Service Requests (here: standard changes)** - fully defined and approved changes, which are individually recorded, but not individually assessed by Change Management. These changes are made routinely. (Note: not all Service Requests are changes.)
- **Requests For Change** - all other requests for modification of the managed infrastructure.

Where do RFCs originate?

RFCs may concern all aspects of the infrastructure within the scope of the ITIL processes. Anyone working with the infrastructure can submit an RFC. We can identify several sources of RFCs, such as:

- **Problem Management** - proposes solutions to eliminate long-term errors to stabilize the provision of services.
- **Customers** - may request more, fewer or other services. These requests may be submitted directly as RFCs, or channeled through Service Level Management or IT Customer Relations Management.

- **Policy** - the tactical and strategic processes of the Service Delivery Set and the Managers Set can lead to RFCs to change the services. For example, Service Level Management, Availability Management and Capacity Management produce annual plans to improve the services, which they may later submit as RFCs.
- **Legislation** - if new regulatory changes are imposed on business activities, or if new requirements are introduced for IT security, Business Continuity and license management. The relevant processes control this.
- **Suppliers** - suppliers issue new releases and upgrades of their products and identify the errors remedied by them. They may also communicate that they no longer support certain versions, or that the performance of a version cannot be guaranteed (e.g. because of the Millennium bug). This may initiate the submission of an RFC by Problem Management or Availability Management.
- **Projects** - a project will often lead to a number of changes. Project management will have to coordinate this effectively with Change Management through the relevant processes, such as Service Level Management, Capacity Management, etc.
- **All other IT personnel** - in principle, anyone can submit proposals to improve the services. Specifically, IT personnel can contribute to the improvement of procedures and manuals.

RFC recording
Here are examples of the information that could be included in an RFC:
- Identification number of the RFC
- Associated problem/known error number (where relevant)
- Description and identification of relevant CIs
- Reason for the change including justification and business benefit
- Current and new version of the CI to be changed
- Name, location and telephone number of the person submitting the RFC
- Submission date
- Estimated resources and timeframes

7.4.2 Acceptance
After recording the RFC, Change Management will make an initial assessment to check if any of the RFCs are unclear, illogical, impractical or unnecessary. Such spurious requests are rejected, stating the reasons. The person who submitted the request should always be given an opportunity to defend his or her request.

A change leads to modification of the data in the CMDB, for example:
- A change in the status of an existing CI
- A change in the relationship between the CI and other CIs
- A new CI, or variation of an existing CI
- A new owner or location of the CI

If the RFC is accepted, the information required for the further processing of the change is included in a change record. Later, the following information will be added to the record:
- Assigned priority
- Assessment of the impact and required costs
- Category
- Recommendations by the Change Manager
- Date and time of authorization
- Planned implementation date of the change

- Backup plans
- Support requirements
- Implementation plan
- Information about the builder and implementers
- Actual date and time of the change
- Date of the evaluation
- Test results and observed problems
- Reasons for rejection of the request (where relevant)
- Scenario and evaluation information

7.4.3 Classification
Once an RFC has been accepted, its priority and category are specified:
- The **priority** indicates how important a change is relative to other RFCs, and it is derived from the urgency and impact of the change. If a change concerns the correction of a known error, then Problem Management may already have assigned the priority code. However, Change Management allocates the final priority code, after consideration of other RFCs being processed.
- Change Management determines the **category** on the basis of impact and resources. This classification determines the further consideration of the request, and therefore indicates the significance of the change.

Determining the priority
Here is an example of a priority code system:
- **low priority** - a change is desirable, but can wait until a convenient time (e.g. the next release, or scheduled maintenance).
- **normal priority** - no great urgency or major impact, but the change should not be deferred. In the CAB meeting it is given a normal priority when allocating resources.
- **high priority** - a serious error affecting a number of users, or an inconvenient error affecting a large group of users, or related to other urgent matters. This change is given the highest priority in the next meeting of the CAB.
- **highest priority** - the RFC concerns a problem that seriously affects the use of essential services by users, or it concerns an urgent IT change (e.g. new function for business reasons, an emergency legislation or a quick fix that cannot wait). Changes with this priority are classified as 'urgent changes'. Urgent changes do not follow the normal procedures, as the required resources are immediately made available. An emergency meeting of the CAB or the IT Steering Committee may be required. Especially for this purpose, a CAB/EC (Emergency Committee) should be installed, with the authority to make emergency decisions. All plans made earlier may be delayed or interrupted.

The codes could be associated with numbers, e.g. low=1/highest=4.

Determining the category
Categories are determined by Change Management, where necessary in consultation with the CAB, which indicates the impact of the change and the demand it makes on the IT organization. Some examples of categories:
- **minor impact** - a change requiring little work. The Change Manager can approve these changes without submitting them to the CAB.
- **substantial impact** - a change that will require significant efforts and which will have a substantial impact on the services. These changes are discussed at a CAB meeting to determine the required efforts and potential impact. Before the meeting, the relevant documentation is

circulated among the CAB members and possibly to specialists and developers.
- **major impact** - a change that will require significant efforts. The Change Manager requires prior authorization from the IT management or IT Steering Committee, after which the change must be submitted to the CAB.

The codes could be associated with numbers, e.g. minor=1/major=3.

Most changes fall into the first two categories. In addition to the classification, the groups working on the solution, and services affected by the change must also be specified.

7.4.4 Plans

Change Management plans the changes using a change calendar, or Forward Schedule of Change (FSC). The FSC contains details of all approved changes and their planning. Members of the CAB advise on the planning of changes, as the availability of personnel, resources, costs, affected service aspects, and the customer all have to be considered. The CAB acts as an advisory committee. Change Management has a delegated authority, as it acts on behalf of the IT management. Major changes may have to be approved by the IT management, before being presented to the CAB. This change approval can consist of three aspects:
- **Financial approval** - cost/benefit analysis and budget
- **Technical approval** - impact, necessity and feasibility
- **Business approval** - approval by the users of the required functions and impact

For effective planning, Change Management has to maintain contact with the project offices and all others in the organization who build and implement the changes. Moreover, careful consideration must be given to communicating the change planning effectively, possibly in the form of a Forward Schedule of Changes (FSC).

Change policy

RFCs can be combined in a single release. In that case, a single back out will suffice if something goes wrong. Such a bundled release should be considered as a single change, even if it comprises several changes. Releases can be planned with a functional objective for the business. They can cover hardware and software, and are implemented by Release Management. It is advisable to define a policy for this area and to communicate it to the IT organization and the customers (see also Release Management). The policy should aim to avoid unnecessary disruption to the user ('digging up the road every week').

In consultation with the affected IT departments, the CAB can specify regular time windows for implementing changes at a time which minimizes the impact on service. Suitable times could be at the weekend or outside regular office hours. Similarly, periods can be established during which few or no changes are allowed, such as during office hours or the end of the financial year when all user departments are closing their books.

CAB meetings

Information about the planning of a change should be distributed before the CAB meeting. Relevant documents and information about the points on the agenda should also be circulated in advance of the meeting.

The CAB should have a number of fixed items on the agenda of its meetings, including:
- Unauthorized changes
- RFCs which must be assessed by the members of the CAB

- Authorized changes that have not been submitted to the CAB
- Open and closed changes
- Evaluations of past changes

Estimating the impact and resources
When estimating the required resources and impact of the change, the members of the CAB, the Change Manager and all others involved (identified by the CAB) should consider the following aspects:
- Capacity and performance of the affected service(s)
- Reliability and recoverability
- IT Services Continuity Management plans
- Back-out plans
- Security
- Impact of the change on other services
- Recording and approval
- Required resources and costs (support and maintenance)
- Number and availability of required specialists
- Required cycle time of the change
- New resources to be purchased and tested
- Impact on operations
- Any conflicts with other changes

CAB members can also advise on the priority.

7.4.5 Coordination
Approved changes are communicated to the relevant product specialists who can then build and integrate the changes. The changes are tested before being implemented. Release Management can play an important role in building, testing and implementing approved changes. Appropriate attention should be given to communication to support changes.

Building
Not all changes have a specific building phase. For example, standard changes such as relocating a PC can be planned and implemented immediately.

Building may include the creation of a new software version, with new documentation, manuals, installation procedures, a back-out plan, and hardware changes. Change Management provides control and coordination, and is supported by Release Management and line management, which should work to ensure that there are appropriate resources to implement the plans.

A back-out procedure will have to be written as part of the delivery of a change to reverse the change if it does not provide the required result. Change Management should not approve the change if there is no back-out procedure. If the change impacts the user environment, then a communication plan will have to be written. An implementation plan is also drawn up during the building phase.

Performance indicators show to what extent the Change Management process is successful in effectively and efficiently dealing with changes, with the smallest possible adverse impact on the agreed service level. These indicators cover issues such as:
- The number of changes completed per time unit, by category

- Rate at which changes are implemented
- Number of rejected changes
- Number of incidents resulting from changes
- Number of back-outs related to changes
- Cost of the implemented changes
- A correlation between estimated resources and timeframes against actuals
- Number of urgent changes

Testing
The back-out procedure, change implementation, and envisaged result of the change should all be thoroughly tested. Consideration should be given to the criteria defined earlier by the CAB. In most cases, a separate test environment or test laboratory will be needed for testing. Early stages of testing can be carried out by the builders, but the change should not be implemented without some independent testing. This usually takes two forms - **user acceptance testing** where the business community (usually the customer of the change) tests the functionality of the change, and **operational acceptance** testing where those having to support and maintain the changed infrastructure perform an independent test. This will include technical support areas and the Service Desk. They will test support documentation, back-up and restore procedures etc. Clear instructions are also required for monitoring the quality of the test, and documenting the test results.

Implementing
Anyone in the relevant department who is responsible for the management of the IT infrastructure may be asked to implement a change to that infrastructure. Change Management ensures that the change is on schedule. There must be a clear communication plan indicating who has to be informed of the change, for example the users, Service Desk, Network Management, etc.

If a change cannot be adequately tested, it may be possible to apply the change to a small pilot group of users, and to evaluate the results before implementing it on a larger scale.

7.4.6 Evaluation
With the possible exception of standard changes, implemented changes should be evaluated. Where necessary, the CAB decides if any follow-up is needed. The following matters should be considered:
- Did the change lead to the required objective?
- Are the users satisfied with the result?
- Were there any side effects?
- Were the estimated costs and efforts exceeded?

If the change was successful, the RFC can be closed. The results are included in the Post Implementation Review (PIR) or change evaluation. If the change was not successful, then the process is restarted where it went wrong, using a modified approach. Sometimes it is better to roll back the action and to create a new or modified RFC. Continuing with an unsuccessful change often makes matters worse.

Procedures with an automatic time limit can help to ensure that change evaluations are not neglected. Depending on the nature of the change, an evaluation can be carried out after a few days, or after a few months. For example, a change to a PC that is used every day can be evaluated after a few days, while a change to a system which is only used once every week can only be evaluated after three months.

7.4.7 Implementing urgent changes

However good the planning is, there may be changes that demand absolute priority. Urgent changes are very important and have to be carried out as soon as possible. In most cases, resources devoted to other activities have to be diverted to these changes. Urgent changes can have a serious impact on the planned work. Hence, the objective is that the number of urgent or unexpected changes (priority 'highest') should be minimized. Some preventive measures include:

- Ensuring that changes are requested in time, before they become urgent.
- When remedying errors due to a poorly prepared change, the situation should not be rolled back beyond a previous version, the Previous Trusted State. Afterwards, an improved implementation of the change should be prepared carefully.

Despite the above measures, urgent changes may still occur, and they require procedures to deal with them quickly, without Change Management losing control of the process. If there is time, the Change Manager can organize an emergency meeting of the CAB/EC. If there is no time or if the request is made outside office hours, then there must be an alternative method for obtaining authorization. This doesn't have to be a face-to-face meeting, but could be a telephone conference call instead.

An example is mentioned in the Incident Management process, where an emergency fix can be applied to solve a serious incident. If the matter is very serious and delay is unacceptable, the urgent RFC procedure may have to be followed.

There may also be insufficient time for the normal tests. For example, a workstation controls a large machine that mixes starch used in making pills at a pharmaceutical manufacturer. If the workstation is not recovered within one hour of failing, the starch mixture hardens, and it takes two people two weeks to remove the hardened material manually with hammers and chisels. In the meantime, the company is losing thousands of dollars per hour because it is not manufacturing its pills. In such a case, the Change Manager will have to assess the risks, and decide on the implementation of the change. Afterwards, all the required stages of the normal process must be completed to ensure that any tests that were skipped are still carried out, and that the files are updated (change records and the CMDB), to ensure that "what changed"? is traceable.

7.5 Process control

7.5.1 Management reports

Change Management aims to strike a balance between flexibility and stability. Reports can be provided on the following issues to show the current situation of the organization:

- Number of changes implemented in a period (overall and per CI-category)
- List of the causes of changes and RFCs
- Number of successfully implemented changes
- Number of back-outs and their reasons
- Number of incidents related to implemented changes
- Graphs and trend analysis for relevant periods

Performance indicators show to what extent the Change Management process is successful in effectively and efficiently dealing with changes, with the smallest possible adverse impact on the agreed service level. These indicators cover issues such as:

- The number of changes completed per time unit, by category
- Rate at which changes are implemented
- Number of rejected changes
- Number of incidents resulting from changes
- Number of back-outs related to changes
- Cost of the implemented changes
- The number of changes within resource and time estimation

7.6 Costs and problems

7.6.1 Costs
- **Personnel costs** - In most cases, there are already personnel coordinating the changes. Still, additional personnel costs may be incurred in fulfilling the Change Manager task and setting up the Change Advisory Board. However, to some extent these costs will be offset by the release of the coordination effort already provided within the organization. In many cases, Change Management is introduced to improve the service quality, and the additional costs incurred are classified as quality costs. After a successful introduction the change coordination costs are offset by a reduction in the cost of solving incidents and problems.
- **Tool costs** - The costs of hardware and software have to be determined in advance. Often, when introducing several processes, an integrated tool is purchased for Change Management, Problem Management, Configuration Management and Incident Management. When dealing with complex IT environments, it becomes almost impossible to control these management processes without such tools.

7.6.2 Problems
The following problems may be encountered when introducing Change Management:
- Paper-based systems are too difficult to use and will present too many problems.
- There may be resistance against an umbrella Change Management authority that monitors all aspects of the IT infrastructure. In that case, IT personnel will have to be trained to become aware that all components of the IT infrastructure can have a significant impact on each other, and that changes applied to configurations require overall coordination.
- There may be attempts to implement changes without going through the agreed procedures. It is absolutely essential that there be an organizational reaction to such attempts. The integrity of the Change Management process depends on full compliance. Staff member complaints about and suggestions for improving the Change Management processes are to be tolerated and welcomed, respectively, but non-compliance must be dealt with decisively, or the entire process will be undermined.
- Other means of ensuring compliance with Change Management procedures include:
  - Undertaking regular audits, possibly by an independent auditor, to assess compliance with the Change Management procedures.
  - Management supervision of internal and external support staff and developers.
  - Ensuring control of all CIs and versions by protecting the CMDB and arranging for Configuration Management to undertake regular Configuration Audits.
  - Ensuring that Incident Management reports if users have access to hardware and software that is not included in the CMDB.
  - Incorporating the conditions and procedures in contracts with external suppliers.
  - Appointing a highly experienced Change Manager with a broad experience and sufficient business (this aspect is often underestimated) and technological knowledge. Getting the right person in the role is crucial and should not be overlooked as is often the case.

7.6.3 Suggestions

Some problems can be addressed by implementing the following suggestions:

- Ensure that each change follows the complete procedure.
- Communicate with all IT personnel and all suppliers to ensure that they accept Change Management, and do not try to implement changes without coordination.
- Ensure that changes are being evaluated.
- Work with Configuration Management to ensure that CI changes are entered in the CMDB.

Chapter 8

Release Management

8.1 Introduction

As organizations become increasingly dependent on IT processes the effective monitoring and protection of these processes also becomes more important. As the rate of change also keeps increasing, there is a growing need for controlling the process of change.

Changes to the IT infrastructure occur in a complex, distributed environment. In modern client/-server applications this often affects both the clients and the servers. The release and implementation of hardware and software demands careful planning in these cases. A release is a set of new and/or changed Configuration Items which are tested and introduced into the live environment together. A release is defined by the RFC that it implements. Release Management takes a planned project approach to implementing changes in IT services, and addresses all, technical or non-technical, aspects of the changes.

Release Management aims to ensure the quality of the production environment, by using formal procedures and checks when implementing new versions. Release Management is concerned with implementation, unlike Change Management that is concerned with verification. Release Management works closely with Configuration Management and Change Management, to ensure that the common CMDB is updated with every release. Release Management also ensures that the contents of releases in the Definitive Software Library (DSL) are updated. The CMDB also keeps track of hardware specifications, installation instructions, and network configurations. Stocks of hardware, particularly standardized basic configurations, are stored in the Definitive Hardware Store (DHS). However, in general, Release Management is primarily concerned with software.

In large projects in particular, Release Management should be part of the overall project plan to ensure funding. An annual fixed budget can be allocated to routine activities such as minor changes. Although costs will be incurred when setting up the process, these are minor compared to the potential costs associated with poor planning and control of software and hardware, such as:
• Major interruptions due to poorly planned software releases
• Duplication of work because there are copies of different versions
• Inefficient use of resources because nobody knows where the resources are
• Loss of source files, which means that software has to be purchased again
• No virus protection, which means that entire networks need decontamination

8.1.1 Basic concepts

Releases
Releases comprise one or more authorized changes. The first subdivision is based on the release level. Releases are often divided into:
• **Major releases:** major rollout of new hardware and software, generally with significantly increased functionality. These releases often eliminate a number of known errors, including work-arounds and quick fixes.
• **Minor software releases and hardware upgrades:** these generally include a number of minor improvements and fixes of known errors. Some may have been implemented as emergency fixes earlier but are now comprehensively dealt with in the release. Such a release also ensures that the 'Previous Trusted State', the starting point for all tests, is updated.
• **Emergency fixes:** normally implemented as a quick fix for a problem or known error.

Release Units

When dealing with hardware, the question arises if only complete PCs will be changed or if cards and hard disk drives (or even RAM and processors) will be changed separately. In terms of software, changes can be made at the system, suite, program or module level. A good example is a DLL (Dynamic Link Library) in the Windows environment, which is often used by several programs. Sometimes, a new DLL version is provided with a package, which may require retesting and re-installation of all other software packages. This process also develops policies on the minimum content of a release.

Release identification

Copies of software items can be distributed from the DSL to the relevant environments:
- **Development environment:** the development of a new version can be based on an earlier version from the DSL. The version number is incremented with each new version. Software may only be changed in the development environment.
- **Test environment:** the environment for testing versions. Often divided into technical tests by developers, functional tests by users, implementation tests by release builders, and possibly a final acceptance test by users and the management organization.
- **Production environment:** the live environment where information systems are made available to users.
- **Archive:** holds older versions of software items that are no longer used.

As several releases may be available, they are given unique identifiers. The release identification should refer to the relevant CI and include a version number of two or more digits, for example:
- **Major releases:** Payroll system v.1, v.2, v.3, etc.
- **Minor releases:** Payroll system v.1.1, v.1.2, v.1.3, etc.
- **Emergency fix releases:** Payroll system v.1.1.1, v.1.1.2, v.1.1.3, etc.

Figure 8.1 shows the testing and possible modification of each new version before its release. As part of the release, the old version is archived should a back out be necessary.

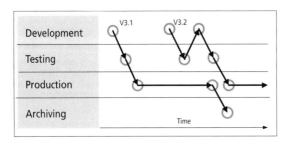

Figure 8.1 Release management version release

Figure 8.2 illustrates a back out.

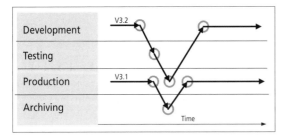

Figure 8.2 Release management back out (source: OGC)

Release types

The number of changes that can be developed, tested and implemented within a given period should be estimated. A Package Release, a combination of a number of changes in a single roll-out, can become too complex for safe implementation.

The rapid development of new hardware and software versions in the market means that a release may be outdated before it can be released. On the other hand, frequent changes can adversely impact the service.

Change Management has to decide about the number of changes that can be included in a release, and how the rollout will be implemented. Change Management can select one of the following options:

- **Delta Release:** a Delta Release only includes changed hardware and software. This often relates to an emergency fix or a quick fix. The disadvantage of this type of release is that it is not always possible to test all links with the rest of the environment, and that modules, that are no longer called by the software, are not deleted. A Delta Release is appropriate if the software can be isolated from the rest of the IT environment. The advantage of a Delta Release is that setting up the test environment takes less work.
- **Full Release:** a Full Release means that a program is distributed in its entirety, including modules that were not changed. This approach is particularly advisable when it is not entirely clear what has been changed. The software and hardware will be tested more thoroughly and there will be fewer incidents after implementation. When preparing a Full Release it is easier to judge if the expected performance criteria will be met. The advantage of a Full Release is that a number of changes can be implemented simultaneously. The preparation will be easier as standard installation scripts can be used. During installation, the program environment can also be cleaned up. However, a Full Release requires more preparation and resources than a Delta Release.
- **Package Release:** a Package Release or bundle of releases emphasizes longer periods of stability for the users. Fixing minor software errors, which the users can live with, and incorporating new functions are activities that can often be combined effectively. Similarly, scheduled upgrades, for example to third party software such as systems software and office applications are appropriate for Package Releases.

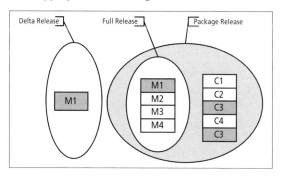

Figure 8.3 Release types

Definitive Software Library (DSL)

The Definitive Software Library (DSL) is a secure repository that holds the definitive authorized versions (master copies) of all sofware CIs. The DSL may be physically in many locations and comprise of a number of secure media vaults and fireproof safes. Release Management covers the life cycle of software from the time it is incorporated in the DSL. Releases are configured with the known good software secured in the DSL. Installation scripts are then developed and CDs may be burned at decentralized environments.

The DSL may include several versions of the same software, including archived versions, documentation and source code. Hence, the DSL should be backed up regularly, as it not only contains the current version but also the back-out versions. If there are several sites with local management, then each site will have a copy of the DSL for rolling out software.

Definitive Hardware Store (DHS)
The Definitive Hardware Store contains spares and stocks of hardware. These are spare components and assemblies that are maintained at the same level as their counterparts in the live environment. The hardware in the DHS is used to replace or repair similar configurations in the IT infrastructure. Details of the composition of these configurations should be included in the CMDB.

Configuration Management Database (CMDB)
During all Release Management activities, it is advisable to check information about CIs in the CMDB. As software versions are incorporated in the DSL, and hardware versions are incorporated in the DHS, the CMDB details are also updated. To support Release Management, the CMDB should contain details about:
- Contents of planned releases, including hardware and software CIs with reference to the original RFC
- Hardware and software CIs which may be impacted by a release
- Details of the physical location of hardware covered by the release

8.2 Objectives
Release Management manages and distributes software and hardware versions used for production, which are supported by the IT department, to provide the required service level.

The objectives of Release Management include:
- Planning, coordinating and implementing (or arranging the implementation) of software and hardware
- Designing and implementing efficient procedures for the distribution and installation of changes to IT systems
- Ensuring that the hardware and software related to changes are traceable and secure, and that only correct, authorized, and tested versions are installed
- Communicating with users and considering their expectations during the planning and roll-out of new releases
- Determining the composition and planning of a rollout, together with Change Management
- Implementing new software releases and hardware in the operational infrastructure, under control of Change Management, and supported by Configuration Management. A release may include any number of related CIs, and not only hardware and software but also documentation such as reports, plans and user and support manuals.
- Ensuring that the original copies of software are securely stored in the Definitive Software Library (DSL) and that the CMDB is updated; the same applies with respect to the hardware in the DHS

8.2.1 Advantages
Together with effective Configuration Management and Change Management, Release Management helps to ensure that:
- The software and hardware in live use are of high quality, as they are developed and tested under quality control before being released.

- The risk of errors in software and hardware combinations or release of an incorrect version is minimized.
- The business carefully handles its software investments, which it largely depends on.
- There are fewer separate implementations, and each implementation is thoroughly tested.
- The risk of incidents and known errors occurring is reduced by testing and controlling implementation.
- The users are more involved in the testing of a release.
- A release calendar is published in advance; hence, user expectations are more in-line with the releases.
- The business has a central software and hardware designing and building, or procurement facility, followed by the distribution to the site.
- The business can standardize software and hardware versions between sites, to facilitate support.
- The risk of illegal software is reduced, along with the risk of incidents and problems due to the wrong or infected software or hardware versions being introduced into the live environment.
- Unauthorized copies and incorrect versions are more easily detected.

8.3 The process

The Release Management process includes the following activities:
- Release policy and planning
- Release building and configuration
- Testing and release acceptance
- Rollout planning
- Communication, preparation and training
- Release distribution and installation

These activities are not really chronological. Release policy and planning is maybe done each 6 months or year, while other activities are done maybe daily.

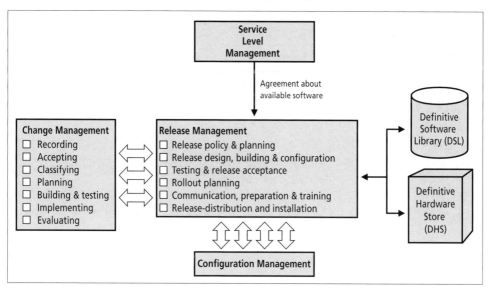

Figure 8.4 Release Management

Successful Release Management depends upon the input from and cooperation with the other ITIL processes (Figure 8.4). The major interfaces are with the following processes.

8.3.1 Configuration Management

Configuration Management is responsible for recording the available software and hardware versions in the CMDB as basic configurations. The software added to the DSL and the hardware for the DHS are recorded in the CMDB at an agreed level of detail. The status monitoring provided by Configuration Management indicates the status of each CI, for example 'live use', 'in development ', 'being tested', 'in stock' or 'archived'.

8.3.2 Change Management

Distribution is controlled by Change Management. Change Management is also responsible for ensuring adequate testing of the release. Change Management also decides how many changes may be combined in a release. Change Management describes the procedures to ensure that changes are authorized, including the impact analysis and analysis of the required resources. In most cases, the Release Manager is responsible for implementing software and hardware changes, and generally sits on the Change Advisory Board.

8.3.3 Service Level Management

An IT service generally consists of providing infrastructure hardware together with standard software or software developed in-house. Release Management is responsible for making hardware and software available and for managing it. Release Management monitors the agreements about the availability of software made in the Service Level Management process.

8.3.4 Release Management activities

Figure 8.5 shows the Release Management activities and their links with the life cycle of a change.

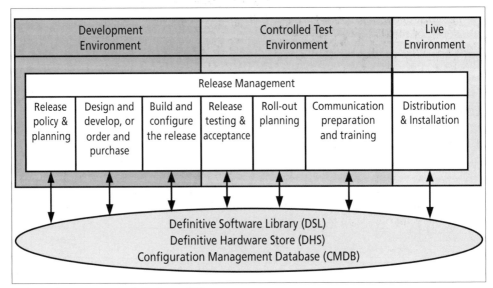

Figure 8.5 Release Management activities (source: OGC)

8.4 Activities

8.4.1 Release policy and planning

The Release Manager develops a release policy defining how and when releases are configured. Major releases can be planned ahead, together with the release identification or version number, so that the addition of changes can be considered at appropriate times.

The Release Manager also specifies at what level CIs can be distributed independently of each other (release units). This depends on:
- The potential impact of the release on other components.
- The number of person-hours and cycle time to build and test isolated changes compared with the effort associated with collecting them and implementing them simultaneously.
- The difficulty of the installation at the user sites. It may be easier to install a full program because standard techniques are available for that.
- The complexity of the dependencies between the new software, hardware, and the rest of the IT infrastructure - the easier it is to isolate software or hardware, the easier it is to test it.

Before a release can be planned, information has to be collected about the product life cycle, products to be handed over, description of the relevant IT service and service levels, authorization for the relevant RFCs, etc.
The following issues are considered when planning a release:
- Coordinating the content of the release
- Drawing up the release schedule
- Agreeing the schedule, sites and organizational units
- Site visits to determine the hardware and software actually in use
- Drawing up a communication plan
- Agreeing on roles and responsibilities
- Obtaining detailed quotes and negotiating with suppliers about new hardware, software and installation services
- Drawing up back-out plans
- Drawing up a quality plan for the release
- Planning the acceptance of the release by the management organization and users

The results of this activity are part of the plan for the change, and include plans for the release, test plans and acceptance criteria.

8.4.2 Design, building and configuration

It is advisable to develop standard procedures for designing, building and configuring releases. A release may be based on sets of components (CIs) developed in-house or purchased from third parties and configured. Installation instructions and instructions for configuring releases should also be treated as part of the release, and should be included as CIs under the control of Change Management and Configuration Management.

It is advisable to set up and test all hardware and software in a 'laboratory' before installation on site. The software and hardware components of a release should be carefully configured and recorded such that they are reproducible. Operating instructions should be drawn up to ensure that the same set of components is combined every time. Often, standardized hardware is reserved which is only used for compiling or creating images. Preferably, this part of the process should be automated to make it more reliable. Naturally, the software and hardware required for this is also covered by Release Management. In software development environments, this activity is known as Build Management and comes under responsibility of Release Management.

Back-out plan
A back-out plan at the level of the entire release defines the activities needed to recover the service if something goes wrong with the release. Change Management is responsible for drawing up back-out plans, however Release Management should help to ensure that the back-out plans are practical. Particularly when implementing a Package Release combining several RFCs, it can be necessary to coordinate the different back-out plans for the release. If something goes wrong with a Full Release or a Delta Release, then it is advisable to roll the release back completely to the Previous Trusted State. If a release cannot be rolled back fully, then there should also be Disaster Recovery plans to restore the service.

It is advisable to fulfill the requirements of the back-out plan in advance, such as making backups and providing a spare server. To address the case where the implementation could take longer than expected, and where that delay would endanger the normal provision of services, the back-out plan should also include deadlines to show when a back-out should be started to restore the service in time (for example before Monday morning, 7:00 AM). A back-out plan should be included in the risk analysis of the change, and the users must accept the plan.

The actual building of the release can include compiling and linking software modules, or filling databases with test data or data such as zip code tables, tax rates, time zones and currency tables as well as user information. This is often handled by automated installation scripts, which are stored in the DSL together with the back-out plans. Complete releases should be identified in the CMDB as standard configurations, to facilitate their configuration in future. Test plans cover the testing and acceptance of the quality of the software, hardware, procedures, operating instructions and rollout scripts before the release, and possibly also the evaluation test after the release. The installation scripts should also be tested. The information needed for this activity includes:
• Definition of the release
• Release schedule
• Instructions for configuring and building the release
• Description of items to be purchased or licensed, and the schedule
• Automated installation scripts and test plans
• Source copies of the software for incorporation in the DSL
• Back-out plans

8.4.3 Testing and release acceptance
The most common cause of unsatisfactory changes and releases is inadequate testing. To avert this, before implementation, the release should undergo a functional test by representatives of the users and an operational test by IT management personnel who will consider the technical operation, functions, operational aspect, performance, and integration with the rest of the infrastructure. The tests should also cover the installation scripts, back-out procedures, and any changes to the management procedures. A formal acceptance of each step should be submitted to Change Management. The last step is approving the release for implementation.

Change Management must arrange the formal acceptance by the users and sign-off by the developers, before Release Management can start the rollout.
Releases should be accepted in a controlled test environment, which consists of basic configurations into which it can also be decomposed. This baseline situation for the release should be

detailed in the release definition. The relevant basic configurations should be recorded in the CMDB. If the release is not accepted then it is sent back to Change Management.

The results of this activity include:
- Tested installation procedures
- Tested release components
- Known errors and shortcomings in the release
- Test results
- Management and support documentation
- List of affected systems
- Operating instructions and diagnostic tools
- Contingency plans and tested back-out plans
- Training program for personnel, managers and users
- Signed acceptance documents
- Change authorization for the release

8.4.4 Implementation planning

The release plan drawn up during the preceding stages is now supplemented with information about the implementation activities.

Rollout planning includes:
- Drawing up a schedule and list of tasks and required human resources
- Making a list of the CIs to be installed and to be phased out, and the way in which they are phased out
- Drawing up an activity plan for each implementation site, considering the available release times, and for an international organization, the time zones
- Mailing release memos and other communications to relevant parties
- Drawing up plans for the purchase of hardware and software
- Purchasing, securing storage, and identifying and recording all new CIs in the CMDB for this release
- Scheduling meetings with management, management departments, Change Management, and user representatives

There are several ways to implement a rollout:
- The release can be rolled out in full - the Big Bang approach
- The release can be rolled out in stages, combining several options:
  - Functional increments, where all users get new functions at the same time
  - Site increments, where groups of users are dealt with
  - Evolutionary, where the functions are expanded in stages

8.4.5 Communication, preparation and training

Personnel who communicate with customers (Service Desk and Customer Relations Management), operational personnel, and representatives of the user organization should be aware of the plans, and how they can affect routine activities. This can be implemented through joint training sessions, cooperation, and joint involvement in release acceptance. Responsibilities should be communicated, and it should be verified that everyone is aware of them. If the release is rolled out in stages, then users should be made aware of that by informing them about the plans and when they can expect the new functions.

Changes to the Service Level Agreements (SLA), Operational Level Agreements (OLA) and Underpinning Contracts (UC) should be communicated in advance to all relevant personnel.

8.4.6 Release distribution and installation

Release Management monitors the logistics processes for purchase, storage, transport, delivery, and hand-over of software and hardware. The process is supported by procedures, records, and accompanying documents such as packing slips, so that it can provide reliable information to Configuration Management. The hardware and software storage facility should be secure and accessible only to authorized personnel.

It is advisable to use automated tools for software distribution and installation where possible. This will reduce the time required for distribution, and increase the quality, while requiring fewer resources. Often, these tools will also facilitate verification of a successful installation. Before undertaking any installation, it is advisable to check if the environment where the release will be made fulfills the conditions, such as sufficient disk space, security, environmental controls or limitations like air conditioning, floor space, UPS / power, etc.

After installation, the information in the CMDB should be updated to facilitate verification of any license agreements.

8.5 Costs and problems

8.5.1 Costs

Release Management costs include:
- Personnel costs
- Storage costs for the DSL and DHS, building, testing and distribution environments
- Costs of software tools and required hardware

8.5.2 Problems

The following problems may be encountered:
- **Resistance to change** - initially, there are may be resistance among personnel used to the old familiar methods. For example they may find it difficult to accept that for some activities they will receive instructions from another area. To address their concerns, they will need to be informed about the advantages of the ITIL approach.
- **Bypassing Release Management** - unauthorized software may introduce viruses in the organization, adversely affect services, and make support more difficult. Firm action should therefore be taken against personnel and users, particularly in the PC environment, who attempt to use unauthorized software.
- **Urgent fixes** - Release Management may not be bypassed, even if an urgent change is needed.
- **Distribution** - if software is to be released at several sites, then it should be ensured that this is synchronized, to prevent version differences between sites.
- **Testing** - without an adequate test environment it may be difficult to assess new versions or new software properly before the release.

Chapter 9
Service Desk

9.1 Introduction

The Service Desk plays an important role in user support. A full blown Service Desk serves as the front office for the other IT departments, and can deal with many customer queries without needing to contact specialist personnel. For the user, the Service Desk provides the single point of contact with the IT organization which ensures that they find the right person to help them with their issue or request. In other words, the users need not endlessly look for somebody who can solve their problems. Often, the Service Desk also follows up on calls originating from within the IT organization. For example incidents that are detected within the department (automatically or by personnel), and calls for service that come from within the IT organization.

This chapter is different from the rest of the book in that here we focus on a function, organizational unit, or a department, whereas the rest of the book deals with processes. The subject is included here because the Service Desk plays an essential role in IT Service Management. To indicate the broader activities, we speak of a Service Desk instead of a Help Desk, as we did for a long time. A Help Desk normally was involved in the incident process, whereas the Service Desk covers a broader range of support activities.

The Service Desk handles activities related to a number of basic ITIL processes:
• The primary process is **Incident Management** as many incidents are recorded (logged) and monitored by the Service Desk, and many Service Desk calls are related to incidents. This includes coordinating third-party activities involved in incident handling.
• The Service Desk may be charged with installing software and hardware and may therefore have a role in **Release Management** or **Change Management.**
• If, when recording an incident, the Service Desk verifies the details of the caller and their IT resources, then the Service Desk plays a role in **Configuration Management.**

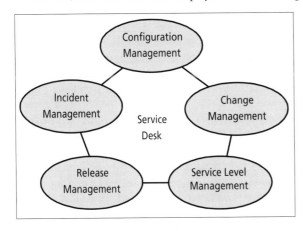

Figure 9.1 Service Desk processes

• The Service Desk may undertake activities concerning standard requests, such as installing LAN connections and relocating workstations in which case it will contribute to the evaluation of changes and be involved in **Change Management.**
• The Service Desk can inform users about the supported products and services they are entitled to. If the Service Desk is not authorized to meet a request then it should politely inform the user of this and notify **Service Level Management** of the request.

The Service Desk handles activities related to a number of other ITIL processes as well, e.g. Infrastructure Management (Operations). The Service Desk maintains the contacts with customers through promotion and providing information about the services. The Service Desk is an excellent tool for the daily contacts with users to monitor customer satisfaction.

9.2 Objectives

The objective of the Service Desk is to support the provision of the services that have been agreed upon by guaranteeing access to the IT organization and undertaking a range of support activities (from various processes).

By serving as an initial point of contact, the Service Desk reduces the workload on other IT departments by intercepting irrelevant questions and questions which are easily answered. The Service Desk acts as a filter that only lets calls through to second and third-line support where this is actually necessary. As an initial point of contact it always acts professionally when dealing with users and ensures that they do not have to search endlessly for a solution.

9.3 Structure

9.3.1 Accessibility

One of the major tasks of the Service Desk is ensuring the accessibility of the IT organization. Users should be encouraged to call the Service Desk if they have any questions or need any support. The way calls are processed can be monitored with reports produced by the PABX.

To make a reliable impression, the Service Desk should be consistent and efficient in customer contacts. This can be supported by procedures based on questionnaires and standard responses, for example using scripts.

A number of different media can be used to improve accessibility, although telephone and e-mail contacts are the most common. Voice mail, fax, Internet gateways, and automatically generated messages (e.g. text messages to mobile phones, or pagers) can also be used.

9.3.2 Business support

Calls can be divided into incidents concerning the technical infrastructure, incidents and questions about the use of an application, questions about the status of the services (incident progress), standard changes, and other requests. Depending on the type of Service Desk, it may deal with all calls or only with technical problems and requests while the ('pay the bills') customer provides application support. In the latter case, the customer department using the application has an application contact, a business operations support desk. This will try to answer questions from users and only route technical questions to the Service Desk of the IT organization. That way, the Service Desk will not be overloaded with questions related to the use of applications.

9.3.3 Structural options

There are several options for the structure of the Service Desk. Common approaches include:
- **Centralized Service Desk** as a single point of contact for all users, possibly with a separate Service Desk close to the users for business applications (split function Service Desk).
- **Local (distributed) Service Desks** at a number of sites. Normally, dividing the Service Desk across a number of sites will make it more difficult to manage.

- **Virtual Service Desk** where the location is immaterial due to the use of communications technology.

Centralized Service Desk

Figure 9.2 shows a split function Centralized Service Desk. If the IT organization is responsible both for providing the service (the Information System) and supporting the use of the Information System then it is best if the user can approach the Service Desk as a single point of contact. In that case, the IT Service Desk is responsible for call acceptance and recording, progress monitoring and escalation. Here, the business operations support function is part of the IT Service Desk or it is the responsibility of a support team managed by the Service Desk. This requires a common incident recording system.

If the IT organization is not responsible for business operations support, then the business operations support desk will represent the users when the IT service provider's support is required.

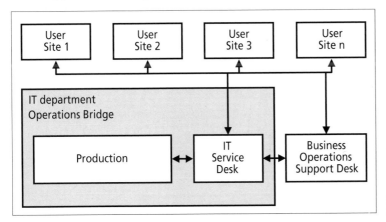

Figure 9.2
Split function Service Desk

This approach can be combined with an operations bridge (a physical concentration of operational management activities, e.g. a Service Desk in combination with an Operations department) to provide direct communication between the Service Desk and operational management (Production, Operations), where Production includes Network Management, Computer Operations, etc. This direct communication facilitates a rapid response if there are errors that cannot be resolved immediately by the Service Desk. Ideally, the departments should be located in close proximity to each other.

Distributed Service Desk

Distributed Service Desks are split across a number of sites, in different buildings or even in different countries. Figure 9.3 shows an example of the structure of a distributed Service Desk. There is a further choice between:

- **A central point of contact,** which routes calls through to local support. The central Service Desk can serve as the initial point of contact for users and specialize in incident recording. Modern call routing software increases the effectiveness of the Service Desk in resolving incidents.
- **Local points of contact** with a central Service Desk to track and monitor incidents. This approach is often used if the local organization has its own language and culture. It is also used when the organization has a substantial number of custom applications in each line of business. For example, a chemical company has over three hundred categories of custom applications, and a thousand applications overall. With this level of customization, the only practical

solution is to distribute the Service Desk function out to each line of business, as knowledge 'on the ground' is required to resolve many incidents. Local responsibility for support costs can also motivate this structure.

- **A call center.** This option is becoming increasingly popular and is often used by suppliers. A central telephone number, usually toll-free, provides access to a voice response menu where the user can select the subject about whom they need assistance, such as e-mail or Office applications. The call is then routed to a specialist support team. These support teams may be in different geographical areas, but the user will not be aware of this.

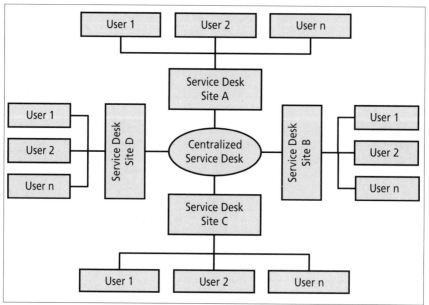

Figure 9.3 Distributed Service Desk with central control (source: OGC).

Virtual Service Desk

A modern, specialized version of the distributed Service Desk is the virtual Service Desk. This consists of a number of local Service Desks who appear to form one unit as modern telecommunication technology and networks make the location immaterial. The Service Desk and support can now be located anywhere. Using a number of sites in different time zones around the world ('follow the sun support') can provide support around the clock. The disadvantage of a virtual Service Desk is that it is more difficult to provide on-site support.

Lately, we see "self-help" as a form of providing "automated" Service Desk functionality. Self-help in the form of, for instance, web access to the knowledge database (look for known errors) and incident records (check status etc.) is an important way to reduce cost and empower the end user community.

9.3.4 Service Desk personnel

Service Desk personnel requirements are determined by the mission and structure of the Service Desk. Here are some examples of missions and the associated human resource requirements:

- **Call center:** this type of support unit records calls only and does not provide a solution. The calls are routed to specialist departments that deal with them. In some cases, the recording and routing of calls can be automated using voice response systems.

- **Unskilled or call recording Service Desk:** calls are recorded, described in general terms, and immediately routed. The Service Desk is largely a dispatching function, and for the calls it is expected to handle, it needs extensive standardized procedures, scripts for dealing with calls, discipline, and an experienced manager. The advantage of this approach is that incident recording is standardized. The disadvantage is that the response time is longer and first-call resolution rates are much lower than with a skilled Service Desk.
- **Skilled Service Desk:** this type of Service Desk has greater skills and experience than the previous type. Using documented solutions it can resolve many incidents, while some incidents are routed to support teams. First call resolution rates are generally much higher than with a Help Desk.
- **Expert Service Desk:** this type of Service Desk has specialist knowledge of the full IT infrastructure and the expertise to resolve most incidents independently.

9.3.5 Service Desk technology
There are many technical options for setting up a Service Desk. Apart from an effective Service Management tool, they include:
- Integrating service management tools with systems management tools
- Communication technology such as Computer Telephony Integration (CTI) or Voice Over Internet Protocol (VOIP)
- Interactive Voice Response systems (IVR)
- E-mail
- Fax servers (fax via e-mail or the Internet)
- Forwarding calls to pagers, mobile phones, laptop and palmtop computers
- Knowledge, search and diagnostic tools (knowledge base, case based reasoning)
- Automated systems management and network tools
- Intranet and Internet self-service platforms

9.4 Activities

9.4.1 Responding to calls
A call means that a user contacts the Service Desk. All calls should be logged to facilitate progress monitoring and provide metrics for process control.

There are two call categories:
- **Incidents:** in essence all calls, except those relating to standard changes:
  - *Error reports:* true faults and complaints about the service
  - *Service Requests:* Service Requests are classified in ITIL as incidents, but do not involve a failure in the IT infrastructure. Service Requests also do not fall into the Change Management category. Examples include, "How do I?" questions, requests for information, e.g. status inquiries, documentation or advice, requests for password resets, batch job runs, file restores or database extracts, requests for consumables (including replacement of a mouse, keyboard, etc., if these are not CIs), supply of documentation e.g. user manuals, etc.
- **Changes:** in most cases these will be standard Requests For Change (RFC). In some cases, the Service Desk will also be responsible for relocating hardware. A standard change is in fact a routine change to the infrastructure that follows an established path, and is the accepted solution to a specific requirement or set of requirements. Examples include an upgrade of a PC in preparation for the use of specific software, setting up PC, software and network connections for new hires, straightforward standard installations and standard orders for workstations,

peripherals and local applications. The key difference between a Service Request and a standard change is that the former is a request for service logged as an incident that does not involve a change to the IT Infrastructure, whereas the latter is logged as a change and does involve a change to the infrastructure.

Note: ITIL considers both call types (error reports and Service Requests) to be 'incidents', since these calls are treated rather similarly. On the other hand, ITIL allows for isolated procedures for Service Requests, that are separated from the Incident Management process.

9.4.2 Providing information
The Service Desk should serve as the main source of information to users. This can be done passively (e.g. by providing a bulletin board), or actively (e-mails, on-screen log-in messages, or screen saver messages). All efforts should be made to inform users about current or expected errors, preferably before they are affected. The Service Desk should also provide information about new and existing services, provisions of the Service Level Agreements (SLAs) and order procedures and costs.

9.4.3 Supplier liaison
The Service Desk is often responsible for contacts with maintenance suppliers. This covers the repair and replacement of printers, workstations and, in some cases, telecommunications equipment. This type of maintenance may be involved in handling incidents in the pure sense (disturbances) as well as incidents in terms of changes and service requests.

9.4.4 Operational management tasks
Making back-ups and restores, providing LAN connections, disk space management on local servers, creating accounts, authorizing and resetting passwords.

9.4.5 Infrastructure monitoring
On the Service Desk, tools can be used to estimate the impact of faults affecting essential equipment, such as routers, servers and gateways, mission-critical systems, applications, and databases. Often, these tools can detect faults and inform Incident Management automatically when a fault has occurred or is threatening. It is not necessary that these tools are used at the Service Desk, since this is a primary task of "Operations", that should be feeding the information to the Service Desk.

9.5 Effectiveness
The satisfaction of the customer or user is the major indicator of Service Desk effectiveness. Some Key Performance Indicators are:
- Is the telephone answered quickly (e.g. 90% of the calls answered within X seconds)?
- Are calls routed to second level support within X minutes (if they cannot be resolved at the Service Desk)?
- Is the service restored within an acceptable time and in accordance with the SLA?
- Are users advised in time about current and future changes and errors?

Some performance indicators can only be measured by means of a customer survey, e.g.:
- Is the telephone answered courteously?
- Are users given good advice on how to prevent incidents?

9.5.1 Management reports

The Service Desk should regularly (e.g. every six months) verify if it meets the defined standards. Appropriate metrics include:

- Percentage of incidents which could be closed without resorting to other levels such as second or third-line support or suppliers.
- The number of calls handled per workstation/user and the total for the Service Desk.
- Average incident resolution time, by impact, or time to realize a service request. Both the cycle time and the time actually spent on the case should be specified.
- PABX reports on the average answer time, number of calls prematurely terminated by users, average call duration, and relative metrics per Service Desk agent.

Standards can be set for those metrics, which are then used to monitor improvement or deterioration of the service. The Service Desk effectiveness can also be measured through regular surveys in the customer organization.

9.5.2 Critical success factors

If it is difficult to reach the Service Desk, the users will not contact it and instead try to resolve errors themselves, or find someone in the organization who can help them. Thus, Service Desk performance should be brought to the required level before running a publicity campaign.

If users try to contact specialists directly they should be referred to the Service Desk.

There should be good SLAs and OLAs and a service catalog to ensure that the support provided by the Service Desk has a clear focus.

Chapter 10

Service Level Management

10.1 Introduction

Service Level Management is the process of negotiating, defining, measuring, managing and improving the quality of IT services at an acceptable cost. All of this must take place in an environment of rapidly changing business needs and rapid changes in technology. Service Level Management aims to find the right balance between quality supply and demand, customer-friendliness, and cost of IT services. It is important that both the provider and the customer realize that a service is being provided and respectively being received. This is formalized by designing, agreeing, and maintaining the Service Level Agreements (SLAs), Operational Level Agreements (OLAs), Underpinning Contracts (UCs) and Service Quality Plans.

10.1.1 Basic concepts

IT Service Providers and Customers

In theory, anyone who obtains IT services is a customer. In most cases, the IT organization will be the provider. As the IT organization itself generally also obtains IT services, and the IT organization is therefore a customer of IT Service Providers at the same time, there can be a complex web of relationships. For example, a software development department can request online services from the central processing department, while that development department also provides software maintenance to ensure the continuity of the same online services. In theory, Service Level Management is a linear process for defining services and concluding agreements, such as Underpinning Contracts (UCs) with external providers, Operational Level Agreements (OLAs) with internal providers, or Service Level Agreements (SLAs) with customers. However, a flexible approach is required, as the distinction between customers and IT Service Providers is often unclear.

In the context of Service Level Management we use the following definitions of customer and provider:
- The **customer** is the representative of an organization who is authorized to make agreements on behalf of that organization about obtaining IT services. Hence, they are not the same as the end-**user** of the IT services.
- The **provider** is the representative of an organization who is authorized to make agreements on behalf of that organization about the provision of IT services.

Service Level Requirements (SLR)

Service Level Requirements covers the detailed definitions of customer needs, and are used to develop, modify and initiate services. The Service Level Requirements can serve as a blueprint for designing a service and its SLA, and may also be used as a design assignment.

Service Specification Sheets (Spec Sheets)

Service Spec Sheets describe the relationship between functionality (as agreed on with the customer, and therefore externally directed from a provider point of view) and technology (implementation within the IT organization, and therefore internally directed) and provide a detailed specification of the service. The Spec Sheets translate Service Level Requirements (external specifications) to technical definitions needed to provide the service (internal specifications). The Spec Sheets also describe any links between the SLAs, the UCs and the OLAs. The Spec Sheets are an important tool to monitor correspondence between the internal and external specifications.

Service Catalog
Developing a Service Catalog can help the IT organization to profile itself and to present itself as an IT Service Provider as opposed to a mere implementer and maintainer of technology. The Service Catalog provides a detailed description of the operational services in the customer's language, along with a summary of the associated service levels which the IT organization can provide to its customers. As such, it is an important communications tool. The Service Catalog can help steer customer expectations, and in this way facilitate the alignment process between service customers and service providers. This document is derived from the external specifications in the Spec Sheets and should therefore be written in the customer's language, and not in the form of technical specifications.

Service Level Agreement (SLA)
A Service Level Agreement is an agreement between the IT organization and the customer, which details the service or services to be provided. The SLA describes the services in non-technical terms, in line with the perception of the customer, and during the term of the agreement it serves as the standard for measuring and adjusting the IT services. SLAs normally have a hierarchical structure, for example general services such as network and Service Desk services are defined for the organization as a whole and approved by management. More specific services, associated with the business activities, are agreed at a lower level in the organization, for example with the business unit management, budget holder or customer representative.

Service Improvement Program (SIP)
The Service Improvement Program is often implemented as a project, defines the activities, phases and milestones associated with improving an IT service.

Service Quality Plan (SQP)
The Service Quality Plan is an important document as it contains all management information needed to manage the IT organization. The Service Quality Plan defines the process parameters of the Service Management processes and operational management. The SLA is "what" we would deliver as opposed to the SQP being "how" we would deliver. It includes targets for each process, in the form of Performance Indicators. For example, for Incident Management it contains the resolution times for various impact levels, and for Change Management it contains the cycle times and costs of standard changes such as a relocation. Reports and reporting intervals are defined for all processes. The Performance Indicators are derived from the Service Level Requirements and are documented in the Spec sheets. If external providers contribute to the provision of services, for example when the Service Desk or PC maintenance are outsourced, then the Performance Indicators are also defined in the Underpinning Contracts.

Operational Level Agreement (OLA)
An Operational Level Agreement is an agreement with an internal IT department detailing the agreements about the provision of certain elements of a service, such as an OLA about network availability or the availability of print servers. For example, if the SLA contains targets for restoring a high priority incident, then the OLAs should include targets for each of the elements in the support chain (targets for the Service Desk to answer calls, escalate etc., targets for Network Support to start to investigate and to resolve network related errors assigned to them, etc.). OLAs support the IT organization providing the services.

Underpinning Contract (UC)
An Underpinning Contract is a contract with an external provider defining the agreements about the provision of certain elements of a service, for example troubleshooting workstations,

or leasing a communications line. This is similar to the external implementation of an OLA. In many organizations, an internal IT department provides the IT services. SLAs and OLAs are often descriptions of what was agreed between internal departments, rather than legal contracts. However, a UC with an external provider will normally be in the form of a formal contract.

10.2 Objectives

Service Level Management ensures that the IT services required by the customer are continuously maintained and improved. This is accomplished by agreeing, monitoring and reporting about the performance of the IT organization, in order to create an effective business relationship between the IT organization and its customers.

Effective Service Level Management improves the performance of the customer's business and results in greater customer satisfaction. Because the IT organization is more aware of what is expected from it and what it provides, it will be better able to plan, budget and manage its services.

Benefits

In general, the introduction of Service Level Management will have the following benefits:
- IT services are designed to meet the expectations, as defined in the Service Level Requirements.
- Service performance can be measured, which means that it can be managed and reported on.
- If the IT organization charges customers for the use of IT services, the customer can draw a balance between the required quality of service and the corresponding costs.
- As the IT organization can specify the services and components required, it can get in control of resource management and costs could be reduced over the long term.
- Improved customer relationships and customer satisfaction.
- Both the customer and the IT organization are aware of their responsibilities and roles, so there will be fewer misunderstandings or omissions.

10.3 The Process

Service Level Management is a process that links the IT service provider and the customer for those services. The Service Level Management process has several objectives:
- To integrate the elements required for the provision of IT services.
- To document the services by clearly describing the elements in various documents.
- To describe the service provided to the customer in a terminology that they understand and can relate to.
- To align IT strategy with the business needs.
- To improve IT Service Delivery in a controlled manner.

Service Level Management has a central role in IT Service Management processes, and has close links with the other Support and Delivery processes. Service Level Management forms a bridge with the customer, as it provides an opportunity to discuss the business needs of the customer without getting bogged down in technical details. The IT organization then translates these business needs into technical specifications and activities within the organization. The extent to which the customer need not be concerned about technology is a good measure of the success of Service Level Management.

Service Level Management demands effective and productive cooperation with customers, as the definition of appropriate service levels requires the contribution and effort of the customer. If the customer (the business) is not familiar with the subjects at hand, then this will have to be addressed first. Figure 10.1 shows the Service Level Management process workflow. It shows two component processes, which are largely parallel: the upper one is about making agreements, and the lower one is about ensuring that these agreements are fulfilled.

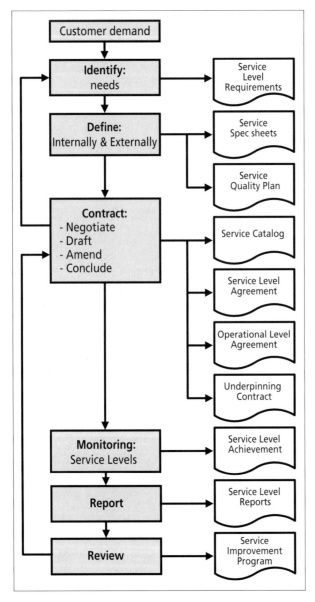

Figure 10.1 Service Level Management process

Service Level Management includes the following activities:
- **Identifying** - identifying the customer's needs, relationship management, and promoting the IT organization. Understanding the business processes and needs of the customer.
- **Defining** - defining the services to be provided to meet the needs and requirements of the customer. These services are defined in Service Level Requirements and Service Spec Sheets. A Service Quality Plan will be created as a result of this activity.

- **Finalizing Contract** - finalizing the contract, i.e. negotiating with the customer about the required service level, in relation to costs involved, and defining it in Service Level Agreements (SLA). Underpinning the SLAs with Operational Level Agreements (OLA) and Underpinning Contracts (UC). Writing or revising the Service Catalog specifying the services available to the customer.
- **Monitoring** - monitoring the service levels.
- **Reporting** - drawing up Service Level Reports. Regularly reporting to the customer and the IT organization about the actual service levels, compared with the Service Level Achievements.
- **Reviewing** - reviewing the service together with the customer to determine opportunities for improvements. A Service Improvement Program may be initiated, if necessary. Frequent communication with the customer about their experience and ideas about the service provided. This may result in new or revised SLAs.

Fully effective Service Level Management requires the introduction of the other Service Support and Service Delivery processes. All the processes contribute to some extent to Service Level Management. When defining a service and the associated service levels, the extent to which the required support processes are introduced should be considered. The relationships between Service Level Management and the other processes are outlined below.

Relationship with the Service Desk

Although the Service Desk is a function, not a process, the relationship between the Service Desk function and the Service Level Management process is a particularly important one. The Service Desk is the initial point of contact for users and, through Incident Management, it aims to recover the agreed service levels as soon as possible in the event of an error. Because of its direct contact with the users of the IT services, the Service Desk can often provide valuable information about the quality perception (user satisfaction) of Service Level Management by the users. Normally, there will be a strong relationship between user satisfaction and customer satisfaction. The Service Desk also plays an important role in assisting with the definition of the response and solution times that will come into effect in the event of service interruption.

Relationship with Availability Management

Availability Management is responsible for realizing and optimizing the availability of the services. Service Level Management provides Availability Management with input about the required availability of the IT services, whereas Availability Management provides information about the actual availability to Service Level Management.

Relationship with Capacity Management

Capacity Management is responsible for managing the capacity of the IT infrastructure. There is a Capacity Plan with details of the current infrastructure usage, and forecasts of the future use. Capacity Management supports Service Level Management by providing information about the impact of a new service or extension of an existing service on the overall capacity. Capacity Management also indicates if the use made of a service is within the agreed limits.

Service Level Management provides information to Capacity Management about the expected current and future use, which Service Level Management has agreed, or is about to agree, with the customer.

Relationship with Incident & Problem Management

Incident Management and Problem Management are good indicators of the effective implementation of the SLA agreements. Incident Management in particular has an important role in restoring the services as soon as possible after an error.

Problem Management aims to optimize the stability of the services by taking permanent measures to ensure that the errors do not recur.
Resolving incidents and problems is essential to providing a high-quality service. Service Level Management uses information from reports provided by these processes when reporting to the customer.

Relationship with Change Management
The SLA can define the changes that can be requested by the customer organization, and the agreements for responding to these changes (whom to address the changes to, cycle time, costs, informing the organization, etc.). A change may also affect the service levels that have been agreed on.

Relationship with Release Management
Many IT services amount to the provision of infrastructure hardware together with custom-made or off-the-shelf software. Release Management monitors the agreements made by Service Level Management regarding the provision of hardware and software. Service Level Management reports on the quality of the IT service on the basis of information from Release Management reports.

Relationship with IT Service Continuity Management
IT Service Continuity Management is concerned with the rapid recovery of IT services in the event of a disaster, and monitors the appropriate measures and procedures. The agreements about this with the customer are made in the Service Level Management process. The measures and costs are then included in the SLA. It may be agreed that in the event of a disaster, certain service levels no longer apply or are temporarily reduced.
Changes to the service and the SLA may require modification of the defined continuity measures and procedures.

Relationship with Security Management
The security measures associated with the IT service can also be essential to effective Service Level Management. Both the IT organization and the customer will have certain security requirements. The corresponding agreements are defined in the SLA. Security Management ensures that the agreed security measures are implemented, monitored, and reported to Service Level Management.

Relationship with Configuration Management
Configuration Management is responsible for entering details of the components (CIs) and documentation (SLA) related to a service in the CMDB, and providing information from this database. Hence, the creation or modification of a service or SLA will affect the CMDB. The Service Desk uses the CMDB to determine the impact of an error on the services, and to check the agreements about the response and solution times. The CMDB is also used to report about the quality of the CIs, so as to enable Service Level Management to report about the quality of the service provided.

Relationship with Financial Management for IT Services
If the customer is charged for services incurred by the IT organization for the service provided,

then this is also included in the SLA. These may be one-time charges, or charges for special or additional services. Financial Management provides Service Level Management with information about the costs associated with providing a service. It also provides information about charging methods, and the rate to be charged to cover the costs of a service.

10.4 Activities
The process steps are described in detail below, including the process workflow and the activities.

10.4.1 Identification
As businesses become more dependent on their IT services, the demand for higher quality IT services is also increasing. The perceived quality of a service depends on the expectations of the customer, the ongoing management of customer perceptions, the stability of the service, and the acceptability of the costs. As such, the best way to provide the appropriate quality is to first discuss the issue with the customer.

Past experiences show that customers are often not clear about their expectations themselves, as they simply assume that certain aspects of the service will be provided, without having any clear agreements. These assumed (implicit) aspects of the IT services are often the cause of much confusion. This once again underlines the need for Service Level Managers to know their customers well, and to help their customers clarify their thinking about what services and service levels they really need, and at what cost.

The requirements of the customer must be expressed in measurable values so that they can contribute to the design and monitoring of IT services. If metrics have not been agreed with the customer, then it cannot be verified if the IT services fulfill the agreements. Service Level Management plays a key part in understanding and defining what the customer wants.

The first step in concluding SLAs about the IT services provided today or in the future should be to identify and define the customer needs in the Service Level Requirements. Besides doing so once within the course of the process, this activity should also be carried out regularly, initiated by reports and reviews, at the request of the customer or for the benefit of the IT organization. This activity may cover either new or existing services.

10.4.2 Definition
Defining the scope and depth of the customer's requirements is considered as a design process within Service Level Management. According to the ISO 9001 model for quality assurance, a design process should include the following steps: design, development, production and installation and maintenance. The design process should be managed to ensure that the results at the end of the process correspond with the requirements of the customer. During the design process, the term 'external' refers to communication with customers, and 'internal' to the technical underpinning within the IT organization. The design process includes a number of steps, from detailing the customer's requirements and defining them in standards, to developing the technical requirements to provide the service.

Defining external standards
The first step of quantifying new or existing IT services is defining or redefining the customer's expectations about the service in general terms. These expectations are formalized in documented Service Level Requirements (SLRs). This should involve the whole customer organization. This step is generally considered as the most difficult part of Service Level Management.

At the beginning of this stage, the Service Level Manager must prepare for the meeting with the customer organization. The first questions to be asked are: 'What is required of the IT service, and what elements should this service consist of?' A service could entail the use of a limited infrastructure, such as a Wide Area Network (WAN). Such a service can contribute to a composite service, such as access to a full information system, including the full underlying infrastructure (WAN, LAN, workstations, applications, etc.)

During these meetings, the users must be divided into groups. The Service Level Manager draws up a list of the user groups, and their requirements and authority. The following information is needed to define the Service Level Requirements:

- A description, from the customer's perspective, of functions to be provided by the service
- Times and days on which the service must be available
- Service continuity requirements
- IT functions needed to provide the service
- References to the current operational methods or quality standards to be considered when defining the service
- A reference to the SLA to be modified or replaced, where relevant

The design stage will produce a Service Level Requirements document, which is signed by the Service Level Manager and the customer. The Service Level Requirements can still be modified while the department is working on the design, procurement and implementation. Such changes may relate to the practicability of the envisaged functions or costs. Both parties must approve any such changes.

Translation to internal standards
During the specification phase, the Service Level Requirements are developed in detail. This stage aims to provide the following information:
- Unambiguous and detailed description of the IT services and required components
- Specification of the way in which the service will be implemented and provided
- Specification of the required quality control procedure

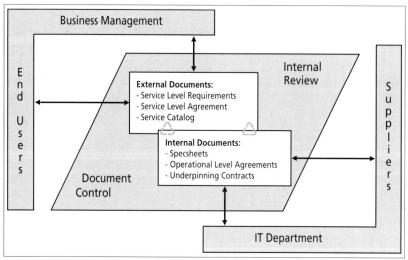

Figure 10.2 Specification stage (source: OGC)

In the specification phase it is recommended to distinguish between elements of the documentation for internal use and those for external use (Figure 10.2). Specifications for external use relate to objectives agreed with the customers, and the design process is controlled by these objectives. These specifications are drawn up in cooperation with the customer organization, and form the input for the specifications for internal use.

Specifications for internal use refer to the internal objectives of the IT organization, which have to be fulfilled to meet customer demands. A separation between internal and external specifications can be most useful once the Service Level Management process is under way. This ensures that the IT organization does not bother its customers with technical details. From that time on, managing the service levels relates to keeping the internal and external specifications aligned. Document Control and Internal Reviews contribute to this by keeping records of related documents, managing versions and organizing regular audits.

Spec sheets (service specifications) describe in detail what the customer wants (external element) and how this will impact the IT organization (internal element). Spec Sheets need not be signed by both parties, however they are subject to Document Control. The Service Catalog can be drawn up on the basis of the service specifications; hence, changes in the service levels can be included immediately in the Spec Sheets and Service Catalog. The SLA is then revised in line with the revised Spec Sheets.

Service Quality Plan
It is recommended to include all management information (key performance indicators) and specifications for internal and external providers in a single document to provide comprehensive information about the contributions made to the IT services by each Service Management process.

10.4.3 Contract
Once the specification phase has been completed, the IT organization has effectively translated the business needs into IT resources and configurations. This information is then used to draw up or modify the following documents.

Service Level Agreement
When developing the SLA structure, it is recommended to first define the general aspects, such as network services for the whole company and developing a general service-based SLA model, before the negotiations begin. The SLAs could have a hierarchical structure, like that of the customer organization, in the form of a framework agreement with a number of tiers. Each tier has its own level of detail. The top tiers include agreements about general services to be provided to the organization. The lower tiers contain information relevant to specific customers.

The structure of a SLA depends on a number of the variables such as:
• **Physical aspects of the organization:**
  - Scale
  - Complexity
  - Geographical distribution
• **Cultural aspects:**
  - Language(s) of the document (for international organizations)
  - Relationship between the IT organization and the customer
  - Charging policy
  - Uniformity of the business activities
  - Profit or non-profit organization

- **Nature of the business activities:**
  - General terms and conditions
  - Business hours - 5 x 8 hours or 7 x 24 hours

Underpinning Contracts and Operational Level Agreements

Any existing UCs or OLAs must be revised during the design process. Everyone involved should be aware of any UCs or OLAs that apply to the provision of a specific service. The Document Control indexes can help clarify the links to the Spec sheets.

Service Catalog

- The following tips can be helpful when writing a Service Catalog:
- Use your customer's language. Avoid technical jargon, and use terminology corresponding to the relevant business.
- Try to look at things from the customer's point of view and use that approach to identify relevant information.
- Provide an attractive layout as the IT organization uses this document to present itself to its customers.
- Ensure that the document is available to the largest number of potential stakeholders, for example by publishing it on an Intranet site or on CD-ROM.

10.4.4 Monitoring

Service Level Management can only be monitored if the service levels are clearly defined in advance and correspond with the externally agreed objectives. The service levels must be measured from the customer's perspective. Monitoring should not be limited to technical aspects, but should also include procedural matters. For example, until the user has been informed that the service has been restored, they will assume that it is unavailable.

Availability Management and Capacity Management generally provide the information about the implementation of the technical objectives associated with the service levels. In some cases, information will also be provided from the Service Support processes, especially to Incident Management. However, measuring internal parameters is insufficient, as this does not relate to the user's perception. Parameters such as response time, escalation time and support must also be measurable. A complete view is only obtained by combining management information from both the systems and Service Management.

10.4.5 Reports

Customer reports (Service Reports) must be provided at the intervals agreed in the SLA. These reports compare the agreed service levels and the service levels that were actually measured. Examples include reports about:

- Availability and downtime during a specified period
- Average response times during peak periods
- Transaction rates during peak periods
- Number of functional errors in the IT service
- Frequency and duration of service degradation (services do not reach the agreed level)
- Average number of users during peak periods
- Number of successful and unsuccessful attempts to circumvent security
- Proportion of service capacity used
- Number of completed and open changes
- Cost of the service provided

10.4.6 Review
Service levels must be reviewed at regular intervals. The following aspects should be considered: Service level agreements since the previous review
- Problems related to the services
- Identification of service trends
- Changes to services within the agreed service levels
- Changes to procedures and estimates of the cost of additional resources
- Consequences of failure to provide the agreed service levels

If the IT services fail to meet the agreed service levels, actions may be agreed for improvement, such as:
- Developing a Service Improvement Program
- Allocating additional personnel and resources
- Modifying the service levels defined in the SLA
- Modifying the procedures
- Modifying Operational Level Agreements and Underpinning Contracts

In many organizations where Service Level Management is being introduced, there are discussions about whether or not to associate sanctions with the failure to meet SLA agreements. This is a difficult issue as Service Level Management is based on the interaction between the IT department and the users of IT services, often within the same organization. In such a situation, where both the IT department and users work towards the same corporate objectives, it is doubtful if sanctions and especially financial penalties contribute to the corporate interests. It would be much better to make agreements based on a common interest about measures to be taken to prevent failure to meet the service levels. However, sanctions may be relevant if the IT service provider obtains a service from an external IT provider. However, in that case there is more likely to be a legally binding contract (UC) than a SLA.

10.5 Process control
A number of critical success factors have to be identified to optimize the process and its control. Performance indicators are also needed to measure and improve the process.

10.5.1 Critical success factors and key performance indicators
The success of Service Level Management depends on the following factors:
- A capable Service Level Manager with both IT and business expertise, and a supporting organization when necessary
- Clear process mission and objectives
- Awareness campaign to provide people with information about the process, develop understanding and gain support
- Clearly defined tasks, authorities and responsibilities within the process, distinguishing between process control and operational tasks (customer contacts)

The following key performance indicators can be used to determine the effectiveness and efficiency of the Service Level Management process:
- Service elements included in SLAs
- Elements of the SLA supported by OLA and UCs
- Elements of the SLAs which are monitored, and where shortcomings are reported
- Elements of the SLAs which are regularly reviewed

- Elements of the SLAs where the agreed service levels are fulfilled
- Shortcomings which are identified and covered by an improvement plan
- Actions which are taken to eliminate these shortcomings
- Trends identified with respect to the actual service levels

10.5.2 Management reports

Management reports, in contrast to service level reports, are not provided for the customer, but to control or manage the internal process. They may contain metrics about actual service levels supported, and trends such as:
- Number of SLAs concluded
- Number of times an SLA was not fulfilled
- Cost of measuring and monitoring the SLAs
- Customer satisfaction, based on survey complaints
- Statistics about incidents, problems and changes
- Progress of improvement actions

10.5.3 Functions and roles

Roles

Service Level Management needs to be controlled by a process manager. This manager should ensure that the process is effective and provides the envisaged benefits. This does not necessarily mean that this role is fulfilled by one person. Many organizations have several Service Level Managers, each being responsible for one or more services or customer groups.

Responsibilities

The Service Level Manager is responsible for:
- Creating and updating the Service Catalog
- Defining and maintaining an effective Service Level Management process for the IT organization, including:
  - SLA structure
  - OLAs with internal providers
  - UCs with external providers
- Updating the existing Service Improvement Program
- Negotiating, concluding and maintaining SLAs, OLAs and UCs
- Reviewing the performance of the IT organization and improving it where necessary

10.6 Problems and costs

10.6.1 Problems

The following problems may be encountered:
- Service Level Management results in a businesslike relationship with the customer and requires that all IT personnel adhere to the agreements. This may require a culture change in the organization.
- Customers may need help specifying the Service Level Requirements.
- It can be quite difficult to express expectations of the customer in terms of measurable standards and associated costs.
- The Service Level Manager should be wary of over-ambitious agreements whilst the planning, measuring and monitoring tools, procedures, Service Quality Plan, and the Underpinning Contracts have not been developed. It is better to use a strategy of gradual improvement.

- The overhead costs associated with monitoring and measuring the service levels are easily underestimated. In a large organization this may require several dedicated staff.
- In practice, many IT organizations start by drafting Service Level Agreements and skip the analysis of the requirements of the customer, the design stage and the development of the Service Quality Plan. This can result in a process which is difficult to manage and which does not provide clear, measurable standards.
- The Service Level Management documents and process could end up becoming ends in themselves, as opposed to a means to a better relationship between the IT service provider and the customer.

10.6.2 Costs

The costs of implementing Service Level Management can be divided into the following categories:
- Personnel costs (Service Level Manager and project team)
- Training costs
- Documentation costs
- Costs of accommodation, hardware and software
- Costs of operational activities related to updating the Service Quality Plan, the Service Level Agreements and the Service Catalog

Chapter 11
Financial Management for IT Services

11.1 Introduction

Most people view IT services as an important contributor to the support of routine business activities, but too few people realize that these services cost money. As the number of users grows, IT budget keeps growing. Customers grow more concerned about IT spending as the budget grows, and less able, without assistance, to map this spending to the business. If charging for IT services is called for, without assistance, the customer finds it difficult to map actual costs per customer to business benefits.

ITIL was developed to structure the management of the IT infrastructure to promote the efficient and economic use of IT resources. One of the objectives was to change over from budget-based organizations with fixed budgets to cost-conscious businesslike organizations.

Quality and costs
Providing IT services to users at a reasonable cost depends on three factors:
- **Quality** - in operational terms of:
  - Capacity
  - Availability
  - Performance
  - Disaster recovery
  - Support
- **Cost** - in terms of:
  - Expenditure
  - Investment
- **Customer requirements** - the cost and quality must be in line with the users' business needs

The first two factors are often in conflict as improving quality normally means increasing costs, while reducing costs normally means decreasing quality. However, these two factors can be balanced by focusing on the customer's needs.

An awareness of the costs associated with providing IT services and applying a realistic charging system for those services, puts the provision of IT services on a solid business footing. Customers will become more aware of the costs and feel that they are being charged a reasonable price, and are therefore less likely to squander IT resources.

11.1.1 Basic concepts
Budgeting
Budgeting involves predicting costs and controlling expenditure. This often starts by preparing a plan with the anticipated customer demand for the services and the related costs.
A forecast can be developed on the basis of historical data, while making allowances for current trends in the business and relying on personal expertise. If there is no historical data available, it may be possible to use similar services as a model.

Accounting
Accounting means monitoring how the IT organization spends its money. It is particularly important to be able to determine costs for each customer, service, activity, etc. Here, understanding the issues is more important than being able to determine the cost to the penny.

Charging

Charging refers to all the activities needed to bill the customer for the services provided to them. Charging includes determining the objective(s) of charging, as well as the algorithm(s) for calculating charges. This requires an effective accounting system that fulfills the need for detail at the different accounting levels: analysis, turning, reporting.

Cost categories

Effective cost control requires an understanding of the nature of the costs. Costs can be classified in several ways.

For each product or service you could determine the costs that contribute to it directly and those that do not:
- **Direct costs:** costs related specifically and exclusively to an IT service. For example activities and materials directly and uniquely associated with a specific service (telephone line rental for Internet access).
- **Indirect costs:** costs that are not specifically and uniquely associated with an IT service. Examples include facilities (e.g. a desk), support services (e.g. network management), and administrative costs (including time).

One option for charging the indirect costs is simply to apportion them between services or customers.

Another option is to use Activity Based Costing (ABC). This method starts with collecting all the overhead costs in an organization and then allocating the costs of activities to the products and services that necessitated these activities.

In essence costs are charged on the basis of criteria other than direct costs. ABC can be a useful charging method if many costs are not directly related to the service volume. Instead of allocating indirect costs arbitrarily, ABC allocates them on the basis of activities carried out for products and services.

Another way to understand costs, is to divide them into fixed and variable costs.
- **Fixed costs** are independent of the production volume; they include investments in hardware, software and buildings. In most cases, the monthly or yearly depreciation and interest are considered, rather than the purchase price. Fixed costs continue even if the production (service) volume is reduced or interrupted.
- **Variable costs** are costs whose levels change in line with changes in the production volume. Examples include external personnel, printer cartridges, paper, heating and electricity. These costs are linked with the services provided; as the production volume increases, the costs will also rise.

A certain distinction relates to capital and operational costs:
- **Capital costs** concern the purchase of assets intended for long-term use within the organization. The costs are depreciated over a number of years. Thus, the costs amount to the depreciation, rather than the purchase price.
- **Operational costs** are day-to-day costs not associated with tangible production resources. Examples include hardware and software maintenance contracts, license costs, insurance premiums, etc.

Cost types

Once the cost accounting structure has been defined (for example by department, service or customer), cost types can be set up for posting cost items in the accounts. The number of cost types will depend on the size of the organization. Cost types should have a clear and recognizable description and structure so that costs are easily allocated.

The cost types then are subdivided into **cost elements.** The charging methods for each cost element can be defined at a later stage. There are six main cost types, some for direct costs and some for indirect costs.

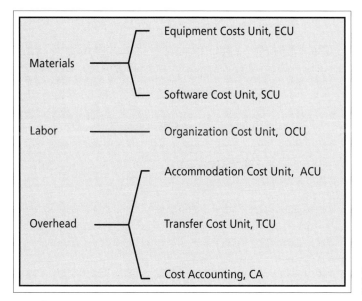

Figure II.I
Cost types and cost elements
(source: OGC)

Examples of these cost types include:
- **Equipment Cost Unit (ECU)** - all IT hardware such as:
  - Servers
  - Disk storage
  - Communications & networks
  - Printers
- **Software Cost Unit (SCU)** - direct and indirect costs to keep the system operating, including:
  - System software
  - Transaction processing software
  - Database management systems
  - System management systems
  - Application development systems
  - Applications
- **Organization Cost Unit (OCU)** - direct and indirect personnel costs, which may be fixed or variable, such as:
  - Salaries
  - Training
  - Travel costs

- **Accommodation Cost Unit (ACU)** - all direct and indirect costs related to housing, such as:
  - Computer rooms
  - Offices
  - Other facilities such as test rooms, training rooms, air conditioning, etc.
- **Transfer Cost Unit (TCU)** - costs associated with goods and services provided by another department. That is, internal charges between departments of an organization.
- **Cost Accounting (CA)** - costs associated with the financial management activities themselves.

II.2 Objectives

Financial Management aims to assist the internal IT organization with the cost-effective management of the IT resources required for the provision of IT services. For this reason, the process aims to break down the IT service costs, and associate them with the various IT services provided. In this way, it aims to support management decisions with respect to IT investment and encourages the cost aware use of IT facilities.

It may be decided to base the charging methods on full cost recovery, recovery with financial support (budgets), or recovery with the objective of making a predefined profit.

Benefits
Once the IT organization has introduced Financial Management, it will be able to:
- Determine the costs of IT services.
- Identify and classify the cost structure.
- Fairly allocate the costs to IT services provided to internal and external customers.
- Introduce charging methods for the use of IT services, where appropriate.
- Operate the IT department as a business unit, where required.
- Recover all costs including capital costs (investment, repayment, depreciation and interest) from the customer.
- Check the charges at regular intervals to determine if they are still realistic and acceptable.
- Shape the behavior of customers and users by building cost awareness and tying costs directly to services.

Because of the diverse nature of the benefits, we make a distinction between Budgeting and Accounting (which are involved with Costing) and Charging.

The main advantage of **Budgeting and Accounting** is that it provides management with better information about the costs of providing IT services. This information enables the IT management to balance costs and quality to provide a financially justifiable service.

Budgeting and Accounting helps the IT Services Manager to:
- Make decisions for each service, based on cost effectiveness.
- Take a businesslike approach to decisions on IT services and the related investments.
- Provide more information to support expenditure, for example by showing the costs of avoiding strategic expenditure.
- Develop budgets and plans on the basis of reliable information.

The main advantage of **Charging** is promoting a businesslike relationship with the customer. A paying customer has rights and can make demands, but will also use resources more carefully if they are aware of the link between the demands they make and the invoice they receive.

Charging enables IT Services Management to:

plans based on cost recovery

during peak times, or sim-
s upon which management

[handwritten: Pick up software from VS]

navior and not lead to a sit-
For example, it may not be
al rates, even if these users
vironment for negotiation.
g IT facilities.

hus, the IT organization is
ity and cost-effectiveness of
organizations also increas-
ookshops, for example, put
orld. This increases the scale
nation about the costs. Cost
ded and the reasonable costs
ore businesslike, and putting

or the flexibility provided by

ding updating relevant infor-

decisions can be taken with

s activities.

Financial Management supports a business in planning and realizing its business objectives. It must be used consistently throughout the business, with a minimum of conflict, to optimize its efficiency. In an IT organization, Financial Management is implemented through three major processes: Budgeting, Accounting and Charging. This cycle is illustrated in Figure 11.2.

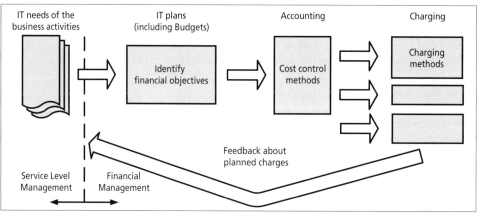

Figure II.2 The financial cycle (source: OGC)

Financial Management for IT Services interacts with almost all the other IT Service Management processes, but has particular dependencies and responsibilities with respect to the processes discussed below.

Relationship with business processes
Service Level Management is important in terms of defining the vision, strategy and planning in line with the business processes (Figure 11.3). Although these activities fall outside the scope of Financial Management, they make an important contribution to this area. This is because the business has a vision of the future, which is used to define measurable objectives which affect all business units and which can also be used to set measurable objectives for the IT organization.

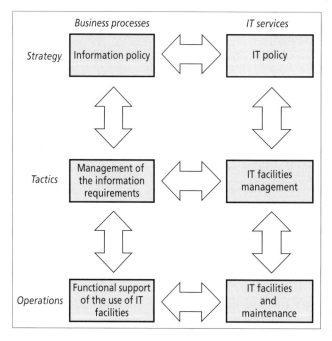

Figure II.3
Relationship with the business processes

Hence, the IT strategy should be based on the business objectives. As the IT organization becomes more familiar with the business, opportunities will be created for the cost effective use of new IT technology. The IT costs of implementation and operation have to be compared with the business advantages in terms of reduced operating costs and increased turnover.

Relationship with Service Level Management
The SLA defines the expectations of the customer and obligations of the IT management organization. The costs incurred to fulfill the customer's requirements have a major impact on the form and scale of services agreed with the customer. The Financial Manager of the IT organization confers with the Service Level Manager about issues such as the costs of meeting current and future business requirements, the Charging policy of the organization and its effect on customers, and how the policy affects customer behavior.

The more a SLA allows different service levels for different customers, the more important and the greater the potential benefits of Charging for IT services. This will also increase the overhead resulting from the Budgeting, Accounting and Charge-back processes.

Relationship with Capacity Management
The provision of capacity and availability will be influenced by cost information. It may be necessary to discuss the cost of provision of increased capacity and improved availability with the customer or the business as a whole. Information on the cost versus business benefit may influence the decision on whether to purchase additional capacity or improve availability.

Relationship with Configuration Management
Configuration Management specifies, identifies, and records all changes to all infrastructure components. The use of information, including cost information in the CMDB facilitates the collection of historical cost data. Configuration Management can also be used to reconcile asset data with data from financial systems.

II.4 Activities

II.4.1 Budgeting
The objective of Budgeting is planning and controlling the activities of an organization. Corporate and strategic planning concerns the long-term objectives of a business. Budgets define the financial plans for the objectives during the period covered by the budget. These periods normally range from one to five years.

Budgeting methods
One of the following methods is selected, depending on the financial policy of the business:
- **Incremental budgeting** - last year's figures are used as the basis for the new budget. This is then adjusted to reflect the expected changes in activities, costs and prices.
- **Zero-Base budgeting** - this method starts with a blank piece of paper: the Zero Base. Past experience is ignored. This requires managers to justify all their resource needs in terms of costs in their budget. This means that every expense has to be evaluated and decided if it should be made, as well as what the cost should be. Obviously, this method is much more time-consuming, and it is therefore normally only used every few years. The incremental method is used for the years in between.

Budgeting process

Budgeting starts by identifying the key factors that limit the growth of the company. In many businesses, this is the sales volume; however, it could also be a lack of space or materials. Often, financial constraints determine the budget. This process includes defining the following secondary budgets (we will ignore the approval processes used in every business):

• **Sales and marketing budget** - if the sales volume determines the budget, then the marketing department is responsible for a large part of the process. An accurate assessment and analysis of the customers, markets, sales regions, products, etc. is essential for drawing up a good budget.
• **Production budget** - the production budget provides detailed information about the services to be provided: quantities, delivery times, person-hours required, materials required, etc.
• **Administrative budgets** - based on the service to be provided, you have to determine the overhead budgets for the relevant departments such as production, sales and distribution, research and development, etc.
• **Cost and investment budgets** - the cost budget results from the plans in the above budgets. The investment budget identifies the expenditure associated with the replacement and purchase of the means of production. Investment projects initiated in the preceding year may also affect the investment budget.

Budget period

The financial (fiscal) year would be an obvious choice for the budget period. For a regular comparison between the actual and budget figures, the budget period is then divided into months or another regular period, such as four-week windows.

Some businesses not only draw up a detailed one-year budget, but also a general forecast for a three or five-year period. This informs senior management about the expectations over a longer period.

II.4.2 Accounting

To be able to run an IT organization as a business, it is essential that all the costs that IT is responsible for are identified and understood. Costs have to be determined, even if they will not be charged to customers. Costs can only be controlled if they are clearly understood. This is not so much about identifying minor costs, but primarily about the different ways in which costs can be structured. This increases the understanding of the way in which money is spent.

One of the primary Accounting activities is defining the cost elements. This structure is fixed for one year, after which it can be modified. In most cases, a cost accounting method will have been selected when introducing a cost element structure to the business. Thus, the cost element structure should be compatible with the methods adopted by the business. In many cases, costs are recorded for each department, customer or product. However, ideally the structure should reflect the services provided. Even when the process is not used for charging, it is often useful to base the cost type structure on a service structure, such as that used in a service catalog.

Business application Accounts	Business application Relationship Management	Business application Marketing data
Terminal Emulator IBM environment		Terminal Emulator other environment
Intranet, Extranet and Internet Information Services		
Groupware Mail & directory services		
General business applications		
Office applications		
File Services & Print Services		
Operating system Windows 98		Operating system Windows NT 4.0
Workstation Baseline-A Powerful desktop PC	Workstation Baseline-B Standard desktop PC	Workstation Baseline-C Laptop PC
Networking services (LAN & WAN)		

Figure 11.4
Example of a service structure

In the example of Figure 11.4 there is a hierarchical structure of the service elements created by the IT organization to provide the services. In this structure, the lower-level service elements support the higher-level service elements. The higher the position of an element in this structure, the more relevant its function is to the business.

After defining the service elements, cost elements have to be defined which are then subdivided into cost units for personnel, hardware, software and overheads.

The advantage of structuring cost elements in line with service elements is that expenditure on the hardware, software and support of the service becomes clearly visible. In addition to a structure based on direct costs as shown in Figure 11.4, it may also be decided how to allocate indirect costs to the services. The more detailed the service structure, the easier it will be to understand the costs. Alternatively, the catalog could only list three standard workstations that include everything. In this case, the diagram would only have three columns and far fewer cost elements. This may be clearer, but it would also provide less detailed information. For example there would be no clear cost element that network support should be allocated to and it would therefore be impossible to the determine the support required for the network.

Budgets for the coming year are then drawn up for each service and cost element, on the basis of past experience and estimates of growth for the coming year. These budgets are monitored every month to identify any new developments such as unexpected growth, and to respond in accordance with the business policy where appropriate.

11.4.3 Charging

Keeping cost records is obviously not a new concept, but it is becoming increasingly important. However, charging for internal costs is a relatively new development. Internal charging is an effective tool to encourage users to use the IT resources more carefully. However, charging for IT services is not that useful if the budget holders in the customer organizations are not charged for other services, such as the telephone, accommodation, mailroom, catering and personnel administration. In other words, charging should be compatible with the financial policies of the organization. If charging is found to be appropriate, then budget holders can address operational costs, which they can pass on in the price of their products and services.

Normally, charging is introduced to recover all the costs incurred. In that case, the IT organization operates as a business unit. This is only feasible if the actual operating costs of the IT services are known.

Charging Policy
It is useful to address charging policies before setting a rate.
There are a number of charging policies. The appropriate method can be selected depending on the objectives of Financial Management. Alternatively, when introducing charging in stages, a different policy might be used for each stage. The charging policies are:
- **Communication of Information** - customer managers are informed about the charges to make them aware of the costs of the use of IT services by their departments. There are two options for this:
  - Calculating the costs associated with each business unit and informing the managers concerned.
  - As above, but including the charges to be passed on, based on a specific charging method.
- **Pricing Flexibility** - rates are determined and charged on an annual basis. If the service provider takes the initiative to invest in a service because it is used more frequently, the contract can include a clause for charging the additional costs. The alternative is to offer excess capacity to other potential customers.
- **Notational Charging** - the costs are invoiced, but need not be paid. This method enables the IT organization to gain experience with the process and correct any mistakes in the charging system. It also gives the customer an opportunity to get used to charging. However, this charging method is only useful if eventually the costs will indeed be recovered, otherwise cost awareness will fall.

Rates
It is often difficult to set a rate for a service. Setting rates include the following activities:
- Deciding on the objective of charging
- Determining direct and indirect costs
- Determining market rates
- Analyzing the demand for services
- Analyzing the number of customers and the competition

To determine the rate for a service, the organization should first determine the objective and the intended benefit for customers and IT personnel.

Price is one of the four Ps in marketing: Product, Price, Promotion and Place. The price is not only relevant in terms of recovering the costs incurred, but also affects the demand for the product. A flexible pricing strategy can be used to promote products or to phase them out. A new service with few customers could be subsidized by the revenue from other services. The costs of a service must be clearly identified before the pricing strategy can be selected.

There is a wide range of pricing policies, such as:
- **Cost Plus** - exists in several forms, all of which are based on charging the costs incurred plus a profit margin (cost + % mark-up). The costs and profit margin can be defined in a number of ways, such as:

- Full costs including a profit margin.
- Marginal costs plus a margin (sufficient to cover the average fixed costs, costs per item, and return on capital). For example, if the availability of the LAN/WAN is included in the charges for a network connection, then this element need not be included in other LAN services.
- One of the above methods, with a margin of 0%.
- **Going Rate** - for services where there are already price agreements.
- **Target Return** - services whose price was determined in advance.
- **Market rate - (what the market will bear)** - prices which match those charged by external suppliers.
- **Negotiated Contract Price** - these prices are discussed with the customer. If the customer requests a new service then it is negotiated whether they have to bear all the investment costs, or only a proportion.

Volume discounts can be granted for services that can be provided at a lower price if the volume increases. To spread the demand on the systems, peak and off-peak rates can be used.

11.4.4 Reporting
Depending on the charging policy, the actual use of IT services is either invoiced or communicated to the customer. The costs are addressed in the regular meetings with the customer under the Service Level Management process. Hence, Service Level Management is provided with the following information:
- IT services expenditure per customer
- Difference between the actual and estimated charges
- Charging and Accounting methods used
- Any disputes about charges, with the causes and solutions

11.5 Process control
Accounting forms part of the overall IT Service Management structure and should be managed by a Financial Manager. This manager is responsible for the implementation and day-to-day management of the Accounting and Charging system and reports to IT management. The Financial Manager need not be part of the IT organization. Reports, critical success factors and performance indicators can be used to optimize Financial Management.

11.5.1 Management reports
The Financial Management process must provide regular reports to the IT management about issues such as:
- Overall costs and benefits of the IT services
- Cost analysis for each IT department, platform, or other relevant unit
- Costs associated with the Financial Management system
- Planning of future investments
- Opportunities for cost reduction.

11.5.2 Critical success factors and performance indicators
Before introducing Financial Management, the users, personnel, and IT management must be informed of the objective of its introduction, and the costs, benefits and potential problems associated with the introduction.
Critical success factors for the introduction of an effective charging system include:
- Users must be aware of which services they are charged for.

- Users must be aware of the charging methods so that they can control their costs (for example through agreements or reports in terms of quantifiable performance units).
- The cost monitoring system must provide details and justification of expenditure.
- IT Service Management must provide balanced systems offering effective IT services at reasonable costs.
- IT management must be fully aware of the impact and costs of the introduction of Financial Management and be fully committed to it.
- Configuration Management must provide relevant information about the structure of the services to set up an appropriate accounting system.

The following performance indicators can help to control the process:
- Accurate cost-benefit analysis of the services provided
- Customers consider the charging methods reasonable
- The IT organization meets its financial targets
- The use of the services by the customer changes
- Timely reporting to Service Level Management

II.5.3 Functions and roles
Some IT organizations have their own Financial Managers, while other organizations have agreements with the financial department, which cooperates closely with IT management. Like any other process, Financial Management must have a process owner responsible for the development and maintenance of the financial system.

The IT Financial Manager who is responsible for the process must work on equal terms with the management of the other processes and the financial department to draw up guidelines for the Budgeting, Accounting and Charging systems.

II.6 Problems and costs

II.6.1 Problems
The following problems may be encountered:
- The activities required for recording and monitoring costs are often a new discipline for IT personnel, and little has been written on the subject
- Monitoring, calculating and charging costs often requires information about the planning of non-IT services, such as buildings for which it is often impossible to obtain planning details
- It is difficult to find personnel who are familiar with both IT and accounting
- If the corporate strategy and objectives for the development of Information Systems have not been clearly formulated and documented then it becomes difficult to consider the necessary investments
- The opportunities provided by the process are often insufficiently understood, resulting in insufficient cooperation
- Lack of management commitment can mean that the process is not taken seriously by the organization

II.6.2 Costs

The costs of this process can be divided into two categories:

- Administrative and organizational costs associated with planning, introducing and carrying out the process
- Costs of the necessary tools, such as an application with hardware and a database.

Chapter 12

Capacity Management

12.1 Introduction

Capacity Management aims to provide the required capacity for data processing and storage, at the right time and in a cost effective way. It is a balancing act. Good capacity management eliminates panic buying at the last minute, or buying the biggest box possible and crossing your fingers. Both of these situations are costly. Many data centers, for example, perpetually run at 30% to 40% or more of unused capacity. This isn't so bad when you have a handful of servers. But when you have thousands of servers, as many enterprise IT shops do, these percentages mean vasts sums of money are being wasted.

Capacity Management addresses the following issues:
- Can the purchase cost of processing capacity be justified in the light of business requirements, and is the processing capacity used in the most efficient way (cost versus capacity)?
- Does the current processing capacity adequately fulfill both current and future demands of the customer (supply versus demand)?
- Is the available processing capacity performing at peak efficiency (performance tuning)?
Precisely when should additional capacity be brought on board?

To implement its objective, Capacity Management needs a close relationship with business and IT strategy processes. Hence, this process is both reactive (measuring and improving) and proactive (analyzing and forecasting).

12.1.1 Basic concepts

Important concepts in Capacity Management include:
- **Performance Management:** measuring, monitoring and tuning the performance of IT infrastructure components.
- **Application Sizing:** determining the hardware or network capacity to support new or modified applications and the predicted workload.
- **Modeling:** using analytical or simulation models to determine the capacity requirements of applications and determine the best capacity solutions. Modeling allows various scenarios to be analyzed and the "what-if" questions addressed.
- **Capacity Planning:** developing a Capacity Plan, analyzing the current situation (preferably using scenarios) and predicting the future use of the IT infrastructure and resources needed to meet the expected demand for IT services.

12.2 Objectives

Capacity Management aims to consistently provide the required IT resources at the right time (when they are needed), and at the right cost, aligned with the current and future requirements of the customer.

Thus, Capacity Management needs to understand both the expected business developments affecting the customer, as well as anticipating technical developments. The Capacity Management process has an important role in determining returns on investment and cost justifications.

Advantages

The advantages of Capacity Management are:

- Reduced risks associated with existing services as the resources are effectively managed, and the performance of the equipment is monitored continuously.
- Reduced risks associated with new services as Application Sizing means that the impact of new applications on existing systems is known. The same applies with respect to modified services.
- Reduced costs, as investments are made at the appropriate time, neither too early nor too late, which means that the purchasing process does not have to deal with last-minute purchases or over-purchases of capacity well in advance of when they are needed.
- Reduced business disruption through close involvement with Change Management when determining the impact on the capacity and preventing urgent changes resulting from incorrect capacity estimates.
- More reliable forecasts the longer Capacity Management is used, which means that customer requests can be responded to more quickly.
- Higher efficiency as demand and supply are balanced at an early stage.
- Managed, or even reduced, capacity-related expenses as the capacity is used more efficiently.

These advantages will improve the relationship with the customer. Capacity Management confers with the customer at an early stage, and anticipates the requirements. The relationships with suppliers will also be improved. Purchasing, delivery, installation and maintenance agreements can be planned more effectively.

12.3 The process

Like many of the ITIL processes, Capacity Management goes back to the days of mainframe computers. Unfortunately, this means that some people think Capacity Management is therefore only relevant in mainframe environments. This is reinforced by the great reduction in hardware costs in recent years. This has resulted in simply buying hardware with excess capacity without considering Capacity Management. The danger here is that the largest source of costs, risks, and possible problems in IT are not in the hardware itself. In other words, the unnecessary proliferation of hardware creates a management problem that is much more expensive than the hardware itself.

Implementing Capacity Management will help prevent unnecessary investments and ad-hoc capacity changes, as the latter aspect in particular can adversely impact the provision of services. These days the cost of IT does not so much come from the investments in capacity, as from managing it. For example, an excessive increase in storage capacity will impact tape back-up operations and it will take longer to find files stored on the network. This example illustrates an important aspect of Capacity Management: good Capacity Management is perhaps the most important ingredient in changing the perception (and reality) of an IT organization from an overhead group to a service provider. With good capacity management in place, the IT service provider will see, for example, that the eighteen strategic initiatives that are slated for IT this year will render the current backup solution obsolete. With this knowledge in mind, the Capacity Manager can ensure that the true cost of these initiatives is seen-i.e., that the cost of the new backup solution is apportioned across the eighteen initiatives. This is proactive. If, instead, there is no capacity management, the IT organization reacts only when the backup window is being exceeded. In this case, the customer sees the IT organization as an overhead, coming "begging for money", simply because IT was not proactive in setting expectations and assigning costs up front.

Capacity Management aims to prevent surprises and rushed purchases by making better use of the available resources, and to increase capacity at the right time, or control the use of the resources. Capacity Management can also help coordinate the capacities of different aspects of a service to ensure that costly investments in certain components are used efficiently.

Today's IT infrastructures are extremely complex. This increases the capacity dependencies between components. Thus, it is increasingly difficult to meet the service levels agreed with the customer. A professional IT organization should therefore take an integrated approach to Capacity Management.
Figure 12.1 shows the main Capacity Management activities.

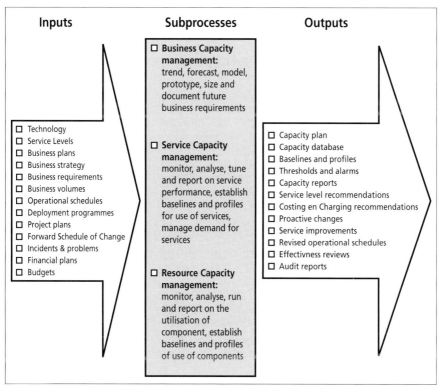

Figure 12.1 Capacity Management process (source: OGC)

Capacity Management has three subprocesses, or levels of analysis where capacity can be considered:
- **Business Capacity Management** - the objective of this subprocess is to understand the future user needs. This can be done by obtaining information from the customer, e.g. from strategic plans or by undertaking trend analysis. This sub-process is primarily proactive. It has strong links with Service Level Management in terms of the definition and negotiation of service agreements.
- **Service Capacity Management** - the objective of this subprocess is to determine and understand the use of IT services (products and services provided to customers). You have to understand the performance and peak loads to ensure that appropriate service agreements can be made and guaranteed.
- **Resource Capacity Management** - the objective of this subprocess is to determine and under-

stand the use of the IT infrastructure. Examples of resources include network bandwidth, processing capacity, and disk capacity. Potential problems have to be detected early to manage these resources effectively. You also need to be abreast of technical developments. Actively monitoring trends is an important activity within this subprocess.

As Capacity Management and the business's needs are related, Capacity Management is an essential element of the planning process. However, the support it provides to operational processes should not be underestimated. The links with the other Service Management processes are discussed below.

Relationship with Incident Management
Incident Management informs Capacity Management about incidents due to capacity problems. Capacity Management can provide scripts for Incident Management to diagnose or solve capacity problems.

Relationship with Problem Management
Capacity Management supports Problem Management in both its reactive and proactive roles. Capacity Management tools, information, knowledge and expertise can be used to support Problem Management at various stages.

Relationship with Change Management
Capacity Management can be part of the CAB. Capacity Management can provide information about the need for capacity and the potential impact of a change on the provision of the service. The information about the changes is input for the Capacity Plan. Capacity Management can submit RFCs during the development of the plan.

Relationship with Release Management
Capacity Management supports distribution planning when the network is used for automatic or manual distribution.

Relationship with Configuration Management
There is a close connection between the Capacity Database (CDB) and the CMDB. The information provided by Configuration Management is essential for developing an effective CDB.

Relationship with Service Level Management
Capacity Management advises Service Level Management about the feasibility of service levels (for example response and cycle times). Capacity Management measures and monitors performance levels and provides information for checking and where necessary changing the agreed service levels and associated reports.

Relationship with Financial Management for IT Services
Capacity Management supports investment budgeting, cost/benefit analysis, and investment decisions. Capacity Management also provides essential information for charging capacity-related services, such as the allocation of the network capacity.

Relationship with IT Service Continuity Management
Capacity Management specifies the minimum capacity needed to continue the service in the event of a disaster. The capacity needs of IT Service Continuity Management should be constantly reviewed to ensure that they reflect day-to-day changes to the operating environment.

Relationship with Availability Management

Capacity Management and Availability Management are closely connected. Performance and capacity problems can result in the loss of the IT services. In fact, the customer may consider poor performance to be equivalent to unavailability. Because of the many dependencies, the two processes need to be coordinated effectively. They both use many of the same tools and techniques such as Component Failure Impact Analysis (CFIA) and Fault Tree Analysis (FTA).

12.4 Activities

The Capacity Management activities are described below for each subprocess.

12.4.1 Business Capacity Management

Business Capacity Management includes the following activities.

Developing the Capacity Plan

The Capacity Plan describes the current capacity of the IT infrastructure and the expected changes in the demand for IT services, replacement of outdated components, and technical developments. The Capacity Plan also defines the changes needed to provide the service levels agreed in the SLAs at an acceptable cost. The Capacity Plan therefore describes not only the expected changes, but also the associated costs. A plan should be drawn up every year, and it should be checked every quarter to confirm it's validity.

In a way, the Capacity Plan is the most important output of Capacity Management. The outputs often include an annual plan that is synchronized with the budget or investment plan, a long-term plan, and quarterly plans with details of the scheduled capacity changes. This provides a coherent set of plans, where the level of detail increases as the planning horizon approaches.

Modeling

Modeling is a powerful Capacity Management tool and is used to forecast the behavior of the infrastructure.

The tools available to Capacity Management range from estimating to extensive prototype testing. The former is cheap and often adequate for routine activities. The latter is usually only appropriate for large-scale implementation projects.

Between these two extremes, there are a number of techniques that are more accurate than an estimate, and cheaper than an extensive pilot. In order of increasing cost they include:
• Trend analysis (cheapest)
• Analytical modeling
• Simulation
• Baseline assessment (benchmark) (most accurate)

Trend analysis can be used to obtain load information, but cannot be used to predict response times. Analytical modeling and simulation have their own advantages and disadvantages. For example, simulation can be used to accurately predict the performance of a host, possibly as an element of Application Sizing. However, it is a time-consuming method. Analytical mathematical models usually take less time, but the outcome is less reliable. A baseline means that an actual operating environment is created, for example at the supplier's computer center. This environment fulfills the performance requirements and is used for 'what if' or change simulations, such as 'what happens when an application component is transferred to another computer system?' or 'what happens if we double the number of transactions?'

Application Sizing
Application Sizing considers the hardware needed to run new or changed applications, such as applications under development or undergoing maintenance, or which may be purchased at the request of the customer. These predictions include information about the expected performance levels, necessary hardware, and costs.

This discipline is particularly relevant during the initial product development stages. Clear information about the required hardware and other IT resources and expected costs at this stage is valuable to management. This discipline also contributes to the drafting of a new SLA.
Application Sizing can require a significant effort for large or complex environments. First, Capacity Management agrees the Service Level Requirements to be fulfilled by the product with the developers. Once the product has reached the hand over and acceptance stage, it is verified if the agreed Service Levels can be fulfilled in terms of the CPU, I/O, network, disk and memory usage.

One of the results of Application Sizing is the workload characteristics. These can be used to predict what the needed capacity will be, if for instance the number of users would grow 25%. Other workload characteristics are the capacity requirements over time (peaks per day/week/year and future growth.)

12.4.2 Service Capacity Management and Resource Capacity Management
These subprocesses include the same activities, however the emphasis is different. Service Capacity Management addresses the provision of IT services., while Resource Capacity Management addresses technology, required to deliver on those services .
These activities are illustrated in Figure 12.2.

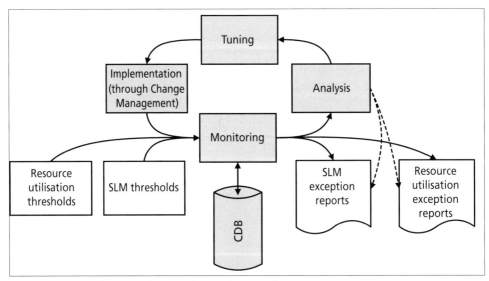

Figure 12.2 Management of resources and service performance (source: OGC)

Monitoring

Monitoring the infrastructure components aims to ensure that the agreed service levels are achieved. Examples of resources to be monitored include CPU utilization, disk utilization, network utilization, number of licenses, etc. (i.e. there are only ten free licenses available).

Analysis

The monitoring data has to be analyzed. Trend analysis can be used to predict future utilization. This may initiate efficiency improvements or the acquisition of additional IT components. Activity analysis requires a thorough understanding of the overall infrastructure and business processes.

Tuning

Tuning optimizes systems for the actual or expected workload on the basis of analyzed and interpreted monitoring data.

Implementation

The objective of implementation is to introduce the changed or new capacity. If this means a change, the implementation involves the Change Management process.

Demand Management

Demand Management aims to influence the demand for capacity. Demand Management is about moving demand. A simple example: a user is running a poorly-written SQL report in the middle of the day, knocking other users out of the database and creating an inordinate amount of traffic. The Capacity Manager suggests creating a job to run the report overnight so the user has it on his desk in the morning.

We distinguish between short-term and long-term demand management:

- **Short-term demand management** - where a recurring lack of capacity is threatened in the near future, and where additional capacity is not easily available.
- **Long-term demand management** - where the cost of upgrades cannot be justified, although there are certain periods (e.g. between 10:00 AM and noon) when there may be insufficient capacity.

Demand Management provides important inputs for drawing up, monitoring and possibly adjusting both the Capacity Plan and the Service Level Agreements.

Demand Management can also involve differential charging (i.e. different charges at peak and off-peak times) to influence customer behaviour.

Populating the Capacity Database (CDB)

Creating and populating the CDB means collecting and updating technical information, and business information, and all other information relevant to Capacity Management. It may not be feasible to store all capacity information in a single physical database. Network and computer system managers may use their own approaches. Often, the CDB refers to a collection of sources with capacity information.

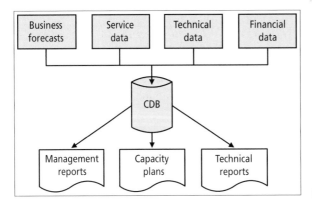

Figure 12.3 CDB information sources

12.5 Process control

Capacity Management is most effective if it is closely linked with the other planning processes, such as Availability Management, and with Application Development activities. This will encourage Capacity Management to take a proactive approach.

12.5.1 Management reports

The management reports provided by the Capacity Management process include, on the one hand, process control information in terms of Capacity Plan characteristics, resources used to implement the process and the progress of improvement activities, and on the other hand, exception reports about issues such as:

• Discrepancies between the actual and planned capacity utilization
• Trends in the discrepancies
• Impact on service levels
• Expected increase/decrease of the capacity utilization in the short term and long term
• Thresholds that, when reached, will require the acquisition of additional capacity.

12.5.2 Critical success factors and performance indicators

• Capacity Management depends on the following critical success factors:
• Accurate business forecasts and expectations
• Understanding of the IT strategy and planning and its accuracy
• Appreciation of technical developments
• Cooperation with other processes

The success of Capacity Management is determined by the following key performance indicators:

• **Predictability of the customer demand:** identification of workload developments and trends over time, and the accuracy of the Capacity Plan.
• **Technology:** options for measuring the performance of all IT services, the pace of implementing new technology, and the ability to continually achieve the agreements laid down in the SLA, even when using older technology.
• **Cost:** reduction in the number of rushed purchases, reduction in unnecessary or expensive overcapacity, and the drawing up of investment plans at an early stage.
• **Operations:** reduction in the number of incidents due to performance problems, the ability to meet customer demand at all times, and the extent to which the Capacity Management process is taken seriously.

12.5.3 Functions and roles

The role of the Capacity Manager is to manage the process and to ensure that the Capacity Plan is developed and maintained, and to ensure that the Capacity Database is up to date.

The System, Network and Application Managers all have important roles in Capacity Management. Not only are they responsible for optimizing the performance, but they are also expected to use their expertise to translate the business demand into system load profiles, and from there to determine the required capacity.

12.6 Problems and costs

12.6.1 Problems

Potential problems in Capacity Management include:

- **Unrealistic expectations** - designers, management and customers often have unrealistic expectations based on a lack of understanding of the technical possibilities of applications, computer systems or networks. One of the tasks of Capacity Management is to guide these expectations, for example by making designers aware of the impact of their design (e.g. for a database) on the capacity and performance. The effect of Capacity Management can also be overestimated, particularly with respect to tuning the system and scheduling the workload. If the operation of systems requires extensive tuning it is likely that the design of the application or database is poor. In general, tuning cannot be used to obtain a higher level of performance than the system was originally designed for. Most large systems have scheduling algorithms that are generally more effective than intervention by system managers. And of course, there is a cost associated with tuning - it makes no sense for a highly paid engineer to garner a 3% performance improvement after a weeks' worth of effort when a $100 stick of memory would produce a 10% improvement. There is a larger cost to over-reliance on tuning - the cost of managing systems which are not, within reason, 'plain vanilla'. Highly 'tweaked' parameters on different boxes, applications, or databases means unintended consequences, and adds delays across all service management processes, in maintenance, troubleshooting, etc.
- **Lack of appropriate information** - it is often difficult to obtain required information, for example for the Capacity Plan. It maybe difficult to obtain reliable information about the expected workload, as the plans of the customer are not known or almost unknown, at least not in detail. This is also difficult for the customer, as product life cycles are getting shorter and shorter. The only solution is to make the best possible estimate and to update the estimate frequently when more information becomes available.
- **Supplier input** - if there is no historical data (for example when a new system is purchased), Capacity Management often has to depend on the information provided by suppliers. Suppliers normally use benchmarks to provide information about their systems, but because of the major differences between testing methods it is often difficult to compare information and it can be misleading about the actual performance of the system.
- **Implementation in complex environments** - implementation in complex distributed environments is difficult because the magnitude of technical interfaces creates a large number of performance dependencies.
- **Determining the appropriate level of monitoring** - monitoring tools often provide many options and may encourage investigations in excessive detail. When purchasing and using these tools, it should be decided in advance at what level monitoring should be carried out.

These problems are relevant to Capacity Management of computer systems as well as networks or large printing systems and PABX systems. This can be even more challenging if several departments are responsible for these domains, which may lead to conflicts about Capacity Management responsibilities.

12.6.2 Costs

The costs of setting up Capacity Management must be estimated during the preparation. The costs can be divided into:

- Purchase of hardware and software tools such as monitoring tools, Capacity Management Database (CDB), modeling tools for simulations and statistical analysis, and reporting tools
- Project management costs associated with the implementation of the process
- Personnel, training and support costs
- Facilities and services

Once the process has been set up, there are recurring costs of personnel, maintenance contracts, etc.

Chapter 13
IT Service Continuity Management

13.1 Introduction
Many managers consider IT Service Continuity Management (ITSCM) as a luxury, for which they need no resources. However, statistics show that disruptive disasters are actually quite common.

Disaster - an event that affects a service or system such that significant effort is required to restore the original performance level.

Hence, a disaster is much more serious than an incident. A disaster is a business interruption. That means that all or part of the business is not "in business" following a disaster. Familiar disasters include fire, lightning, water damage, burglary, vandalism and violence, large-scale power outages, and hardware failure. Terrorist attacks, such as on the World Trade Center in New York, are becoming more common. The Internet can also lead disasters, such as Denial of Service (DoS) attacks that disrupt the communications of an entire organization. Some companies could have prevented serious problems by thinking about and developing Business Continuity Plans. Furthermore, businesses are becoming increasingly dependent on IT services, which means that the impact of the loss of services also increases and becomes less acceptable. In fact, for many companies, doing business is equivalent to using IT, and without IT they cannot create any revenue. It is therefore essential to consider how business continuity can be safeguarded. Since the publication of the Contingency Planning module by the CCTA there have been many changes in IT, and the way it is used by organizations. Traditional contingency planning used to be part of the remit of the IT organization. However, at present IT is much more closely integrated with many aspects of the business. Where the traditional contingency planning process was primarily reactive (what to do in the event of a disaster), the new IT Service Continuity Management process emphasizes prevention, i.e. avoiding disasters.

13.2 Objectives
The objective of IT Service Continuity Management is to support the overall Business Continuity Management (BCM) by ensuring that required IT infrastructure and IT services, including support and the Service Desk, can be restored within specified time limits after a disaster. ITSCM can have a number of different aims. As ITSCM is an integral part of BCM, the scope of ITSCM should be defined on the basis of the business objectives. When assessing the risks it can then be decided if they are within or outside the scope of the ITSCM process.

Benefits
As businesses are becoming increasingly dependent on IT services, the cost of failing to plan, and the benefits of planning can only be identified through a risk analysis. Once the risk to the business, rather than just the risk to the IT services has been identified, investments can be made in prevention measures and measures to deal with disasters, such as recovery plans. The guidelines of this chapter can be used to limit and manage the impact of disasters.
If a disaster does occur, businesses with an ITSCM process have the following advantages:
• They can manage the recovery of their systems.
• They lose less time and offer better continuity to the users.
• They minimize the interruption to their business activities.

13.3 The process

IT Service Continuity Management is responsible for:
- Assessing the impact of the disruption of IT services following a disaster
- Identifying services critical to the business that require additional prevention measures
- Defining periods within which services have to be restored
- Taking measures to prevent, detect, prepare for and migitate the effects of disasters or to reduce their impact
- Defining the approach to be used to restore the services
- Developing, testing and maintaining a recovery plan with sufficient detail to survive a disaster and to restore normal services after a defined period

As the business operations as a whole and IT are becoming more and more enmeshed, both areas are described within the ITIL scope:
- **Business Continuity Management (BCM)** covers risk analysis and management so that the organization can ensure the minimum required production capacity or provision of service at all times. The BCM aims to reduce risks to an acceptable level and develops plans for restoring business activities if they are interrupted by a disaster.
- **IT Service Continuity Management (ITSCM)** is the process of dealing with disasters affecting IT services and maintaining services to allow the business to continue to operate.

IT Service Continuity Management is part of the overall Business Continuity Management and depends on the information provided by the BCM process. The availability of IT services is ensured by combining risk reduction measures (e.g. installing reliable systems) and providing recovery options (e.g. backup systems and redundant systems). Its successful implementation requires support throughout the organization, management commitment and the cooperation of all personnel.

IT Service Continuity Management interacts with all the other IT Service Management processes and particularly with the following.
- **Service Level Management** provides information about the IT service obligations.
- **Availability Management** supports ITSCM by developing and implementing prevention measures.
- **Configuration Management** defines baseline configurations and the IT infrastructure to provide ITSCM with information about the infrastructure to be restored after a disaster.
- **Capacity Management** ensures that the business requirements are fully supported by the appropriate IT resources.
- **Change Management** ensures that all ITSCM plans are correct and up-to-date by involving ITSCM in all changes that may affect prevention measures and recovery plans.

13.4 Activities

Figure 13.1 shows the ITSCM activities. The numbers refer to the subsections of section 13.4 under which the activities are described.

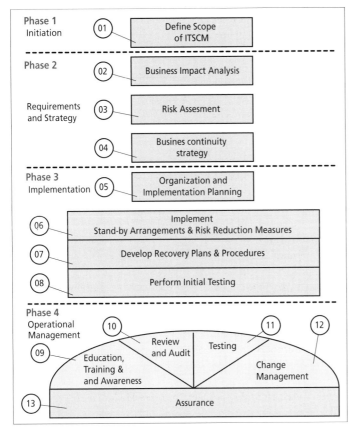

Figure 13.1 ITSCM process model
(based on the OGC model)

13.4.1 Determining the scope of ITSCM

The organization as a whole should be considered when initiating ITSCM, and the following activities must be undertaken:

- **Defining the policy** - the policy should be defined as soon as possible and communicated throughout the organization so that all those concerned are aware of the need for ITSCM. Management has to demonstrate its commitment.
- **Defining the scope and relevant areas** - insurance requirements, quality standards such as the ISO-9000 series, Security Management standards such as BS7799, and general business policy principles are used to select the approach and methods for risk assessment and Business Impact Analysis. The appropriate management structure and process structure for coping with disasters are also identified.
- **Allocating resources** - setting up an ITSCM environment will require a significant investment in personnel and resources. Training must also be provided to ensure that personnel are prepared to implement Stage 2 of the ITSCM process (Requirements and Strategy).
- **Setting up the project organization** - it is advisable to use formal project management methods, for example PRINCE2, supported by planning software.

13.4.2 Business Impact Analysis

Before analyzing the IT services, it is advisable to identify the reasons for the company to include IT Service Continuity Management in Business Continuity Management, and to identify the potential impact of a serious disruption of services. In some cases, the business can survive for some time and the emphasis will be on **restoring services,** in other cases the business cannot operate without IT services and the emphasis will be on **prevention.** Most businesses will have to strike a balance between the two extremes.

Potential reasons include:
• Protecting business processes
• Rapid service recovery
• Surviving competition
• Maintaining market share
• Maintaining profitability
• Protecting the reputation perceived by customers

The above reasons may well be combined. In the financial industry, such as currency trading, the loss of market information means that the business will lose money as trading (the main business process) is interrupted. Furthermore, if there is a statutory requirement to record all trading activity using a specified system, then trading can continue in the event of disruption to that system, but sooner or later a statutory requirement will be infringed and fines may be imposed (profit and need for rapid service recovery). In both cases, the company may lose customers and market share.

Service analysis

Once the reasons for initiating ITSCM have been identified, an analysis is made of the IT services that are essential to the business (e.g. information systems, office applications, accounting applications, e-mail, etc.) and which must be available in accordance with the Service Level Agreements. For some nonessential services, it may be agreed to provide an emergency service with limited capacity and availability. The service levels during disaster recovery may only be modified in agreement with the customer. For critical services, a balance has to be struck between prevention and recovery options.

Infrastructure

A service analysis is followed by an assessment of the dependencies between services and IT resources. Availability Management information is used to analyze the extent to which IT resources perform a critical function in supporting the IT services discussed earlier. Capacity Management provides information about the required capacity. It is also determined to what extent these services may be disrupted, from the loss of service to its restoration. Later, this information will be used to identify the recovery options for each service.

13.4.3 Risk assessment

There are no official disaster statistics, but some disasters worldwide include:

Poison gas	Tokyo Metro, Japan (March 1995)
Power outage	Auckland, New Zealand (December 1997)
Earthquakes	Los Angeles, USA (January 1994)
	Kobe, Japan (January 1995)
Terrorist attacks	World Trade Center, New York, USA (February 1993)
	Bishopsgate, London, England (April 1993)

	Oklahoma City, Oklahoma, USA (April 1995)
	Docklands, London, England (February 1996)
	Manchester, England (June 1996)
	World Trade Center, New York, USA (September 2001)
Floods	Bangladesh (July 1996)
	Pakistan (August 1996)

A risk analysis can help identify the risks a business is exposed to. Such an analysis will provide management with valuable information by identifying the threats and vulnerabilities and relevant prevention measures. Because maintaining a disaster recovery plan is relatively expensive, the prevention measures should be taken first. Once such measures have been taken against most risks, it is determined if there are any remaining risks that may necessitate a Contingency plan. Figure 13.2 shows the links between Risk Analysis and Risk Management; it is based on the **CCTA R**isk **A**nalysis and **M**anagement **M**ethod (CRAMM).

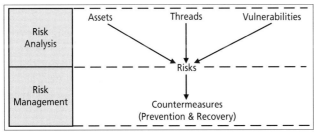

Figure 13.2 The CCTA Risk Assessment Model (source: OGC)

The model supports effective contingency planning by taking a phased approach.

Risk analysis
- First, the relevant **IT components** (assets) must be identified, such as buildings, systems, data, etc. Effective asset identification means that the owner and purpose of each component must be documented.
- The next step is to analyze the **threats** and dependencies and to estimate the likelihood (high, medium, low) that a disaster will occur, for example a combination of an unreliable main power supply and an area with many storms and thunderstorms.
- Next, the **vulnerabilities** are identified and classified (high, medium, and low). A lightning conductor will provide some protection against lightning strikes, but they can still seriously affect the network and the computer systems.
- Finally, the threats and vulnerabilities are evaluated in the context of the IT components, to provide an estimate of the **risks.**

The scope of the process should be considered when estimating the risks; in fact this is part of initiating the ITSCM process (Phase 1). For example, minor problems can be solved by Availability Management measures, and some business risks are outside the scope of ITSCM.

13.4.4 IT Service Continuity Strategy
Most businesses will aim to strike a balance between risk reduction and recovery planning. There is a distinction between risk reduction, business activity recovery activities, and IT recovery options. The relationship between risk reduction (prevention) and recovery planning (recovery options) is discussed below.

Threats can never be fully eliminated. For example, a fire in a building nearby may also damage your building. Reducing one risk might also increase another risk. For example, outsourcing might increase security risks.

Prevention measures

Prevention measures can be taken on the basis of the risk analysis, while carefully considering the costs and risks. The measures may aim to reduce the likelihood or impact of contingencies, and therefore narrow the scope of the recovery plan. Measures can be taken against dust, excessively high or low temperatures, fire, leaks, power outages, and burglary. The remaining risks are then covered by the recovery plan.

The **Stronghold/Fortress Approach** is the most extensive form of prevention. It eliminates most vulnerability, for example by building a bunker with its own power and water supply. However, this may introduce other vulnerabilities such as the risk of network failure, or roadblocks, as off-site recovery will now be even more difficult. The stronghold/fortress approach is suitable for large computer centers that are too complex for a recovery plan. It is vital nowadays to complement a stronghold/fortress approach with a skirmish capability, i.e., an organizational capability to go where the problem is and deal with it promptly before it spirals out of control.

Selecting recovery options

If there are some remaining risks that have not been eliminated by prevention measures, then they will have to be addressed by recovery planning. Recovery options will have to be provided as follows to ensure business continuity:

- **Personnel and accommodation** - how to deal with housing, furniture, transport and travel distances, etc.
- **IT systems and networks** - recovery options are discussed below
- **Support services** - power, water, telephones, post, and courier services
- **Archives** - files, documents, paper-based systems, and reference materials
- **Third parties services** - such as e-mail and Internet service providers

There are a number of options available for the rapid recovery of IT services:

- **Do nothing** - few businesses can afford this approach. It is more likely to indicate a head-in-the-sand attitude. Departments which think that they can survive without IT recovery facilities may give the impression they mean so little to the business that they are dispensable after a contingency. Nevertheless, it could be investigated for each service if this option might be acceptable.
- **Return to a manual (paper-based) system** - this option is normally unfeasible for services critical to the business, as there will be insufficient personnel with experience of using traditional systems. Furthermore, paper-based systems used in the past may no longer be available. However, paper-based systems may be feasible for less important, minor services. Most recovery plans include some paper-based backup routines. For example, the recovery option for a credit card terminal could be the use of paper credit card slips.
- **Reciprocal agreements** - this option can be used if two organizations have similar hardware and agree to provide each other with facilities in the event of a disaster. For this option, the two businesses have to conclude an agreement and ensure that changes are coordinated so that both environments remain interchangeable. Capacity Management should ensure that the reserved capacity is not used for other purposes, or can be released quickly. This option is less attractive nowadays due to the increasing use of online systems such as ATMs and on-line banking as these systems have to be available 24 hours a day, 7 days a week.

- **Gradual recovery (cold stand-by)** - this option can be used by businesses that can manage without IT services for some time, for example 72 hours. It provides an empty computer room at an agreed *fixed facility*, or a mobile computer room delivered to the business's site, the *portable facility*. The computer room is provided with electrical power, air-conditioning, network facilities, and telephone connections. This recovery option can be provided for under contract with an external supplier. Separate agreements will have to be made with suppliers of IT components to ensure that they can be delivered quickly. The advantage of this approach is that the facility is always available. The advantages and disadvantages are different for fixed and portable facilities and relate to issues such as:
  - *Distance to the facility* - few providers offer fixed facilities. These may be remote, a disadvantage which is avoided by the use of a portable facility.
  - *Time* - fixed facility locations are only available for a limited period.
  - *Delay* - in either case, the delivery of the required computer hardware may take some time.
  - *Network* - it is often difficult to provide appropriate network facilities. Connections for a portable facility could be provided in the building used for normal operations.
- **Intermediate recovery (warm stand-by)** - this option provides access to a similar operational environment where the services can continue normally after a short changeover period (24-72 hours). There are three versions of this option:
  - *Internal:* (mutual fallback) if the business has several sites or dedicated test environments that can be used for production. This option provides full recovery with a minimum changeover time. Organizations with several distributed systems often use a variation on this approach, where part of the required capacity is reserved on each system. This spare capacity is monitored by Capacity Management (similar to the reciprocal agreement recovery option).
  - *External:* some service providers provide this option as a commercial service. The costs are divided between the customers. The costs of these arrangements depend on the required hardware and software and the agreed period during which the facility is provided (e.g. 16 weeks). These arrangements are often made to bridge the period needed to set up a cold stand-by facility. This approach is relatively expensive and the facility is likely to be some distance away.
  - *Mobile:* the infrastructure for this option is provided ready-for-use in a trailer. The trailer serves as a computer room and provides environmental control facilities such as air-conditioning. The IT organization must provide a place to park the trailer. Power supply, data and telecommunications connections must be available at dedicated points some distance from the building. The advantages of this option include the short response time and proximity to the business site. This option is only available for a limited number of hardware platforms. Some of the larger hardware suppliers offer this service by providing a number of trailers with standard hardware configurations. At agreed times, for example once every year, the trailer visits the business to test the recovery arrangements. The advantage of this is that it may also be possible to test the impact of an upgrade to a new version of the operating system.
- **Immediate recovery (hot start, hot stand-by)** - this option provides an immediate or very rapid recovery of services in less than 24 hours by providing an identical production environment and mirroring of the data, and possibly even mirroring of the production processes. The latter option is normally developed in close cooperation with Availability Management.
- **Combinations of options** - in many cases, a Contingency plan can provide for a more expensive option to bridge the introduction of a cheaper option. For example, a trailer with operating computer center (mobile hot start) can provide a temporarily solution until portable facilities have been set up and the new host computers have been delivered (mobile cold start). Normal operations are restored after refurbishment of the building and moving the new host computers into the building.

13.4.5 Organization and implementation planning

Once the business strategy has been determined and choices have been made, the ITSCM has to be implemented and the plans for the IT facilities have to be developed in detail. An organization will have to be set up to implement the ITSCM process. This could include management (Crisis Manager), coordination, and recovery teams for each service.

At the highest level there should be an overall plan addressing the following issues:
- Emergency response plan
- Damage assessment plan
- Recovery plan
- Vital records plan (what to do with data, including paper records)
- Crisis Management and PR plans

All these plans are used to assess emergencies and to respond to them. It can then be decided if the business recovery process should be initiated, in which case the next level of plans has to be activated, including the:
- Accommodation and services plan
- Computer system and network plan
- Telecommunications plan (accessibility and links)
- Security plan (integrity of the data and networks)
- Personnel plan
- Financial and administrative plans

13.4.6 Prevention measures and recovery options

This is when the prevention measures and recovery options identified earlier are put into practice. Prevention measures to reduce the impact of an incident are taken together with Availability Management, and may include:
- Use of UPS and backup power supplies
- Fault-tolerant systems
- Off-site storage and RAID systems, etc.

A start should also be made to introduce stand-by agreements. These should cover personnel, buildings and telecommunications. Even during the contingency period a start can be made with restoring the normal situation and ordering new IT components. Dormant contracts can be made in advance with suppliers. This means that signed orders are available for the components to be supplied at an agreed price. When the disaster occurs, the supplier can process the order without having to issue quotations. Such dormant contracts should be updated every year as prices and models will change. The Configuration Management baselines should be considered when updating these contracts.

The following activities can be carried out to set up stand-by agreements:
- Negotiating off-site recovery facilities with third parties
- Maintaining and equipping the recovery facility
- Purchasing and installing stand-by hardware (dormant contracts)
- Managing dormant contracts

13.4.7 Developing plans and procedures for recovery

The plans should be detailed and formal, as a recovery plan requires maintenance and changes must be approved by those concerned. These issues also need to be communicated. The major problems relate to changes in the infrastructure and the agreed service levels. For example, migration to a new midrange platform could mean that there is no equivalent unit at the back-up facility for a warm, external start. For this reason, Configuration Management plays an important role in monitoring the baseline configurations referred to in the recovery plan. The plan should also identify the procedures needed to support it.

Recovery plan

The recovery plan should include all elements relevant to restoring the business activities and IT services, including:

- **Introduction** - describes the structure of the plan and envisaged recovery facilities.
- **Updating** - discusses the procedures and agreements for maintaining the plan, and tracks changes to the infrastructure.
- **Routing list** - the plan is divided into sections, each specifying the actions to be undertaken by a specific group. The routing list shows what sections should be sent to which personnel.
- **Recovery initiation** - describes when and under what conditions the plan is invoked.
- **Contingency classification** - if the plan describes procedures for different contingencies, they should be described here in terms of seriousness (minor, medium, major), duration (day, week, weeks), and damage (minor, limited, serious).
- **Specialist sections** - the plan should be divided into sections based on the six areas and groups covered by the plan:
  - *Administration* - how and when is the plan invoked, which managers and personnel are involved, and where is the control center based?
  - *IT infrastructure* - hardware, software, and telecommunications to be provided by the recovery system, recovery procedures, and dormant contracts for the purchase of new IT components.
  - *Personnel* - personnel required at the recovery facility, possibly transport to the facility, and accommodation if the facility is located far from the business.
  - *Security* - instructions for protection against burglary, fires and explosions at both the home site and the remote site, and information about external storage facilities such as warehouses and vaults.
  - *Recovery sites* - information about contracts, personnel with specified functions, security, and transport.
  - *Restoration* - procedures to restore the normal situation (e.g. the building), conditions under which these procedures are invoked, and dormant contracts.

Procedures

The recovery plan provides a framework for drafting the procedures. It is essential to develop effective procedures, such that anyone can undertake the recovery by following the procedures. These should address:

- Installing and testing hardware and network components
- Restoring applications, databases, and data

These and other relevant procedures are attached to the recovery plan.

13.4.8 Initial testing

Initial testing is a critical aspect of ITSCM. Tests should be performed initially, then following major changes, and then at least annually. The IT department is responsible for testing the effectiveness of the plans and procedures for the IT elements of the plan. Tests may be announced or unannounced.

13.4.9 Training and awareness

Effective training of IT and other personnel and awareness by all personnel and the organization are essential to the success of any IT Services Continuity process.

IT personnel will have to train non-IT personnel in business recovery teams to ensure that they are familiar with the issues so that they can provide support during the recovery operations. The actual contingency facilities, on-site or off-site, should also be covered by the training and tests.

13.4.10 Review and audit

It should be verified regularly if the plans are still up-to-date. This concerns all aspects of ITSCM. In the IT area, such an audit will have to be undertaken every time there is a significant change to the IT infrastructure, such as the introduction of new systems, networks and service providers. Audits must also be carried out if there is any change to the strategy of the IT department or the business. Organizations where rapid and frequent change is common could implement a regular program for verifying the ITSCM concepts. Any resulting changes to the plans and strategy must be implemented under the direction of Change Management.

13.4.11 Testing

The Recovery plan must be tested regularly, rather like an emergency drill on a ship. If everyone has to study the plan when a disaster happens then there are likely to be many problems. The test can also identify weaknesses in the plan or changes that were overlooked. In some cases, changes can be tested beforehand using the recovery facilities before introducing them into the live IT infrastructure.

13.4.12 Change Management

Change Management plays an important role in keeping all the plans current. The impact of any change to the Recovery plan has to be analyzed.

13.4.13 Assurance

Assurance means verifying if the quality of the process (procedures and documents) is adequate to meet the business needs of the company.

13.5 Process control

Effective process control depends on management reports, critical success factors and performance indicators.

13.5.1 Management reports

In the event of a disaster there will be reports about its cause and effect, and how successfully it was dealt with. Any observed weaknesses will be addressed in improvement plans.

The management reports from this process also include evaluation reports of recovery plan tests. These are used for assurance. The process also reports about the number of changes to recovery plans as a result of significant changes elsewhere. Reports may also be issued about new threats.

13.5.2 Critical success factors and performance indicators

The success of IT Service Continuity Management depends on:
- An effective Configuration Management process
- Support and commitment throughout the organization
- Up-to-date, effective tools
- Dedicated training for anyone involved in the process
- Regular, unannounced tests of the recovery plan

Performance indicators include:
- Number of identified shortcomings of the recovery plans
- Revenue lost further to a disaster
- Cost of the process

13.5.3 Functions and roles

The charter of the IT Service Continuity Manager is to implement and maintain the process to ensure that it fulfills the requirements of Business Continuity Management at all times, and to represent the IT Service function within Business Continuity Management.

A number of roles and responsibilities can be identified. There are also differences between the responsibilities during normal and crisis conditions.

Role	Responsibilities during normal conditions	Responsibilities during crisis conditions
Board	Initiating BCM Allocating personnel and resources Defining policies Defining process authority	Crisis management Taking corporate/business decisions
Senior management	Managing the ITSCM process Accepting plans, test reports, etc. Communicating and maintaining awareness Integrating ITSCM within BCM	Coordinating and arbitrating Providing personnel, resources and funding
Management	Undertaking risk analysis Defining deliverables Drafting contracts Managing tests, evaluations and reports	Invoking recovery and continuity mechanisms Leading teams Reporting
Team leaders and team members	Developing deliverables Negotiating services Implementing tests, evaluations and reports Developing and implementing procedures	Implementing the recovery plan

Table 13.1 Examples of ITSCM responsibilities

13.6 Costs and problems

13.6.1 Costs

The major costs associated with the introduction of IT Service Continuity Management are:
- Time and costs for initiating, developing and implementing ITSCM.
- Investment associated with the introduction of risk management and resulting additional hardware, these costs can be reduced if the measures are considered within the scope of Availability Management at the time of designing new configurations.

- Continuing costs of the recovery arrangements that depend on the selected option, such as fees for external hot start contracts, cost of test arrangements, and the period during which the recovery facilities are available.
- Returning operational costs of ITSCM, such as testing, auditing, and updating the plan.

These costs may only be incurred after making a considered choice, and comparing the potential costs associated with not having a recovery plan. Although the costs of maintaining a recovery plan may appear to be high, they are often reasonable compared with the overall expenditure on fire and theft insurance. Furthermore, effective ITSCM may reduce the cost of insurance.

13.6.2 Problems
When implementing the process, the following potential problems should be considered:
- **Resources** - the organization will have to provide additional capacity for a project team to develop and test the plan.
- **Commitment** - the annual costs must be included in the organization's budgets, which requires commitment.
- **Access to recovery facilities** - all options discussed above requires regular testing of the recovery facilities. Thus, the contracts will have to provide the IT organization with regular access to the recovery facilities.
- **Estimating the damage** - certain damage, such as lost reputation, cannot be financially quantified.
- **Budgeting** - the need for expensive contingency facilities is not always understood, or the plans are cut back.
- **No business manager commitment** - this results in a failure to develop ITSCM, although the customer assumes that arrangements have been made.
- **Perpetual Prospectivity** - this is where all or most parts of IT service continuity management are not yet in place and progress is postponed consequently. In such cases, when inquiring about ITSCM, the response will be "yes, we're meeting on that next week...", "we're about to appoint a committee to do just that", etc.
- **Black Boxing** - this is where the IT service provider has abdicated responsibility, as well as given up control for ITSCM readiness: "someone else is handling it". Because the organization has spent a lot of money or has outsourced a portion of their operations to a supplier, the management expects that the money they've spent will ensure their ability to recover, or that the supplier too has plans in place that will help them recover after a business interruption.
- **IT department** - must be guided by the actual wishes and requirements of the business, and not by the IT department's assumptions about them.
- **Familiarity with the business** - it is essential that the business supports the development of ITSCM by identifying essential issues.
- **Lack of awareness** - it is essential that the organization as a whole is aware of the value of ITSCM. Without the awareness and support of all personnel, the process is doomed to failure.

Chapter 14
Availability Management

14.1 Introduction
The pace of technological development keeps increasing. Because of this, within many organizations the hardware and software that is needed keeps expanding and is becoming more diverse, despite of standardization efforts. Old and new technologies have to work together. This results in additional network structures, interfaces and communications facilities. Business operations are becoming increasingly dependent on reliable technology.

A few hours of computer downtime can have a serious impact on the turnover and image of a business, particularly now that the Internet is developing into an electronic marketplace. As the competitors' businesses are only a mouse click away, customer loyalty and satisfaction are now more important than ever. This is one of the reasons why computer systems are now commonly expected to be available 7 days a week, 24 hours a day.

14.1.1 Basic concepts
Figure 14.1 illustrates the basic concepts of Availability Management.

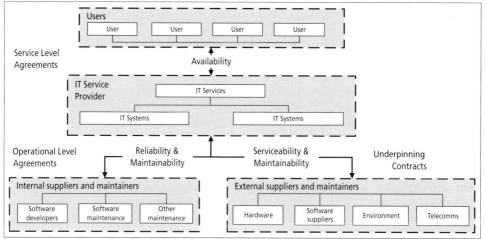

Figure 14.1 Availability Management concepts (source: OGC)

Availability
High availability means that the IT service is continuously available to the customer, as there is little downtime and rapid service recovery. The achieved availability is indicated by metrics. The availability of the service depends on:
• Complexity of the IT infrastructure architecture
• Reliability of the components
• Ability to respond quickly and effectively to faults
• Quality of the maintenance and support organizations and suppliers
• Quality and scope of the operational management processes

Reliability

Adequate reliability means that the service is available for an agreed period without interruptions. This concept also includes resilience. The reliability of a service increases if downtime can be prevented. Reliability is calculated using statistics. The reliability of a service is determined by a combination of the following factors:

- Reliability of the components used to provide the service
- Ability of a service or component to operate effectively despite failure of one or more subsystems (resilience)
- Preventive maintenance to prevent downtime

Maintainability

Maintainability and recoverability relate to the activities needed to keep the service in operation, and to restore it when it fails. This includes preventive maintenance and scheduled inspections. These concepts include the following activities:

- Taking measures to prevent faults
- Detecting faults
- Making a diagnosis, including automatic diagnosis by components themselves
- Resolving the fault
- Recovery after a fault
- Restoring the service

Serviceability

Serviceability relates to contractual obligations of external service providers (contractors, third parties). The contracts define the support to be provided for the outsourced services. As this only concerns a part of the IT service, the term does not refer to the overall availability of the service. If a contractor is responsible for the service as a whole, for example when a Facilities Management contract is concluded, then serviceability and availability are synonymous.

Effective Availability Management requires a thorough understanding of both the business and the IT environment. It is important to be aware that availability cannot simply be "bought": availability has to be included in the design and implementation from the initial design stage. Finally, availability depends on the complexity of the infrastructure, the reliability of the components, the professionalism of the IT organization and its contractors, and the quality of the process itself.

14.2 Objectives

The objective of Availability Management is to provide a cost-effective and defined level of availability of the IT service that enables the business to reach its objectives.

This means that the demands of the customer (the business) have to be aligned with what the IT infrastructure and IT organization is able to offer. If there is a difference between supply and demand then Availability Management will have to provide a solution. Furthermore, Availability Management ensures that the achieved availability levels are measured, and, where necessary, improved continuously. This means that the process includes both proactive and reactive activities. The following premises must be taken into account when developing the process:

- The introduction of Availability Management is essential for obtaining a high degree of customer satisfaction. Availability and reliability determine to a large extent how the customers perceive the service provided by an organization.
- There will always be faults, despite a high degree of availability. Availability Management is

largely responsible for a professional response to such undesirable situations.
- The design of the process demands not only a thorough understanding of IT, but also an appreciation of the processes and services of the customer. The objectives can be realized by combining these two aspects.

Availability Management has a broad scope and includes both new and existing services to customers, relationships with internal and external suppliers, all infrastructure components (hardware, software, networks, etc.) and organizational aspects which may affect availability, such as the expertise of personnel, management processes, and procedures and tools.

14.2.1 Benefits

The major benefit of Availability Management is that the IT services that are designed, implemented and managed, fulfill the agreed availability requirements. A thorough understanding of the business processes of the customer and IT, combined with continuously aiming to maximize the availability and customer satisfaction within the constraints can make an important contribution to realizing an effective service culture. Other benefits of Availability Management include:
- There is a single point of contact and a single person responsible for the availability of products and services.
- New products and services fulfill the requirements and availability standard agreed with the customer.
- The associated costs are acceptable.
- The availability standards are monitored continuously and improved where appropriate.
- Appropriate corrective action is undertaken when a service is unavailable.
- The occurrence and duration of unavailability are reduced.
- The emphasis is shifted from remedying faults to improving service.
- It is easier for the IT organization to prove its added value.

The following ITIL processes have relationships with Availability Management.

Service Level Management
Service Level Management is responsible for negotiating and managing Service Level Agreements, in which availability is one of the most important elements.

Configuration Management
Configuration Management has information about the infrastructure and can provide valuable information to Availability Management.

Capacity Management
Changes in the capacity often affect the availability of a service and changes to the availability will affect the capacity. Capacity Management has extensive information available, including information about the IT infrastructure. Thus, these two processes often exchange information about scenarios for upgrading or phasing out IT components, and about availability trends which may necessitate changes to the capacity requirements.

IT Service Continuity Management
Availability Management is not responsible for restoring business processes after a disaster. This is the responsibility of IT Service Continuity Management. ITSCM provides Availability Management with information about critical business processes. Also, in practice, many measures taken to enhance Availability also enhance IT Service Continuity, and vice versa.

Problem Management
Problem Management is directly involved in identifying and resolving the causes of actual or potential availability problems.

Incident Management
Incident Management specifies how incidents should be resolved. This process provides reports with information about recovery times, repair times, etc. This information is used to determine the achieved availability.

Security Management
Availability Management has close ties with Security Management. The three basic issues in Security Management are:
• Confidentiality
• Integrity
• Availability

Security criteria have to be considered when determining availability requirements. Availability Management can provide valuable information to Security Management, particularly about new services.

Change Management
Availability Management informs Change Management about maintenance issues related to new services and elements thereof, and initiates the Change Management process to implement changes necessitated by availability measures. Change Management informs Availability Management about scheduled changes (FSC).

14.3 The process
Where possible, essential components are duplicated and fault detection and correction systems are used to meet high availability standards. Often, automatic fallback systems will operate in the event of a fault. However, organizational measures also need to be taken and can be provided by introducing Availability Management.

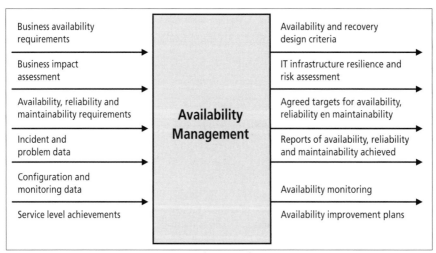

Figure 14.2 Availability Management inputs and outputs (Source: OGC)

Availability Management can start once the business has clearly indicated its availability requirements for the service. It is an ongoing process that only ends when a service is phased out.
The **inputs** of the Availability Management process (Figure 14.2) are:
- Business availability requirements
- Impact assessment for all business processes supported by IT
- Availability, reliability and maintainability requirements for the IT components in the infrastructure
- Data about faults affecting services or components, generally in the form of incident and problem records and reports
- Configuration and monitoring data about the services and components
- Achieved service levels, compared with the agreed service levels for all services covered under the SLA

Outputs:
- Availability and recovery design criteria for new and improved IT services
- Technology needed to obtain the required infrastructure resilience to reduce or eliminate the impact of faulty infrastructure components
- Availability, reliability and maintainability guarantees of infrastructure components required for the IT service
- Reports about the achieved availability, reliability and maintainability
- Availability, reliability and maintainability monitoring requirements
- An Availability Plan for the proactive improvement of the IT infrastructure

14.4 Activities
Availability Management includes a number of key activities that concern planning and monitoring.
These activities are:
- **Planning**
  - Determining the availability requirements
  - Designing for availability
  - Designing for recoverability
  - Security issues
  - Maintenance management
  - Developing the Availability Plan
- **Monitoring**
  - Measuring and reporting

These key activities are discussed below.

14.4.1 Determining the availability requirements
This activity must be undertaken before a SLA can be concluded and should address both new IT services and changes to existing services. It must be decided at the earliest possible stage if and how the IT organization can fulfill the requirements.
This activity should identify:
- Key business functions
- Agreed definition of IT service downtime
- Quantifiable availability requirements
- Quantifiable impact on the business functions of unscheduled IT service downtime

- Business hours of the customer
- Agreements about maintenance windows

Clearly defining the availability requirements at an early stage is essential to prevent confusion and differences in interpretation at a later stage.

The customer's requirements must be compared with what can be provided. If there is a mismatch, then the cost impact of this will have to be determined.

14.4.2 Designing for Availability

Vulnerabilities that affect the availability standards should be identified as early as possible. This will prevent excessive development costs, unplanned expenditure at later stages, Single Points Of Failure (SPOF), additional costs charged by suppliers, and delayed releases.

A good design, based on the appropriate availability standards, will make it possible to conclude effective maintenance contracts with suppliers. The design process employs a range of techniques such as Component Failure Impact Analysis (CFIA, see section 14.4.9) to identify SPOFs, CRAMM (see the chapter on IT Service Continuity Management) and simulation techniques.

If the availability standards cannot be met, the best option is to determine if the design can be improved. The use of additional technology, other methods, a different release strategy, a better or different design, and development tools may provide opportunities to meet the standards.

If the requirements are particularly demanding then the use of other fault tolerance technology, other service processes (incident, problem, and Change Management), or additional Service Management resources may be considered. The financial resources available largely determine the options and choices.

14.4.3 Designing for Maintainability

As completely uninterrupted availability is rarely feasible, periods of unavailability must be considered. When an IT service is interrupted it is important that the fault is quickly and adequately solved, and that the agreed availability standards are fulfilled. Designing for recoverability involves issues such as an effective Incident Management process with appropriate escalation, communication, and backup and recovery procedures.

The tasks, responsibilities and authority should be clearly defined.

14.4.4 Key security issues

Security and reliability are closely linked. A poor information security design can affect the availability of the service. High availability can be supported by effective information security. During the planning stage, the security issues should be considered and their impact on the provision of services should be analyzed.

Some of the issues include:
- Determining who is authorized to access secure areas
- Determining which critical authorizations may be issued

14.4.5 Maintenance management

Normally, there will always be scheduled windows of unavailability. These periods can be used for preventive action, such as software and hardware upgrades. Changes can also be implemented during these windows. In the 24-hour economy, however, it is becoming more and more difficult to determine appropriate maintenance windows. The definition, implementation, and verification of maintenance activities have developed into major issues in Availability Management.

Maintenance must be carried out when the impact on services can be minimized. This means that it must be known in advance what the maintenance objectives are, when the maintenance should be undertaken and what maintenance activities are involved (this could be based on CFIA). This information is essential for Change Management and other activities.

14.4.6 Measuring and reporting

Measuring and reporting are important Availability Management activities as they provide the basis for verifying service agreements, resolving problems, and defining proposals for improvement.

> *If you don't measure it, you can't manage it.*
> *If you don't measure it, you can't improve it.*
> *If you don't measure it, you probably don't care.*
> *If you can't influence it, then don't measure it.*

The life cycle of an incident includes the following elements:
- **Occurrence of the incident:** the time at which the user becomes aware of the fault, or when the fault is identified by other means (technically or physically).
- **Detection:** the service provider is informed of the fault. The incident status is now 'reported'. The time this took is known as the detection time.
- **Response:** the service provider needs time to respond. This is known as the response time. This time is used for diagnosis, which can then be followed by repair. The Incident Management process includes Acceptance and Registration, Classification, Matching, Analysis, and Diagnosis.
- **Repair:** the service provider restores the components that caused the fault.
- **Service recovery:** the service is restored. This includes activities such as configuration and initialization, and the service is restored to the user.

Figure 14.3 illustrates the periods that can be measured.

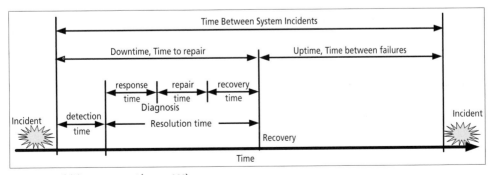

Figure 14.3 Availability measurement (source: OGC)

As the figure shows, the response time of the IT organization and any external contractors is one of the factors determining the downtime. As this factor can be controlled by the IT organization and directly affects the service quality, agreements about it can be included in the SLA. The measurements can be averaged to give a good impression of the relevant factors. The averages can be used to determine the achieved service levels, and to estimate the expected future availability of a service. This information can also be used to develop improvement plans.

The following metrics are commonly used in Availability Management:
- **Mean Time to Repair - MTTR:** average time between the occurrence of a fault and service recovery, also known as the downtime. It is the sum of the detection time and the resolution time. This metric relates to the recoverability and serviceability of the service.
- **Mean Time Between Failures - MTBF:** mean time between the recovery from one incident and the occurrence of the next incident, also known as uptime. This metric relates to the reliability of the service.
- **Mean Time Between System Incidents - MTBSI:** mean time between the occurrence of two consecutive incidents. The MTBSI is the sum of the MTTR and MTBF.

The ratio of the MTBF and the MTBSI indicates if there are many minor faults or just a few major faults.

Availability reports may include the following metrics:
- Rate of availability (or unavailability) in terms of MTTR, MTBF and MTBSI
- Overall uptime and downtime
- Number of faults
- Additional information about faults which actually or potentially result in a higher than agreed unavailability.

The problem with availability reporting is that the presented metrics may not correspond with the customer's perception. It is therefore important to report about availability from the customer's perspective. The report should primarily provide information about the availability of the service for essential business functions, application services, and the availability of the data (business view), rather than information about the availability of technical IT components. Reports should be written in a language the customer can understand.

14.4.7 Developing the Availability Plan

The Availability Plan is one of the major products of Availability Management. It is a long-term plan concerning availability over the next few years. It is not the implementation plan for Availability Management.

The plan should be a living document. Initially it should describe the current situation, and at a later stage it can be expanded to include improvement activities for existing services and guidelines, as well as plans for new services and guidelines for maintenance. A comprehensive and accurate plan requires liaison with areas such as Service Level Management, IT Service Continuity Management, Capacity Management, and Financial Management for IT Services and Application Development (directly or through Change Management).

14.4.8 Tools
To be efficient, Availability Management must use a number of tools for the following activities:
- Determining downtime
- Recording historical information
- Generating reports
- Statistical analysis
- Impact analysis

Availability Management uses information from the Incident Management records, the CMDB, and the Capacity Database. Information may be stored in a dedicated Availability Management Database (AMDB).

14.4.9 Methods and techniques
There is now a broad spectrum of Availability Management methods and techniques to support planning, improvement and reporting. The most important of these are discussed below.

Component Failure Impact Analysis (CFIA)
This method uses an availability matrix with the strategic components and their roles in each service. An effective CMDB, which defines the relationships between services and production resources, can be most helpful when developing this matrix.

An example of a CFIA matrix in Figure 14.4 shows that the Configuration Items which are marked with 'X' for many services are important elements of the IT infrastructure (horizontal analysis), and that services which are frequently marked with 'X' are complex and sensitive to faults (vertical analysis). This method can also be applied to dependencies on third parties (Advanced CFIA).

Configuration Item:	Service A	Service B
PC #1	B	B
PC #2		B
Cable #1	B	B
Cable #2		B
Outlet #1	X	X
Outlet #2		X
Ethernet segment	X	X
Router	X	X
WAN link	X	X
Router	X	X
Segment	X	X
NIC	A	A
Server	B	B
System software	B	B
Application	B	B
Database	X	X

X = Fault means service is unavailable
A = Failsafe configuration
B = Failsafe, with changeover time
" " = No impact

Figure 14.4 CFIA matrix (source: OGC)

Fault Tree Analysis (FTA)

Fault Tree Analysis is a technique used to identify the chain of events leading to failure of an IT service. A separate tree is drawn for every service, using Boolean symbols. The tree is traversed from the bottom up. FTA distinguishes the following events:

- **Basic Events:** inputs in the diagram (circles) such as power outages and operator errors. These events are not investigated.
- **Resulting Events:** nodes in the diagram, resulting from a combination of earlier events.
- **Conditional Events:** events that only occur under certain conditions, such as an air conditioning failure.
- **Trigger Events:** events that cause other events, such as an automatic shutdown initiated by a UPS.

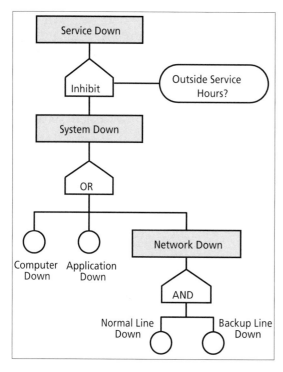

Figure 14.5 Fault Tree Analysis (source: OGC)

Events can be combined with logical operations, such as:

- **AND operation:** the Resulting Event will occur if all inputs occur simultaneously.
- **OR operation:** the Resulting Event will occur if one or more of the inputs occur.
- **XOR operation:** the Resulting Event will occur if only one of the inputs occurs.
- **Inhibit operation:** the Resulting Event will occur if the input conditions are not fulfilled.

CCTA Risk Analysis and Management Method (CRAMM)

This method is discussed in the chapter on IT Service Continuity Management.

Availability calculations

The metrics discussed above can be used to conclude service availability agreements with the customer. These agreements are included in the Service Level Agreement. The formula below may be used to determine if the achieved availability fulfilled the agreed availability requirement:

$$\% \text{ Availability} = \frac{\text{Achieved uptime}}{\text{Agreed uptime}} * 100\%$$

Figure 14.6 Availability formula (source: OGC)

The achieved uptime amounts to the difference between the agreed uptime and the achieved downtime. Example: if it were agreed that the service should have a 98% availability on working days from 07.00 to 19.00 h, and the service was down for two hours during this window, then the achieved uptime (availability percentage) would be:

$$(5 \times 12 - 2)/(5 \times 12) \times 100\% = 96.7\%$$

System Outage Analysis (SOA)
SOA is a technique which can be used to identify the causes of faults, to investigate the effectiveness of the IT organization and its processes, and to present and implement proposals for improvement.

The characteristics of an SOA are:
- It has a broad scope: it is not limited to the infrastructure, but also covers processes, procedures, and cultural aspects.
- Issues are considered from the customer's perspective.
- It is jointly implemented by representatives of the customer and the IT organization (SOA team).

The benefits include a more efficient approach, direct communication between the customer and the supplier, and a broader base for proposals for improvement.

Technical Observation Post (TOP)
When using the TOP method, a dedicated team of IT specialists focuses on a single aspect of availability. This method may be appropriate where routine tools provide insufficient support. The TOP can also combine the expertise of designers and system managers.

The key aspects of this method are an efficient, effective and informal approach that quickly leads to results.

14.5 Process control

14.5.1 Reporting
The availability reports for the customer were discussed above. The following metrics can be reported for process control:
- Detection times
- Response times
- Repair times
- Recovery times
- Successful use of appropriate methods (CFIA, CRAMM, SOA)
- Extent of process implementation: services, SLAs and customer groups covered by SLAs

Some metrics can be determined for each service, team or infrastructure domain (network, computer center, and workstation environment).

14.5.2 Critical success factors and performance indicators

The critical success factors for Availability Management are:
- The business must have clearly defined availability objectives and wishes.
- Service Level Management must have been set up to formalize agreements.
- Both parties must use the same definitions of availability and downtime.
- Both the business and the IT organization must be aware of the benefits of Availability Management.

The following performance indicators show the effectiveness and efficiency of Availability Management:
- Percentage availability (uptime) per service or group of users
- Downtime duration
- Downtime frequency

14.5.3 Functions and roles

The organization can establish the role of Availability Manager to define and control the process. The task of the Availability Manager could include the following elements:
- Defining and developing the process in the organization
- Ensuring that IT services are designed such that the achieved service levels (in terms of availability, reliability, serviceability, maintainability, and recoverability) correspond with the agreed service levels
- Reporting
- Optimizing the availability of the IT infrastructure to provide a cost-effective improvement of the service provided to the business

14.6 Problems and costs

14.6.1 Problems

Most problems concern the organization. Problems to be expected include:
- Senior management divides responsibility for availability between several disciplines (line managers, process managers).
- Each manager feels responsible for his or her own area, and there is no overall coordination.
- IT management fails to understand the added value provided to the incident, problem, and Change Management processes.
- The current availability level is considered sufficient.
- There is no support for appointing a single, responsible process manager.
- The process manager does not have the required authority.

Even with sufficient management support, problems may still arise due to:
- Underestimating resources
- Lack of effective measurement and reporting tools
- Lack of other processes such as Service Level Management, Configuration Management, and Problem Management

These problems can be solved with good management support, the right person with full responsibility for the process, appropriate tools, and rapid and effective resolution of existing problems.

If Availability Management is used inefficiently the following problems may arise:
• It will be difficult to define appropriate availability standards.
• It will be more difficult to guide internal and external suppliers.
• It will be difficult to compare the costs of availability and unavailability.
• If availability standards were not considered during the design, later modification to meet these standards may be many times more expensive.
• Availability standards are not fulfilled which may lead to failure to meet the business objectives.
• Customer satisfaction may be reduced.

Aiming for an excessively high availability is another potential problem. Costs will rise sharply, disproportionate to the benefits. There is always likely to be downtime. Availability Management plays an important role in resolving these undesirable events.

14.6.2 Costs
The costs of Availability Management include:
• Cost of implementation
• Personnel costs
• Facilities costs
• Measuring and reporting tools

Availability Management should identify the investment needed to improve the availability early. A cost/benefit analysis should be carried out in all cases. In general, the costs will rise as the required availability increases. Finding the optimum solution is an important task of Availability Management. Experience shows that the optimum can often be reached with limited resources, rather than requiring significant investment.

The discussion of the costs and benefits can be guided by asking what the costs will be if we completely ignore Availability Management and reach a situation where the agreed availability requirements are not fulfilled. This will have the following impact on the customer:
• Reduced productivity
• Reduced turnover and profit
• Recovery costs
• Potential claims from third parties, etc.

The following aspects are difficult to quantify but are equally important:
• Loss of goodwill and customers
• Loss of reputation and trust
• Loss of personnel motivation and satisfaction

The Availability Management process can contribute to the objectives of the IT organization in these areas by providing the required services at an acceptable and justifiable cost.

Chapter 15

Security Management

15.1 Introduction

Business processes can no longer operate without a supply of information. In fact, more and more business processes consist purely of one or more information systems. Information Security Management is an important activity that aims to control the provision of information and to prevent unauthorized use of information.

For many years, Information Security Management was largely ignored. However, this is changing. Security is now considered as one of the main management challenges for the coming years. The interest in this discipline is increasing because of the growing use of the Internet and e-commerce in particular. More and more businesses are opening electronic gateways into their business. This introduces the risk of intrusion, and raises some important questions for businesses. What risks do we want to cover, and what measures should we take now and in the next budgeting round? Senior Management has to take decisions and these decisions can only be taken if a thorough risk analysis is undertaken. This analysis should provide input to Security Management to determine the security requirements.

Business requirements for security affect IT service providers and should be laid down in Service Level Agreements. Security Management aims to ensure that the security aspects of services are provided at the level agreed with the customer at all times. Security is now an essential quality aspect of management.

Security Management integrates security in the IT organization from the service provider's point of view. The Code of Practice for Information Security Management (BS 7799) provides guidance for the development, introduction and evaluation of security measures.

15.1.1 Basic concepts

Security Management comes under the umbrella of Information Security, which aims to ensure the safety of information. **Safety** refers to not being vulnerable to known risks, and avoiding unknown risks where possible. The tool to provide this is **security.** The aim is to protect the value of the information. This value depends on confidentiality, integrity and availability.
- **Confidentiality:** protecting information against unauthorized access and use.
- **Integrity:** accuracy, completeness and timeliness of the information.
- **Availability:** the information should be accessible at any agreed time. This depends on the *continuity* provided by the information processing systems.

Secondary aspects include privacy (confidentiality and integrity of information relating to individuals), anonymity, and verifiability (being able to verify that the information is used correctly and that the security measures are effective).

15.2 Objectives

In recent decades, almost all businesses have become more dependent on information systems. The use of computer networks has also grown, not only within businesses but also between them, and between businesses and the world outside. The increasing complexity of the IT infrastructure means that businesses are now more vulnerable to technical failures, human error, intentional human acts, hackers and crackers, computer viruses, etc. This growing complexity requires a unified management approach. Security Management has important ties with other processes. Some security activities are carried out by other ITIL processes, under the supervision of Security Management.

Security Management has two objectives:
- To meet the security requirements of the SLAs and other external requirements further to contracts, legislation and externally imposed policies
- To provide a basic level of security, independent of external requirements

Security Management is essential to maintaining the uninterrupted operation of the IT organization. It also helps to simplify Information Security Service Level Management, as it is much more difficult to manage a large number of different SLAs than a limited number.

The process input is provided by the SLAs that specify security requirements, possibly supplemented by policy documents and other external requirements. The process also receives information about relevant security issues in other processes, such as security incidents.

The output includes information about the achieved implementation of the SLAs, including exception reports and routine security planning.

At present, many organizations deal with Information Security at the strategic level in information policy and information plans, and at the operational level by purchasing tools and other security products. Insufficient attention is given to the active management of Information Security, the continuous analysis and translation of policies into technical options, and ensuring that the security measures continue to be effective when the requirements and environment change. The consequence of this missing link between the strategic and the operational level is that, at the tactical management level, significant investments are made in measures that are no longer relevant, at a time when new, more effective measures ought to be taken. Security Management aims to ensure that effective Information Security measures are taken at the strategic, tactical and operational levels.

15.2.1 Benefits
Information Security is not a goal in itself; it aims to serve the interests of the business or organization. Some information and information services will be more important to the organization than others. Information Security must be appropriate to the importance of the information. Tailor-made security is developed by striking a balance between security measures and the value of the information, and threats in the processing environment. An effective information supply, with adequate Information Security is important to an organization for two reasons:
- **Internal reasons:** an organization can only operate effectively if correct and complete information is available when required. The level of Information Security should be appropriate for this.
- **External reasons:** the processes in an organization create products and services that are made available to the market or society, to meet defined objectives. An inadequate information supply will lead to substandard products and services which cannot be used to meet the objectives and which will threaten the survival of the organization. Adequate Information Security is an important condition for having an adequate information supply. The external significance of Information Security is therefore determined in part by the internal significance.

Security can provide significant added value to an information system. Effective security contributes to the continuity of the organization and helps to meet its objectives.

15.3 The process

Organizations and their information systems change. Checklists such as the Code of Practice for Information Security Management are static and insufficiently address rapid changes in IT. For this reason, Security Management activities must be reviewed continuously to ensure their effectiveness. Security Management amounts to a never-ending cycle of plan, do, check, and act. The activities undertaken by Security Management, or undertaken in other processes under the control of Security Management are discussed below.

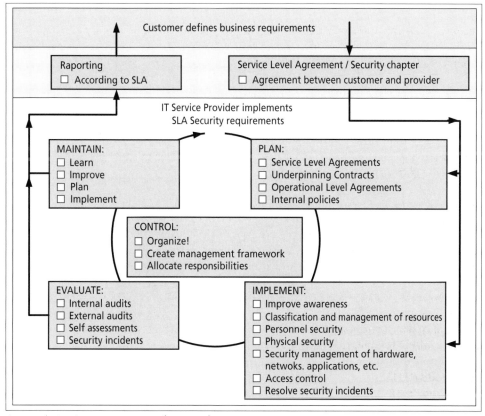

Figure 15.1 the Security Management process (source: OGC)

Figure 15.1 shows the Security Management cycle. The customer's requirements appear at the top right, as input to the process. The security section of the Service Level Agreement defines these requirements in terms of the security services and the level of security to be provided. The service provider communicates these agreements to the organization in the form of a Security Plan, defining the security standards or Operational Level Agreements. This plan is implemented, and the implementation is evaluated. The plan and its implementation are then updated. Service Level Management reports about these activities to the customer. Thus, the customer and the service provider together form a complete cyclical process. The customer can modify requirements on the basis of the reports. And the service provider can adjust the plan or its implementation on the basis of these observations, or aim to change the agreements defined in the SLA. The control function appears in the middle of Figure 15.1. This diagram will now be used to discuss the Security Management activities.

15.3.1 Relationships with other processes

Security Management has links with the other ITIL processes (see Figure 15.2). This is because the other processes undertake security-related activities. These activities are carried out in the normal way, under the responsibility of the relevant process and process manager. However, Security Management gives instructions about the structure of the security-related activities to the other processes. Normally, these agreements are defined after consultation between the Security Manager and the other process managers.

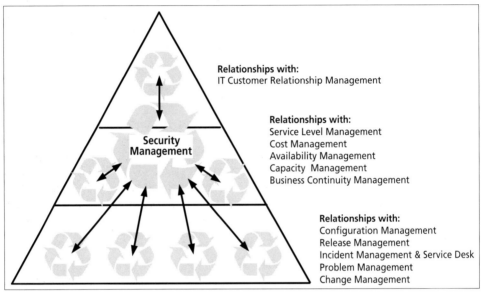

Relationships with:
IT Customer Relationship Management

Relationships with:
Service Level Management
Cost Management
Availability Management
Capacity Management
Business Continuity Management

Relationships with:
Configuration Management
Release Management
Incident Management & Service Desk
Problem Management
Change Management

Figure 15.2 Security Management's relationships with other processes (source: OGC)

Configuration Management

In the context of Information Security, Configuration Management is primarily relevant because it can classify Configuration Items. This classification links the CI with specified security measures or procedures.

The classification of a CI indicates its required confidentiality, integrity and availability. This classification is based on the security requirements of the SLA. The customer of the IT organization determines the classification, as only the customer can decide how important the information or information systems are to the business processes. The customer bases the classification on an analysis of the extent to which the business processes depend on the information systems and the information. The IT organization then associates the classification with the relevant CIs. The IT organization must also implement this set of security measures for each classification level. These sets of measures can be described in procedures. Example: 'Procedure for handling storage media with personal data'. The SLA can define the sets of security measures for each classification level.

The classification system should always be tailored to the customer's organization. However, to simplify management it is advisable to aim for one unified classification system, even when the IT organization has more than one customer.

In summary, classification is a key issue. The CMDB should indicate the classification of each CI. This classification links the CI with the relevant set of security measures or procedure.

Incident Management

Incident Management is an important process for reporting security incidents. Depending on the nature of the incident, security incidents may be covered by a different procedure than other incidents. It is therefore essential that Incident Management recognize security incidents as such. Any incident that may interfere with achieving the SLA security requirements is classified as a security incident. It is useful to include a description in the SLA of the type of incidents to be considered as security incidents. Any incident that interferes with achieving the basic internal security level (baseline) is also always classified as a security incident.

Incidents reports are generated not only by users, but also by the management process, possibly on the basis of alarms or audit data from the systems.

It is clearly essential that Incident Management recognize all security incidents. This is to ensure that the appropriate procedures are initiated for dealing with security incidents. It is advisable to include the procedures for different types of security incidents in the SLA plans and to practice the procedure. It is also advisable to agree a procedure for communicating about security incidents. It is not unusual for panic to be created by rumors blown out of proportion. Similarly, it is not unusual for damage to result from a failure to communicate in time about security incidents. It is advisable to route all external communications related to security incidents through the Security Manager.

Problem Management

Problem Management is responsible for identifying and solving structural security failings. A problem may also introduce a security risk. In that case, Problem Management must involve Security Management in resolving the problem. Finally, the solution or workaround for a problem or known error must always be checked to ensure that it does not introduce new security problems. This verification should be based on compliance with the SLA and internal security requirements.

Change Management

Change Management activities are often closely associated with security because Change Management and Security Management are interdependent. If an acceptable security level has been achieved and is managed by the Change Management process, then it can be ensured that this level of security will also be provided after changes. There are a number of standard operations to ensure that this security level is maintained. Each RFC is associated with a number of parameters that govern the acceptance procedure. The urgency and impact parameters can be supplemented by a security parameter. If an RFC can have a significant impact on Information Security then more extensive acceptance tests and procedures will be required.

The RFC should also include a proposal for dealing with security issues. Again, this should be based on the SLA requirements and the basic level of internal security required by the IT organization. Thus, the proposal will include a set of security measures, based on the Code of Practice.

Preferably, the Security Manager (and possibly also the customer's Security Officer) should be a member of the Change Advisory Board (CAB).

Nevertheless, the Security Manager need not be consulted for all changes. Security should normally be integrated with routine operations. The Change Manager should be able to decide if they or the CAB need input from the Security Manager. Similarly, the Security Manager need not necessarily be involved in the selection of measures for the CIs covered by the RFC. This is because the framework for the relevant measures should already exist. Any questions should only relate to the way in which the measures are implemented.

Any security measures associated with a change should be implemented at the same time as the change itself, and be included in the tests. Security tests differ from normal functional tests. Normal tests aim to investigate if defined functions are available. Security tests not only address the availability of security functions, but also the absence of other, undesirable functions as these could reduce the security of the system.

In terms of security, Change Management is one of the most important processes. This is because Change Management introduces new security measures into the IT infrastructure, together with changes to the IT infrastructure.

Release Management
All new versions of software, hardware, data communications equipment, etc. should be controlled and rolled out by Release Management. This process will ensure that:
- The correct hardware and software are used.
- The hardware and software are tested before use.
- The introduction is correctly authorized using a change.
- The software is legal.
- The software is free from viruses and that viruses are not introduced during its distribution.
- The version numbers are known, and recorded in the CMDB by Configuration Management.
- The rollout is managed effectively.

This process also uses a regular acceptance procedure which should include Information Security aspects. It is particularly important to consider security aspects during testing and acceptance. This means that the security requirements and measures defined in the SLA should be complied with at all times.

Service Level Management
Service Level Management ensures that agreements about the services to be provided to customers are defined and achieved. The Service Level Agreements should also address security measures. The objective is to optimize the level of service provided.
Service Level Management includes a number of related security activities, in which Security Management plays an important role:
1. Identification of the security needs of the customer. Naturally, determining the security needs is the responsibility of the customer as these needs are based on their business interests.
2. Verifying the feasibility of the customer's security requirements.
3. Proposing, discussing and defining the security level of the IT services in the SLA.
4. Identifying, developing and defining the internal security requirements for IT services (Operational Level Agreements).
5. Monitoring the security standards (OLAs).
6. Reporting on the IT services provided.

Security Management provides input and support to Service Level Management for activities 1 - 3. Activities 4 and 5 are carried out by Security Management. Security Management and other processes provide input for activity 6. The Service Level Manager and the Security Manager decide in consultation who actually undertakes the activities.

When defining a SLA it is normally assumed that there is a general basic level of security (baseline). Additional security requirements of the customer should be clearly defined in the SLA.

Availability Management
Availability Management addresses the technical availability of IT components in relation to the availability of the service. The quality of availability is assured by continuity, maintainability and resilience. Availability Management is the most important process related to availability. As many security measures benefit both availability and the security aspects confidentiality and integrity, effective coordination of the measures between Availability Management, IT Service Continuity Management, and Security Management is essential.

Capacity Management
Capacity Management is responsible for the best possible use of IT resources, as agreed with the customer. The performance requirements are based on the qualitative and quantitative standards defined by Service Level Management. Almost all the activities of Capacity Management affect availability and therefore also Security Management.

IT Service Continuity Management
IT Service Continuity Management ensures that the impact of any contingencies is limited to the level agreed with the customer. Contingencies need not necessarily turn into disasters. The major activities are defining, maintaining, implementing, and testing the contingency plan, and taking preventive action. Because of the security aspects, there are ties with Security Management. On the other hand, failure to fulfill the basic security requirements may be considered itself as a contingency.

15.3.2 Security section of the Service Level Agreement
The Service Level Agreement (SLA) defines the agreements with the customer. The Service Level Management process is responsible for the SLA (see also Chapter 10). The SLA is the most important driver for all ITIL processes.

The IT organization indicates to what extent the requirements of the SLA are achieved, including security requirements. The security elements addressed in the SLA should correspond to the security needs of the customer. The customer should identify the significance of all business processes (see Figure 15.3).

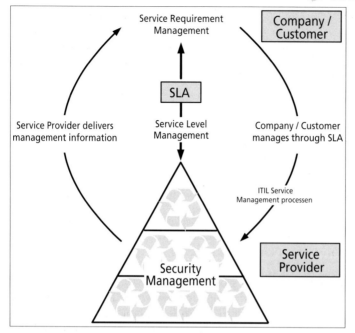

Figure 15.3 Relationships between the processes (source: OGC)

These business processes depend on IT services, and therefore on the IT organization. The customer determines the security requirements (SLA Information Security requirements, not included in Figure 15.3) on the basis of a risk analysis. Figure 15.4 shows how the security elements of the SLA are defined.

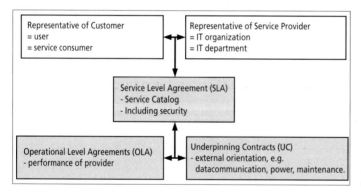

Figure 15.4 Developing the security section of the SLA (source: OGC)

The security elements are discussed between the representative of the customer and the representative of the service provider. The service provider compares the customer's Service Level Requirements with their own Service Catalog, which describes their standard security measures (the Security Baseline). The customer may have additional requirements.

The customer and provider compare the Service Level Requirements and the Service Catalog.

The security section of the SLA can address issues such as the general Information Security policy, a list of authorized personnel, asset protection procedures, restrictions on copying data, etc.

15.3.3 The security section of the Operational Level Agreement

The Operational Level Agreement is another important document. It describes the services provided by the service provider. The provider must associate these agreements with responsibilities within the organization. The Service Catalog gives a general description of the services. The Operational Level Agreement translates these and general descriptions into all services and their components, and the way in which the agreements about the service levels are assured within the organization.

Example: the Service Catalog refers to 'managing authorizations per user and per individual'. The Operational Level Agreements details this for all relevant services provided by the IT organization. In this way, the implementation of the measure is defined for the departments providing UNIX, VMS, NT, Oracle services, etc.

Where possible, the customer's Service Level Requirements are interpreted in terms of the provider's Service Catalog, and additional agreements are concluded where necessary. Such additional measurements exceed the standard security level.

When drafting the SLA, measurable Key Performance Indicators (KPI) and criteria must also be agreed for Security Management. KPIs are measurable parameters (metrics), and performance criteria are set at achievable levels. In some cases it will be difficult to agree on measurable security parameters. This is easier for availability, which can generally be expressed numerically. However, this is much more difficult for integrity and confidentiality. For this reason, the security section of the SLA normally describes the required measures in abstract terms. The Code of Practice for Information Security Management is used as a basic set of security measures. The SLA also describes how performance is measured. The IT organization (service provider) must regularly provide reports to the user organization (customer).

15.4 Activities

15.4.1 Control - Information Security policy and organization

The Control activity in the center of Figure 15.4 is the first subprocess of Security Management and relates to the organization and management of the process. This includes the Information Security management framework. This framework describes the subprocesses: the definition of security plans, their implementation, evaluation of the implementation, and incorporation of the evaluation in the annual security plans (action plans). The reports provided to the customer, via Service Level Management, are also addressed.

This activity defines the subprocesses, security functions, and roles and responsibilities. It also describes the organizational structure, reporting arrangements, and line of control (who instructs who, who does what, how is the implementation reported). The following measures from the Code of Practice are implemented by this activity.

Policy:
- Policy development and implementation, links with other policies
- Objectives, general principles and significance
- Description of the subprocesses
- Allocating functions and responsibilities for subprocesses
- Links with other ITIL processes and their management

- General responsibility of personnel
- Dealing with security incidents

Information Security organization:
- Management framework
- Management structure (organizational structure)
- Allocation of responsibilities in greater detail
- Setting up an Information Security Steering Committee
- Information Security coordination
- Agreeing tools (e.g. for risk analysis and improving awareness)
- Description of the IT facilities authorization process, in consultation with the customer
- Specialist advice
- Cooperation between organizations, internal and external communications
- Independent Information Systems audit
- Security principles for access by third parties
- Information Security in contracts with third parties

15.4.2 Plan

The Planning subprocess includes defining the security section of the SLA in consultation with Service Level Management, and the activities in the Underpinning Contracts related to security. The objectives in the SLA, which are defined in general terms, are detailed and specified in the form of an Operational Level Agreement. An OLA can be considered as the security plan for an organizational unit of the service provider, and as a specific security plan, for example for each IT platform, application and network.

The Planning subprocess not only receives input from the SLA but also from the service provider's policy principles (from the Control subprocess). Examples of these principles include: 'Every user should be uniquely identifiable', and 'A basic security level is provided to all customers, at all times.'

The Operational Level Agreements for Information Security (specific security plans) are drafted and implemented using the normal procedures. This means that, should activities be required in other processes, there will have to be coordination with these processes. Any required changes to the IT infrastructure are made by Change Management using input provided by Security Management. The Change Manager is responsible for the Change Management process.

The Planning subprocess is discussed with Service Level Management to define, update and comply with the security section of the SLA. The Service Level Manager is responsible for this coordination.

The SLA should define the security requirements, where possible in measurable terms. The security section of the agreement should ensure that all the customer's security requirements and standards can be verifiably achieved.

15.4.3 Implement

The Implementation subprocess aims to implement all the measures specified in the plans. This subprocess can be supported by the following checklist.

Classification and management of IT resources:
- Providing input for maintaining the CIs in the CMDB
- Classifying IT resources in accordance with agreed guidelines

Personnel security:
- Tasks and responsibilities in job descriptions
- Screening
- Confidentiality agreements for personnel
- Training
- Guidelines for personnel for dealing with security incidents and observed security weaknesses
- Disciplinary measures
- Increasing security awareness

Managing security:
- Implementation of responsibilities, implementation of job separation
- Written operating instructions
- Internal regulations
- Security should cover the entire life cycle; there should be security guidelines for system development, testing, acceptance, operations, maintenance and phasing out
- Separating the development and test environments from the production environment
- Procedures for dealing with incidents (handled by Incident Management)
- Implementation of recovery facilities
- Providing input for Change Management
- Implementation of virus protection measures
- Implementation of management measures for computers, applications, networks and network services
- Handling and security of data media

Access control:
- Implementation of access and access control policy
- Maintenance of access privileges of users and applications to networks, network services, computers, and applications
- Maintenance of network security barriers (firewalls, dial-in services, bridges and routers)
- Implementation of measures for the identification and authentication of computer systems, workstations and PCs on the network

15.4.4 Evaluate

An independent evaluation of the implementation of the planned measures is essential. This evaluation is needed to assess the performance and is also required by customers and third parties. The results of the Evaluation subprocess can be used to update the agreed measures in consultation with the customers, and also for their implementation. The results of the evaluation may suggest changes, in which case an RFC is defined and submitted to the Change Management process.

There are three forms of evaluation:
• Self-assessments: primarily implemented by the line organization of the processes
• Internal audits: undertaken by internal IT auditors
• External audits: undertaken by external IT auditors

Unlike self-assessments, audits are not undertaken by the same personnel that act in the other subprocesses. This is to ensure that the responsibilities are separated. Audits may be undertaken by an Internal Audit department.
Evaluations are also carried out in response to security incidents.

The main activities are:
• Verifying compliance with the security policy and implementation of security plans
• Performing security audits on IT systems
• Identifying and responding to inappropriate use of IT resources
• Undertaking the security aspects of other IT audits

15.4.5 Maintenance
Security requires maintenance, as the risks change due to changes in the IT infrastructure, organization and business processes. Security maintenance includes the maintenance of the security section of the SLA and maintenance of the detailed security plans (Operational Level Agreements).

Maintenance is carried out on the basis of the results of the Evaluation subprocess and an assessment of changes in the risks. These proposals can either be introduced into the Planning subprocess, or included in the maintenance of the SLA as a whole. In either case, the proposals can result in the inclusion of activities in the annual security plan. Any changes are subject to the normal Change Management process.

15.4.6 Reporting
Reporting is not a subprocess, but an output of the other subprocesses. Reports are produced to provide information about the achieved security performance and to inform the customers about security issues. These reports are generally required under agreement with the customer.

Reporting is important, both to the customer and to the service provider. Customers must be correctly informed about the efficiency of the efforts (e.g. with respect to the implementation of security measures), and the actual security measures. The customer is also informed about any security incidents. A list with some suggestions for reporting options is included below.
Examples of scheduled reports and reportable events:

The Planning subprocess
• Reports about the extent of compliance with the SLA and agreed Key Performance Indicators for security
• Reports about Underpinning Contracts and any problems associated with them
• Reports about Operational Level Agreements (internal security plans) and the provider's own security principles (e.g. in the baseline)
• Reports about annual security plans and action plans

The Implementation subprocess
• Status reports about the implementation of Information Security. This includes progress

reports about the implementation of the annual security plan, possibly a list of measures which have been implemented or are yet to be implemented, training, outcome of additional risk analyzes, etc.
- A list of security incidents and responses to these incidents, optionally a comparison with the previous reporting period
- Identification of incident trends
- Status of the awareness program

The Evaluation subprocess
- Reports about the performance of the subprocess
- Results of audits, reviews, and internal assessments
- Warnings, identification of new threats

Specific reports
To report on security incidents defined in the SLA, the service provider must have a direct channel of communication to a customer representative (possibly the Corporate Information Security Officer) through the Service Level Manager, Incident Manager or Security Manager. A procedure should also be defined for communication in special circumstances.

Apart from the exception in the event of special circumstances, reports are communicated through Service Level Management.

15.5 Process control

15.5.1 Critical success factors and performance indicators
The critical success factors are:
- Full management commitment and involvement
- User involvement when developing the process
- Clear and separated responsibilities

The Security Management performance indicators correspond with the Service Level Management performance indicators, in so far as these relate to security issues covered by the SLA.

15.5.2 Functions and roles
In small IT organizations, several processes may be managed by one person. While in large organizations, several persons will be working on one process, such as Security Management. In this case there is normally one person appointed as Security Manager. The Security Manager is responsible for the effective operation of the Security Management process. Their counterpart in the customer's organization is the Information Security Officer, or Corporate Information Security Officer.

15.6 Problems and costs

15.6.1 Problems
The following issues are essential to the successful implementation of Security Management:
- **Commitment:** security measures are rarely accepted immediately; resistance is more common than acceptance. Users resent losing certain privileges due to security measures, even if these

facilities are not essential to their work. This is because the privileges give them a certain status. A special effort will therefore have to be made to motivate users, and to ensure that management complies with the security measures. In the field of Security Management in particular, management must set an example ('walk the talk' and 'lead by example'). If there are no security incidents, then management may be tempted to reduce the Security Management budget.

- **Attitude:** information systems are not insecure due to technical weaknesses, but due to the failure to use the technology. This is generally related to attitude and human behavior. This means that security procedures must be integrated with routine operations.
- **Awareness:** awareness, or rather communication, is a key concept. There sometimes appears to be a conflict of interest between communication and security – communication paves the road, while security creates obstacles. This means that implementing security measures requires the use of all communication methods to ensure that users adopt the required behavior.
- **Verification:** it should be possible to check and verify security. This concerns both the measures introduced, and the reasons for taking these measures. It should be possible to verify that the correct decisions have been taken in certain circumstances. For example, it should also be possible to verify the authority of the decision-makers.
- **Change Management:** frequently the verification of continued compliance with the basic level of security wanes over time when assessing changes.
- **Ambition:** when an organization wants to do everything at once, mistakes are often made. When introducing Security Management, the implementation of technical measures is much less important than organizational measures. Changing an organization requires a gradual approach and will take a long time.
- **Lack of detection systems:** new systems, such as the Internet, were not designed for security and intruder detection. This is because developing a secure system takes more time than developing a nonsecure system, and conflicts with the business requirements of low development costs and a short time-to-market.
- **Over-reliance on stronghold/fortress techniques:** More and more frequently security threats come from unanticipated places. Consider the first ILOVEYOU and Nimda virus attacks, and the first instance of Denial of Service (DoS) attacks. While it is important to protect information assets with traditional stronghold/fortress approaches, it has become equally important to have a skirmish capability when it comes to security events. It is analogous to needing both "slow twitch" and "fast twitch" muscles. The organization must have the capability to rapidly put resources on the ground where the trouble is, before that trouble has a chance to spiral out of control.

15.6.2 Costs

Securing the IT infrastructure demands personnel, and therefore money, to take, maintain and verify measures. However, failing to secure the IT infrastructure also costs money (cost of lost production; cost of replacement; damage to data, software, or hardware; loss of reputation; fines or compensation relating to failure to fulfill contractual obligations). As always, a balance will have to be struck.

Quick Couriers

The case study deals with a developing young company that is confronted with all relevant service management issues. At the end of each section some questions are raised as food for thought for the reader.

New York City traffic is now so congested that it is difficult to run a courier service with vans. This is why, after graduation, three friends, Jane, John and Peter, decided to set up a bicycle courier service, and founded Quick Couriers (QC). QC delivers packages in the town center using bicycles.

At first, the founders of Quick Couriers just worked for themselves, but they now have contracts with international courier companies to collect and deliver packages downtown, and can no longer do all the work by themselves. So they now use students who work for them part-time to make package deliveries, using their company's reclining bikes.

Jane is responsible for bookkeeping, invoicing, order processing and maintaining commercial contacts. Quick Couriers has purchased software applications for bookkeeping and relationship management.

John answers the phone, deals with customer inquiries, does courier planning and logistics, and passes messages from couriers on to Jane or Peter.

Peter maintains the bicycles, orders part and tools, does the logistics planning, and instructs the couriers.
The three friends recently reviewed their company's position and defined their vision and policies. The vision is 'Quick Couriers should become synonymous with express delivery in downtown Manhattan and surrounding areas'. To implement this, the company has started an advertizing campaign and is recruiting more couriers. They have plans to equip the couriers with pagers or mobile phones. They have also requested a quotation for an Internet-based system which customers can use to request a courier and to trace their packages. Another option under consideration is the expansion of business operations by opening another office in Brooklyn or Queens. Furthermore, they have decided that it will be critical to the company's future to put the business on a more professional footing. Hence, they have identified the areas that require attention.

A.1 Configuration Management

Peter keeps paper records of the tools, maintenance instructions, bicycles, trailers, parts, ponchos and helmets. If he is ill, or on holiday, his cousin Paul looks after the maintenance.

The business now has twenty delivery units (bicycle and trailer), sixteen of which are in continuous use. The other four are either undergoing maintenance or are available as spares. Quick Couriers uses two models, obtained from different suppliers.

To speed up the maintenance, Peter has made a number of subassemblies of the most expensive and vulnerable components. For example, he has disc brake sets, gear sets, front and rear wheels, and lighting sets. When he has time, he repairs the sets by replacing the worn or broken parts, but sometimes he outsources this work to his neighbour Mary, a bicycle enthusiast who has taken early retirement.

In his workshop, Peter has a row of bins with loose parts, and he has a file to keep track of outstanding orders he has sent to his suppliers. Some parts are exchangeable with those of ordinary modern racing bikes.

The bicycle garage is next to the workshop. Many couriers drop in to collect a new schedule or to get their bicycle repaired.

Due to the increasing volume of business, Peter can no longer manage his paper files and it takes too long to make reports. Jane complains about all the bills for parts and tools and wonders if they could make any savings.

Peter has now installed a database package to track the inventory. He calls the database ConFig. He keeps a printed report of the parts in the workshop. He has also bought a power engraver to label parts in the inventory.

Questions:
1. What initiated the development of this process?
2. Who is involved in this process, apart from Peter himself?
3. Draft the scope and level of detail of the database. Which Configuration Item (CI) attributes are relevant to Peter?
4. What is involved in status monitoring? What is the use of a status history?
5. Give examples of some questions, e.g. about trends, which Peter can answer with the database, but could not earlier.
6. How will Peter fill his database?
7. How can Peter ensure that his database remains up-to-date?
8. What should Peter report to Jane?

A.2 Incident Management & Service Desk

With sixteen couriers permanently on the road, John's workload answering the phone gets higher and higher. He is constantly getting orders from customers, complaints about the late delivery of packages, and messages from couriers whose bicycle has broken down or who cannot make a delivery because the address is incorrect.

John finds it more and more difficult to keep track of everything, and he forgets to return calls. Jane also notices that some orders are forgotten. Bits of paper get lost, and it is unclear who is working on what. While every effort is being made to provide good service, it is also impossible to determine how quickly problems are being resolved. Customers have started to complain about shortcomings in the service, and everyone at the company has the impression that the number of orders is falling.

In the meantime, Peter has faced with an increasing number of routes and packages to be included in the planning. He has set up a database, RoutePlan, for the packages and routes, sorted by zip code. Each courier route covers a number of zip codes and has an optimal sequence. Several couriers may serve the same route.

John has been asked to deal with some of the phone calls on his own. For example, he informs customers about the range of services provided by Quick Couriers, and records complaints. He is also charged with sorting out what has happened to packages, and making sure that the customers are called back. He can now access the RoutePlan database on Peter's computer using a recently installed network segment that links their two computers.

To keep track of all the messages and phone calls, John has set up a new database, TelLog. John uses TelLog to keep track of all phone calls, and to allocate category and priority codes to them.

Questions:
1. What initiated the development of this Service Desk?
2. What type of Service Desk is primarily used for this process?
3. What incident information is relevant to an incident call?
4. Give examples of categories and priorities.
5. Who can John call upon if he cannot solve a problem?
6. Effective communication with the repair workshop is essential. What term is used for this within ITIL?
7. How can Quick Couriers make sure that incident calls are not overlooked, and who is responsible for this?
8. Is Business Operations support provided here? If so, explain how.
9. What information links would you want to create to the other systems, and for what purpose?
10. What should John report to Peter and Jane?

A.3 Problem Management

With RoutePlan for package routing, TelLog for recording calls and ConFig for the stock records, the service has now been improved and the pressure of work has reduced. Quick Couriers now have thirty couriers on the road, and Jane and John have married, on on a bicycle built for two, of course.

John now also uses RoutePlan for route planning. A student looks after the telephone switchboard and can resolve most incidents using the documentation provided by John. The first time a new problem arises, the student asks Peter, John or Jane for help and then documents the solution so it can be easily retrieved the next time. If a courier gets stuck because of a problem with their bike, the student on the switchboard sends a replacement part with the next courier on that route. If the courier cannot fix the problem then Peter uses a trailer to deliver a replacement bike to them.

However, Peter still worries about the number of repairs to the reclining bikes. Racing bikes are fairly fragile and they are in constant use. It all rather depends on how couriers deal with curbs and potholes. Quick Couriers have the impression that brand A suffers less wear than brand B, but they are unsure about this. Some assemblies fail more frequently than others, but it is unclear if this is due to the use, fitting or brand.

Jane worries about the number of packages that are lost. Although they are eventually located, she wants to know how the system can be made foolproof. The couriers receive performance bonuses and there is a prize for the courier who manages the highest average number of deliveries per hour. But Jane still wants information about their efficiency and customer friendliness so that she can provide coaching where necessary.

John has been asked to take a closer look at the data in TelLog, RoutePlan and ConFig to identify the underlying causes. He expects that he will have to combine a lot of historical data and subject it to trend analysis.

Questions:
1. What initiated the development of this process?
2. Who are involved, and what are their roles?
3. What activities does John undertake, and what are the results?
4. What information does John want to obtain from the other systems?
5. Give examples of problems and Known Errors.
6. What are John's responsibilities with respect to Known Errors?
7. What conclusions does Peter report to Jane and John?

A.4 Change Management

John learned quite a bit from his exercise in identifying underlying causes. For example, he found that the disc brakes of one brand wear out more quickly than those of another brand, there are some couriers who damage their bikes more frequently than their colleagues, and some packages are being lost because they are put in the wrong courier's trailer.

John has made some recommendations about these issues. As these recommendations concern the areas covered by Jane and Peter, he discusses the potential impact and amount of work involved with them. Events of the preceding week are discussed at the weekly meetings on Monday morning. As John is expected to present proposals for improvements regularly, he now has a separate agenda and list of action items.

Peter has been asked to test a new type of brake. After that he is going to draw up a maintenance schedule. The brakes can then be replaced gradually on the basis of this schedule. This will be combined with other planned maintenance, to ensure that the bicycles are not withdrawn from service too long or too frequently.

A proposal for a more structured approach to sorting and allocating packages will be tested, and they will have meetings with the couriers whose bikes are often damaged.

Questions:
1. What initiated the development of this process?
2. Who are involved, and what are their roles?
3. What activities are undertaken in the meeting further to John's proposals?
4. Describe how you would test the various proposals, and if a fallback plan would be necessary. What could be included in a test plan?
5. What is involved in planning the modifications? Identify bottlenecks, risks, required resources and expected impact.
6. What will be needed to close the outstanding action items? What other process is involved?

A.5 Release Management

When couriers deliver packages to a customer, they leave their bike outside on the pavement. John has bought some high-quality locks to prevent theft of the bikes. The bicycles also have separate wheel locks and locks for the trailers.

Peter keeps the spare keys in a box in a drawer. Couriers occasionally lose their keys and it is quite a job to find the matching spare key. After some time has passed it has become unclear for which locks the spare keys have also been lost. Quick couriers regularly has to purchase new locks, and now that their fleet of bicycles is expanding, this is getting rather expensive. That is why Peter has decided to improve the management of the keys and their copies.

A set of locks is defined for each bicycle. The locks are numbered and the numbers are entered in ConFig. Peter purchases a key cabinet for storing the original keys and the copies.

Questions:
1. What initiated the development of this process?
2. Who are involved, and what are their roles?
3. What steps have to be taken before a new set of locks can be used?
4. What steps are taken before a new set of key copies can be given to a courier?
5. Would you replace the whole set if just one of the locks fails? What do you call this?
6. What steps would you undertake if only one lock is replaced? What do you call this?

A.6 Availability Management

Quick Couriers is getting more and more work. When a bicycle fails it takes too long before it is repaired, leaving the courier and the packages waiting by the roadside. Also, if a courier is ill, the entire schedule is upset. Customers are starting to complain that deliveries are taking too long.

Jane wants to get a grip on the developments so she can include them in the company's plans. The issues include maintenance, delivery time and personnel. The company's objective is to be able to guarantee the shortest possible delivery times. Some ideas include setting up a mobile repair team, purchasing a telephone switchboard with a menu system, and setting up an order processing and tracing system on the Internet. All these would require a significant investment.

Questions:
1. What initiated the development of this process?
2. Who are involved, and what are their roles?
3. List some assets, threats and vulnerabilities.
4. Use this information to identify the risks.
5. What prevention measures can you think of?
6. List what should be included in the planning in terms of maintenance, suppliers and personnel.

A.7 Capacity Management

The market is changing rapidly, Quick Couriers is getting new customers in other districts, and they are thinking of expanding into Jersey City, NJ, and Newark, NJ, both of which are close to New York City. Peter is also thinking of opening another office in Yonkers, north of New York City and a branch office at John F. Kennedy International airport (JFK).

Jane has empirical information about the staffing levels required for each route. She has used the RoutePlan system to create a report which shows, for each route, how many packages are carried on each day of the week, what time of day each route is busiest, and how many packages fit into a trailer. She has used the average as a baseline, and identified a percentage above and below the baseline for each month and time of day. She wants to use this information for equipment and personnel planning.

Jane uses this information to make a report about the expected expansion and required costs and investment.

Questions:
1. What initiated the development of this process?
2. Who are involved, and what are their roles?
3. Give examples of modeling activities.
4. How can peak loads be accommodated without deploying additional capacity?
5. What activities assist in estimating the resources for starting a new route?
6. What should be included in the capacity plan?

A.8 IT Service Continuity Management

Last week, the building next door to Quick Couriers burned down. That gave Jane, John and Peter a real fright. Their current site is very convenient, and finding accommodation is difficult in New York City. They realized that if their building burned down, it could take months to get back into business.

So Quick Couriers decided to include disaster recovery options in their plans for a new office in the south of New York City. They are also going to consider alternatives in the vicinity of the current location that could be used as a temporary base to serve the routes in the downtown area. The following issues are included in their plan:
• Accommodation
• Accessibility
• Personnel
• Electronic files and computer systems
• Equipment
• Their customers' packages

Questions:
1. What initiated the development of this process?
2. Who are involved, and what are their roles?
3. What are the reasons for the company to maintain a disaster recovery plan?
4. What are the threats, assets and vulnerabilities?
5. Use this information to identify the risks.
6. What preventive measures can be taken, and which risks require off-site disaster recovery facilities?
7. What is the ITIL term for a disaster recovery plan that includes a fallback to the IT facilities of another organization?
8. Identify the issues to be included in a plan to fall back to another site, and describe how this should be tested.
9. How is the plan influenced by the capacity plan and the plans to improve availability (e.g. the new office)?
10. What is the effect of Change Management (Change Advisory Board, CAB)? Give an example for this case study.

A.9 Financial Management

The range of services provided by Quick Couriers is being expanded. There are lower rates for off-peak deliveries, rates for urgent deliveries and volume discounts. Customers can use the Internet to request collection of packages, and to trace the location of their packages. However, some of the Quick Couriers employees have left and set up their own business which has put pressure on the quality and price of services.

The costs related to supporting the service have also increased. The company is becoming increasingly dependent on effective IT facilities. Jane has entered into a contract with an Internet service provider, arranged for a leased line, and Quick Couriers now employ a system manager to ensure that the system keeps running. There is a repair team that is constantly on the road. The administration costs have increased due to the increased number of staff. Investments have been made in buildings, so that now depreciation has become a relevant factor in accounting. Couriers operating express services have to be available at all times, which means that they are sometimes idle.

It is becoming increasingly difficult to set prices that consistently cover the costs. Jane wants to promote certain services (those which their competitors can also provide effectively) by charging lower rates, but must set the price point carefully so the new pricing does not result in an operating loss.

Jane wants to introduce a cost center system to get information about the costs associated with providing each service. Now that she is going to get more information about the costs per service, she hopes to be able to offset the losses on certain services with profits from other services.

Questions:
1. What initiated the development of this process?
2. Who are involved, and what are their roles?
3. Give examples of fixed and variable costs, and direct and indirect costs.
4. Give an example of the service catalog and means of production required for the different services.
5. Make a summary price policy plan.

A.10 Service Level Management

Jane wants the regular customers to commit to their business. For this reason, she wants to maintain better contacts with them and conclude long-term service contracts. Regular customers would pay a fixed monthly amount, instead of paying separately for each package or service. This will provide the company with a regular income which will make it easier to plan services.

Because Quick Couriers have so many bikes on the road, the company is becoming increasingly dependent on the suppliers of parts and other services. For this reason, Jane wants to conclude contracts with them that guarantee delivery times.

Quick Couriers hire a new employee to act as account manager. His task is to translate the customer demands into plans for new or modified services. After concluding the underpinning contracts he can start developing a new catalog.

Questions:
1. What initiated the development of this process?
2. Who are involved, and what are their roles?
3. Describe the function of the account manager.
4. Give an example of a framework agreement with a regular customer.
5. How are the services agreed with the customer guaranteed?
6. What could be included in a Service Quality Plan for the company?
7. If you were the account manager, who would you conclude a SPA (or OLA) with?
8. Who would you report the Service Achievements to?
9. How are changes to under performing services planned?

B1. Acronyms

ACU	Accommodation Cost Unit
AMDB	Availability Management Database
BCM	Business Continuity Management
BSC	Balanced Score Card
CA	Cost Accounting
CAB	Change Advisory Board
CAB/EC	Change Advisory Board/Emergency Committee
CCTA	Central Computer and Telecommunications Agency
CDB	Capacity Database
CFIA	Component Failure Impact Analysis
CI	Configuration Item
CMDB	Configuration Management Database
CMM	Capability Maturity Model
CRAMM	CCTA Risk Analysis and Management Method
CRM	Customer Relationship Management
CSF	Critical Success Factor
CTI	Computer Telephony Integration
DHS	Definitive Hardware Store
DoS	Denial of Service
DSL	Definitive Software Library
ECU	Equipment Cost Unit
EFQM	European Foundation for Quality Management
EXIN	EXamination INstitute
FSC	Forward Schedule of Change
FTA	Fault Tree Analysis
HRM	Human Resource Management
ICT	Information and Communication Technology
ISEB	Information Systems Examination Board
ISO	International Standards Organization
IT	Information Technology
ITIL	Information Technology Infrastructure Library
ITSCM	IT Service Continuity Management
ITSM	IT Service Management
ITSMF	IT Service Management Forum
IVR	Interactive Voice Response
KPI	Key Performance Indicator
LAN	Local Area Network
MTBF	Mean Time Between Failures
MTBSI	Mean Time Between System Incidents
MTTR	Mean Time To Repair
OCU	Organization Cost Unit
OGC	Office of Government Commerce
OLA	Operational Level Agreement
PC	Personal Computer
PI	Performance Indicator
PIR	Post-Implementation Review
RFC	Request For Change
SCU	Software Cost Unit

SIP .... Service Improvement Program
SLA .... Service Level Agreement
SLM .... Service Level Management
SLR .... Service Level Requirements
SMART .... Specific, Measurable, Appropriate, Realistic and Time-bound
SOA .... System Outage Analysis
SPOF .... Single Point Of Failure
SQP .... Service Quality Plan
TCU .... Transfer Cost Unit
TOP .... Technical Observation Post
UC .... Underpinning Contract
UPS .... Uninterruptible Power Supply
VOIP .... Voice Over Internet Protocol
WAN .... Wide Area Network

B2. Further reading

Sources
The following sources for this book can be used to learn more about ITIL. Titles printed in bold were published in 2000 or later.

SUBJECT	TITLE	PUBLISHER	ISBN
Service Support	**Service Support**	OGC / HMSO	0 11 330015 8
Service Delivery	**Service Delivery**	OGC / HMSO	0 11 330017 4
Service Delivery	Security Management	OGC / HMSO	0 11 330014 X
Applications	Software Lifecycle Support	OGC / HMSO	0 11 330559 1
Applications	Testing an IT Service for Operational Use	OGC / HMSO	0 11 330560 5
Management	Customer Liaison	OGC / HMSO	0 11 330546 X
Management	IT Services Organization	OGC / HMSO	0 11 330563 X
Management	Planning and Control for IT Services	OGC / HMSO	0 11 330548 6
Management	Quality Management for IT Services	OGC / HMSO	0 11 330555 9
Management	Business and Management Skills	OGC / HMSO	0 11 330686 5
Business	Guide to Business Continuity Management	OGC / HMSO	011 330675 X
Business	Surviving IT Infrastructure Transitions	OGC / HMSO	0 11 330678 4
Business	Understanding and Improving	OGC / HMSO	0 11 330679 2
Business	Managing Facilities Management	OGC / HMSO	0 11 330526 5
Business	Intro. to Business Continuity Management	OGC / HMSO	0 11 330669 5
Business	In Times of Radical Change	OGC / HMSO	0 11 330678 3
Business	Managing Supplier Relationships	OGC / HMSO	0 11 330562 1
Infrastructure	Computer Installation and Acceptance	OGC / HMSO	0 11 330556 7
Infrastructure	Computer Operations Management	OGC / HMSO	0 11 330539 7
Infrastructure	Management of Local Processors and Terminals	OGC / HMSO	0 11 330550 8
Infrastructure	Network Services Management	OGC / HMSO	0 11 330558 3
Tools	IT Infrastructure Support Tools	OGC / HMSO	0 11 330586 9
Tools	Service Delivery Tools	OGC / HMSO	0 11 330633 4
Misc.	IT Service Management Case Studies	OGC / HMSO	0 11 330676 8
Misc.	Practices in Small IT Units	OGC / HMSO	0 11 330674 1
General	**World Class IT Service Management Guide**	tenHagen&Stam	90 76383 46 4

| General | **The Guide to IT Service Management** | Addison Wesley | 0 20 173792 2 |
| Humor | Not The IT Infrastructure Library | Giggle Productions | 0 95 334690 0 |

B.3 Relevant web sites

OGC	http://www.ogc.gov.uk
ITIL	http://www.itil.co.uk
EXIN	http://www.exin.nl
ISEB	http://www.bcs.org.uk/iseb
itSMF-AU	http://www.itsmf.org.au
itSMF-BE	http://www.itsmf.be
itSMF-CA	http://www.itsmf.ca
itSMF-DE	http://www.itsmf.de (Germany, Switzerland and Austria)
itSMF-NL	http://www.itsmf.nl
itSMF-SA	http://www.itsmf.org.za
itSMF-UK	http://www.itsmf.com
itSMF-USA	http://www.itsmf.net
ITSM PORTAL	http://nl.itsmportal.net
ITIL/ITSM World	http://www.itil-itsm-world.com
The ITIL Tooling Page	http://tools2manage-it.com
ITIL world	http://www.itilworld.com
Loyalist College	http://www.itilexams.com